Biblical Folklore

About the Author

Rev. Dr. Daniel Vincent (*b.* 1952) is an ordained presbyter of the Church of South India, Trichirapalli-Thanjavur Diocese, presently working in the C.S.I. St. Luke's Church at Trichirapally. He is also the Chaplain of the Bishop Heber College, Trichirapally. He has an MA in Journalism, M. Th (Master of Theology) in Mass Communication, Ph.D. in Folklore, and P.G. Diploma in Psychological Counselling. He has to his credit many articles published in various magazines. He has served in the villages for more than 15 years and lived with the village folks.

BIBLICAL FOLKLORE

Rev. Dr. Daniel Vincent, Ph.D

CONCEPT PUBLISHING COMPANY, NEW DELHI-110 059

Cataloging in Publication Data—DK
Courtesy: D.K. Agencies (P) Ltd. <docinfo@dkagencies.com>

Vincent, Daniel, 1952-
Biblical folklore / Daniel Vincent.
p. cm.
Includes bibliographical references (p.)
Includes index.
ISBN 8180693821

1. Folklore in the Bible. 2. Bible.—Criticism, interpretation, etc.
I. Title.

DDC 220.6 22

ISBN 81-8069-382-1

First Published 2007

Published and Printed by
Ashok Kumar Mittal
Concept Publishing Company
A/15-16, Commercial Block, Mohan Garden
New Delhi-110059 (India)
Phones: 25351460, 25351794
Fax: 091-11-25357103
E-mail: publishing@conceptpub.com

I Dedicate this Book

To All My Teachers

to My Parents

and

My Parents in-Law

CHURCH OF SOUTH INDIA
TIRUCHIRAPALLI-THANJAVUR DIOCESE
Diocesan Office, Puthur, Trichy-620017

Rt. Rev. Dr. D. James Srinivasan
BISHOP

FOREWORD

I am extremely pleased to write this foreword to Rev. Dr. Daniel Vincent's book. Dr. Vincent has chosen to take a new look at the Bible and its people from the dimension of its folk elements. The task has led his research to go into the intricacies of many aspects of the people's lives which have moulded their social life style, belief and behaviour. The Bible should certainly have provided a lot of resources for this kind of study by the very fact that the Bible came into being in the present form after several centuries of existence in the form of oral traditions and fragmented writings, growing and changing all the time. This research enterprise is not like picking up a book by a certain author and exploring it with our understanding of folk influence on the author's thinking and writing. Bible has been a dynamically growing literature interacting with the lives of the people for several centuries getting polished by the community's multi-dimensional folk influence on the many authors in their own historical context before it crystallized into the present shape.

Dr. Vincent had rightly chosen to pick up the Bible and see how the writings had been enriched by several generations of the people of God. I am sure the book will receive acknowledgement by researchers, Bible scholars, anthropologists and sociologists and historians.

I wish him God's blessings.

Date : 25.01.2006

Rt. Rev. Dr. D. James Srinivasan
(Bishop)

PREFACE

Folklore is a nascent subject. Although new in origin, it has gained great currency in the academic world. In a way it is an acknowledgment by the academic world of the roots of wisdom found among the people. Folklore is both an art and a science because ancient people have couched their thoughts and reactions and reflections in the forms of ballads, songs and stories.

Often times folklore arose as a reaction to socio-politico situations. Much work has been done so far in the field of folklore but little is the effort made in the direction of the Biblical Folklore. There were many difficulties in attempting a connection between the Bible and Folklore at the very outset. Can a sacred literature, considered to be the Word of God, be brought under the microscopic analysis of folklore? Will not the people who consider the Bible as the Word of God inspired by the Holy spirit object to its being related to folklore? Will it not be a desecration or atleast will it not be sacrilegious?

I had the privilege of refering to folklore in my Master's thesis. There it was an elementary effort, at once a beginning and a prompting. This had been in my mind to make a detailed scientific study of the folklore in the Bible. My job is that of a clergy man who is connected with the Bible everyday. My Scholarship has been related to folklore. At the very outset, I must confess that this was a vast subject with enormous potentialities. To bring the spade of folklore, to explore the Bible was a little difficult for me. But, undaunted I pursued the subject.

There are two advantages which followed from the study. An attempt has been made to make folklore as a tool of analysis. The analytical tool of folklore is employed to analyse a religious book. As a result, the value of folklore is improved. At the same time, the Holy Bible makes God the Speaker and the people as listeners. The Bible Community has faithfully pursued the instruction of God in the form of stories, customs, proverbs, riddles etc. It can be boldly said that this study has helped to make the message of the Bible the Dialogue of God with human beings more understandable.

In India even though a few Christians have done lot of research work on folklore, none have really attempted anything on Biblical folklore. Here the Bible has been analyzed from different angles namely the form, the content etc., and the folks of the Bible are brought under a study. The folklore study of the Bible and people of the Bible has really paid a rich dividend of better understanding of the Bible on the one hand and a superior employment of the folklore analysis on the other.

Rev. Dr. Daniel Vincent

ACKNOWLEDGEMENTS

I thank and praise God, without whose grace I could not be presently achieve this task of publishing this book, which had been one of my life's ambitions. My good Lord and saviour Jesus Christ has enabled me to realize my dream by adding his mercy and grace.

I gratefully acknowledge my deep debt of gratitude to my teachers, especially, my school Head teacher and inspiration, Late Mr. M.P.H. Albert, Dr. S. Saktivel, retired Professor of Folklore Department, Tamil University,Thanjavur, and Late Rev. Dr. C. R. W. David under whom I learnt the basics of Mass Communication theories and to Rev. Prof. D. Chellappa, my Philosopher, guide and my God-father, for his unstinted help and encouragement. My debt to Rt. Rev. Dr. R. Paulraj the Retired Bishop of Tiruchirapally-Thanjavur Diocese and to Rt. Rev. Dr. D. James Srinivasan, the Present Bishop of Tiruchirapally-Thanjavur Diocese for the encouragement they gave me.

I owe my thanks to Mr. Jesudoss Manalan, the Librarian of the Bishop Heber College, Tiruchirapally for his help in bringing this book in to a form.

My stint as the author of this book imposed a heavy burden upon my family, both in the hours of silence and absence. My children Annie, Mercy and Gracy and my wife Jansy bore the brunt of this deprivation patiently and silently, but all the time with smiling faces to encourage me in my work.

Rev. Dr. Daniel Vincent

A-5, 1st Main Road,
Ramalinga Nagar,
Trichy - 620 003
Tamil Nadu
S. India

CONTENTS

Foreword by ***Rt. Rev. Dr. D. James Srinivasan, Bishop*** 7
Preface 9
Acknowledgements 11

1. Introduction 15
2. The Bible and the Bible Community 34
3. Folktales in the Bible 58
4. Proverbs in the Bible 90
5. Riddles in the Bible 133
6. Folk Beliefs in the Bible 151
7. Folk Gods in the Bible 194
8. Folk Music and Songs in the Bible 227
9. Folk Medicine in the Bible 258
10. Folk Games in the Bible 291
11. Conclusion 307

Bibliography 312
Index 323

1

INTRODUCTION

The Holy Bible of the Christians is neither theology, nor history, nor science. It tells about the beliefs, the rites, the events which happened in the course of the history of a community. We can call this community as the Bible community.

For long years, the contents of the Bible has extant then was more oral than written. It was reduced to writting some where in the eighth century B.C. although the Bible speaks of a time very much earlier than that. Even languages have changed over this time. The first volume ever written was actually in a foreign language.

So much so it is likely that many folktales, riddles, proverbs, music, games, medicine etc., must have gained a part in the Bible. This is a humble attempt to make a study of such elements of folklore and highlight them for an analysis.

Folklore of late has earned a position of credibility and accuracy in the field of science. Its approach has become inter-disciplinary, rather multi-disciplinary. Enormous literature have come in the field of folklore, transending the barriers of claims and countries. From the Norseman's tales to Jataka tales, folklore has become a very comprehensive mode of expression in the life and progress of the peoples and nations of the world.

The research question that comes to the mind is "To what extent is the folklore as part of the Bible?". When an analysis of this question is made it is found that there is a body of fundamentalist's thinking which would completely religate the christian people to a far off land alleging thereby that, Christianity is not an ancient religion and therefore they are foreigners.

A study of this type will reveal that such a stance will not bear much probing and cannot be established as true. Not only the

Bible community was ancient in origin, but also there is a striking resemblence between the folklore of Asia and that of the Bible. The similitudes of Biblical folklore with that of the vast array of Asian folklore can go to establish that neither the Bible is foreign nor its followers. Therefore, the study of folklore in the Bible has an object of not only disproving the contention that it is alien, but also to establish the fact that folklore is one sure indicator of establishing its oneness.

Folklore can be summarized in a few definitions. In the words of Don Yodor :

> "This existing thing about folklife is precisely this, that it covers everything. Every phase of life is, traditional or folk society can be studied, with the inter-relationships and functions of part to whole. Not only does the researcher study the verbal acts of folksong, folktale, riddle, etc., which the folklorist has long ago made him province but also agriculture and agranian history, settlement patterns; dialectology or folk speech, folk costume, the folk year, folk religion, folk medicine, folk recreation, folk literature and the folk art and crafts. It is this existing totality of the verbal spiritual and material aspects of culture that we mean by the term `folk life"[1].

Definition of Folklore

New English Dictionary explains this word 'Folklore' as:

"The traditional beliefs, legends and customs, current among the common people, the study of these Popular Antiquities or Popular literature".

The word 'Folklore' was coined by William John Thomas (a well known antiquary and the founder of Notes and Queries) in a letter which appeared in the Athenaeuns. on 22nd August, 1846.

Encyclopaedia of Religion and Ethics defines folklore like this:

> "Folklore consists of customs, rites and beliefs, belonging to individuals among the people, to groups of people, to inhabitants of districts or places, and belonging to them apart from and often times in definite antagonism to the accepted customs, rites and beliefs of the state or the nation to which the people and the groups of people belong"[2].

These customs, rites and beliefs are mostly kept alive by traditions, that almost universal desire to carry on without alteration what one's parents or ancestors performed or professed. They owe their preservation partly to the fact that great masses of the people do not belong to the civilization which towers over them and which is never of their own creation; partly to certain of the people being isolated from centres of thought and culture.

The *Encyclopaedia Brittanica* gives three approaches to Folklore. They are:

(i) Humanistic perspective;
(ii) Anthropological perspective;
(iii) Psychological-psycho analytic perspective.

Humanistic Perspective

The humanistic folklorist sees the materials of folklore in large part as 'oral literature' and the folk as artistic performers of tale or song. Its emphasis is on the narrator.

Anthropological Perspective

The anthropological folklorist examines the materials of folklore using the hypothesis of the social sciences. He looks for cultural norms and values and predictable laws of behaviour that from a consistent pattern in the non-literate society he has closely observed. Folklore to him is an aesthetic product of this society, mirroring its values and offering a projective screen that illuminates its fanatacies. Hence the folkloristic anthropologist frequently reports to an one to one correlation between the value system and the tale repertoire of a given culture, whereas the humanistic folklorist promptly points out that the same tales are found in many parts of the globe of a particular people, even when they have been strongly localised. Its main emphasis is on the cultural norms and values.

Psychological-Psycho Analytic Perspective

The psychological-psycho analytic folklorist views the materials of folklore, neither aesthetically nor functionally but behaviouristically. Myths, dreams, jokes and fairy tales express hidden layers of unconcious wishes and fears. Its main emphasis is on behaviour.

Scholars on Folklore

Various scholars have done a lot of research on folklore. Lot of books and articles have come out regarding. Here are some of the definitions of the scholars.

Jones Balys

> "Folklore is the collection of the old and new generation's traditional creations. We can get them by using the sounds and words in the poetry and prose. It consists of the folk beliefs, superstitions, habits, dances and dramas or kuthus"[3].

William R. Bascom

> "In the anthropological method, we can understand myth, stories, folk stories, proverbs, riddles and ample ideas of the arts and the knowledge about all the above things as folklore. Like the literature, folklore too has the art form. It has the connections with music, dance and handicrafts. But the way of expression will be different"[4].

Aurelio M. Espinosa

> "Folklore is the godown of the society's experience, all the things it had learnt and experienced. These things are different from the scientific knowledge. The roots of folklore have gone deep in human society and has attained a very higher status of culture. Folklore is a branch of the human knowledge. The scientific knowledge helps us to learn, compile and form the folklore and it is the process of learning human life and culture"[5].

Charles Francis Potter

> "Folklore is the living fossil. It refuses to die and is the human society's million years life's experience, cultural and scientific fossils"[6].

P.R. Subramaniam defines folklore as Folk art forms. **Prof. A.M. Paramasivanandham** explains folklore as the oral tradition. **Sankar Sengupta**, in his introduction to **N. Vanamamalai's** book *Studies in Tamil/Folk Literature* defines folklore as :

> "Oral traditional literature which every now and then is taking its shape in the form of stories, sayings, songs, proverbs, riddles, rites, rituals, etc. They are the different parts of folklore"[7].

Keval J. Kumar goes on to say:

> "The folk art forms satisfy the innate desire for self expression, and also satisfy man's need for moral instruction combined with entertainment, as well as for the dramatic and lyrical"[8].

S. Agesthialingam says:

> "The folklore refers to the stories, songs, proverbs and mannerisms which are for research"[9].

D. Lourdu explains :

> "Folklore means the study of the life and the mannerism of village dwellers"[10]. He called it as the 'Nattar Vazakkatrial".

Folklore and Other Disciplines

Folklore has become a separate discipline now. It has also become an 'Inter disciplinary' department. Folklore depicts the people's civilizations, culture, habits, history and day-to-day life. It is intertwined with other disciplines like anthropology, history, psychology, philosophy, sociology and linguistics... Since the relationship is so close between the folklore and the above said disciplines, the folklorist is called a 'social scientist', and he can examine the social-cultural aspects of the human life through folklore. Folklore also helps to understand the religious beliefs of the people, and the primitive religions. Sigmund Freud, a psychologist uses myths and the folk stories to explain the 'Oedipus Complex'. The psycologists accept that folklore expresses the peoples' feelings and emotions.

Folklore and Anthropology

Anthropology is a subject which unreveals the truths like the human evolution, physical anthropology, cultural and social anthropology. Man/woman has got two kinds of inheritance, (i) Biological inheritance and (ii) social inheritance. **S. Sakthivel** points out :

> "Folklore and anthropology have always had well organised and intimate relationship that is not possible to draw exact boundaries between them. Both deal with human aspects of culture"[11].

Andrew Lang considers this folklore as a traditional element and the peoples' beliefs, old stories and habits are considered to be the elements of the tradition. A folklorist examines the life from the birth to death through folk songs of lullaby to lament.

S. Sakthivel argues :

> "The study of all kinds of traditional beliefs, superstitions, arts, crafts, etc., occupies a middle ground and can be claimed as a legitimate subject both for anthropologists and Folklorists"[12].

If one considers anthropology as the whole, folklore forms a part. In order to understand the culture of a group of people or a race, the anthropologist inquire into the songs, stories, ballads, beliefs and habits of that particular group of people. The main interest is shown on the evolution and diffusion. The myths and the stories explain the animism and totemism.

S. Sakthivel says :

> "Another field in which folklorists" work may be of great interest to the anthropologists is the analysis and classification of traditions"[13].

Folklore and Sociology

The science which talks about society is called sociology. **August Comte** (1798-1857) was the first one to use this word. Both the folklorists and the sociologists examine social set up. The proverbs and the stories explain the social relationship based on caste. Folk literature help us to understand the confused relationships between the great traditions. Sociology does not study much about the agriculturists. But folklore focuses all its attention towards village folks, artisans and agriculturists.

One can understand the family relationships and rituals through the lullabys, then can find the social changes through folklore such as the shift in the family system from corporate family to individual family from polygamy to monogamy. The folklore also explains some of the things very clearly such as the habits and rituals related to life, death, etc.. For e.g. the Nalla Thangal story explains the non-sharing of the property to the girls in the family. Proverbs show the conditions of each caste as a picture : For e.g. to show the Chettiyar caste people will not do anything without profit... a proverb says 'Adhayam Illama Chetti Athoda Pogamattan'. (Even if a Chettiyar goes in the current of the river, he will not go, if it doesn't offer him any benefit).

Folklore and History

Folklore stands as one of the historical sources. Especially the folk stories and the folk story songs are very useful in history. So it is right to state that,

> "History and folklore are inseparably intertwined and the product well connected"[14].

Since folklore tells about the past history of man it is called as 'Historical Science'. As the stone carvings, brass plates and written literature stand as evidence and proofs for history, folk literature also stand as evidences. Folklore examines the unwritten heritage of the people. Both the historians and the folklorists are interested in the 'reconstruction' of cultural history. To understand the history, traditions, archeology and comparative literature are important.

"Thus tradition is common to both folklore and history".

Like this the folklore lies at par with history in telling the past events of the political and social life of the country and human beings.

Folklore and Psychology

The study of human behaviour is called psychology. **John Dewey** says that "Psychology is a science which tells the truth about human being". Folklore examines the traditions. In this process we have to examine the changes which occur during the transition period between the old and new traditions. When a folklorist attempts to examine the behaviour, he must also examine the emotions. When one attempts to examine the traditions he has to do on the basis of psychological and anthropological bases. The individuals' behaviour, faith and rituals are safe-guarded by the traditions. This thing can be divided into two, namely traditional way and psychological way. The psychological way examines the origin of faith and its bases. Arts, myths and traditions are the gifts of our ancestors to us. The psychologists believe that the art crafts and myths are of great help to understand the signs. Man's life is made up of environments and traditions. Only imaginations and dreams can change the human beings' routine works and sorrows psychologically. The psychologists consider the folk literature as the field expressing human emotions.

Folklore and Philosophy

Myth which is a part of the folk literature clearly shows us the relationship between folklore and the primitive religion. Even though we don't have a direct relationship between folklore and philosophy, we find the religious faiths of the folk through folklore. A majority of the folk people (rural) believe that their lives are controlled by God. When they meet with good things in their life, they think it is from God, and if anything bad happens, they believe that it is due to the anger of God and offer prayers to their God.

We understand their philosophy of life, their faith, the philosophy of birth and death, their karma, concept and the philosophy of heaven and hell... etc., through folklore.

Folklore and Linguistics

Language is the tool which we use to communicate our ideas to others. We call the research of the language as linguistics. The relationship between folklore and linguistics is very limited. It is not like anthropology or sociology. In the 19th century, when both folklore and linguistics grew into separate disciplines, the scholars of the linguistics showed some interest on folklore:

> "Linguistic methodology provided the model for the folklorists"[15]

Jacob Cream, the father of folklore (1785-1863 A.D) belongs to philology. He used the comparative method in the folklore study, which was originally used in the linguistics study. **Max Muller** (1823-1900) also followed the footsteps of **Jacob Cream** and did his research on the myth. **P.R. Subramaniam** says:

> "None can deny the influence of comparative linguistics and its method in Folklore scholarship"[16].

Since folklore is based on the oral traditions, the linguistic scholars examine the oral traditions of it and write descriptive grammar. The emergence of the structural school proves the relationship between the folklore and the linguistics.

Thus Folklore proves itself as an inter-disciplinary study because of its relationship with other disciplines like anthropology, sociology, psychology, philosophy, history and linguistics.

Current Theories of Folklore

Richard M. Dorson mentions twelve theories as the current theories of folklore. They can be called as methods too.

Historical-Geographical Method

This method is used to trace the origin and the reasons for the spreading of folk stories. The Finnist scholars dismiss anti-diffusionists who affirm that tales cannot cross linguistic and cultural boundaries. The evidence of their monographic studies demonstrates that certain tales and ballads easily leap language walls, more easily even those they pass cultural boundaries. Further, the evidence indicates that the tales move from more advanced to less civilized people. Dorson says:

> "With the expansion of Europe in the 15th and 16th century, European colonizers transported folktales to the continents of North and South America and Africa, but the tales of Africans and American Indians are not found among European peasants. Hence, the areas of origin of

> the widely diffused folktales that have been intensively studied prove to be India and Western Europe with Asia Minor and other zones of Europe as Secondary centres of diffusion"[17].

According to the Finnish method folklore studies to statistical abstracts, summaries, symbols, tables and maps ignoring aesthetic and stylistic elements and the human side of the research.

Historical Reconstructional Method

Certain scholars welcome the use of folklore and folklore materials to recapture vanished historical periods for which other evidence is scanty. Such a method is called historical-reconstructional method.

"Jacob Crimms' thesis powerfully attracted the 19th century British folklorists, but after the insertion of evolutionism into scientific thought following Darwin's publication of the Origin of Species in 1859, a historical reconstructionisam added a preamble of prehistory in its chronology and looked back to a primitive savage rather than to a civilized pagan..."[18].

This method was used by the Japanese folklore scholars for the reconstruction of their primitive animistic religion. The skeptics like Lord Roglan in England and the American anthropologist Robert Lowie reject all historical traditions as mythical or trivial, but others like Hector and Nora Chadwick see a Kernal of historic fact in all great folk epics Dorson says:

> "The resolution of this theory problems lies in an analysis of each individual tradition according to certain criteria, have the tradition carriers resided continuously in the same locality on that visible land marks reinforce the story line? Does the culture institutionalize oral historians? Are the tribal traditions supported by other kinds of evidence-linguistic, ethnological, documentary and by external traditions? If such questions can be answered affirmatively, the presumption of historical trustworthiness increases"[19].

Ideological Method

In the 20th century, there rose an attempt to use folklore for political purposes. If one wants to understand the real culture of a country, he has to explore that particular country's folk literature in the process of the national movements. In Germany and Russia, folklore played a major role. In the freedom struggle of countries like Ireland, Philippines, Cuba and India (Tamilnadu-Kåttabomman Story), folklore played a major role, and it was a great force against the imperialists. In Algeria, the military marching song is in the tune of a folksong and it was a source of encouragement to the soldiers.

"Folklore is an echo of the past, but at the same time it is also a vigorous voice of the present. Folklore has been and continuous to be a reflection and a weapon of class conflict... Lenin declared that folklore must be considered from the social, political point of view as an aid to understand the past"[20].

Functional Method

The aim of this method is to assess the purpose and role of folklore in the culture of a particular race. Most of the scholars in this method are anthropologists. The purpose of their experiment is to know how the folklore functions as a 'Social Institution'.

"Ruth Bandict (a student of Franz Boas, who is the father of American Anthropology) propounded one functional use of folklore in her Zuni Mythology (1935), revising her master who had claimed that tribal narratives mirrored the ethnography of the culture"[21].

Folklore is like the non-formal education among the illiterates. People are advised to live a moral life through proverbs, stories and proverbs are used to correct the persons who go against the laws of the society. Malinowski says :

> "Myth is thus a vital ingredient of human civilization; it is once an idle tale but a hard worked active force; it is not an intellectual explanation or an artistic imaginary but a pragmatic charter of primitive faith and moral wisdom"[22].

Richard M.Dorson points out:

> "Field workers in Africa have pointed out the prevalent use of proverbs in Judicial proceedings. Among the Anang in Nigeria, whom John Messenger observed, a plaintiff secured considerable sympathy in court by employing proverb a habitual thief"[23].

This method talks about the use and the work of folklore in people's life.

Psycho-Analytical Method

This experiment was done mostly on assumptions. Abraham in his book '*Dreams and Myth*' gives a new explanation to the mythical stories of promotheus. Richard M.Dorson explains it like this:

"Lightning brings fire to primitive man, but early man also leaves to make fire by twirling a straight hard stick the 'horer' into a soft round wooden disc. These are obvious genital symbols and Abraham interprets the myth of promotheus to proclaim the masculine power of procreation as a principle of all life"[24].

Sigmund Freud uses folk stories, myths, taboos superstitions to explain the sub-conscious mind. Abraham says the dream is the myth of an individual. If the dream uncovers the infantile desires of one human being, myth reveals psychic expression of the childhood of the race. Infantile desires are not usually disclosed so nakedly. A censor imposed by the super ego screens, the brute wishes of the libidinous and they emerge in dreams and myths in symbolic garb. It is the business of the psycho analytical folklorists to penetrate the vail of the censor and read the true message of the fantasy. Those who analyse the 'fertility ritual' also follow this psycho-analytical method.

Structural Method

The Russian scholar Vladenia Propp is called the father of the structural method, and he purposely introduced his scheme to displace the taxonomy of Antti Arane. In 1928, Propp released a book called "*Morphology of Folktale*", in Russian language. In 1958, an English translation of the same came out in 1968. Alan Dundes gave an introduction to this book and released the second edition. Dundes followed Propp's method and released a book called '*The Morphology of North American Indian Folklore*'. Even though Dundes followed Propp's method, he made some changes, Dorson says :

> "Dundes made certain reinforcements of Propp's agenda. For Propp's colourless term 'function' he substituted 'Motifeme'—a coinage derived from the linguist Kenneth Pike and he proposed 'allomotif' to designate motify occurring as part of the motifeme"[25].

Another anthropologist Levistrauss followed Propp did some research on the folk behaviours, using the structural method, having the linguistics as the base. He did some experiment on the myths in his thesis '*The Structural Study of Myth*'. In Tamil, P. R. Subramaniyam was the first one to use this structural method in his research on Lullabys and lament songs.

Oral Formulaic Method

Literary students of folklore have responded with growing enthusiasm to the oral formulaic theory of folk expressions. In studying oral epic with the mind to distinguish it from written epic, the factors which we have found of most help thus far have been the formula, which involves a study of the line; entanglement, which involves a study of the way in which are line is linked with another and the theme which involves a study of the structure of the poem as a whole.

Kailasapathy Points Out

> "... this kind of oral formulaic method is seen in the Sangam period's poetry"[26].

Cross Cultural Method

The anthropologists Andrew Lang and Edwin Sidney Hertland did their research on the basis that human beings' culture attains the civilized stage step by step from barbarianism. Regarding Frazer's work, Dorson says:

> "In his twelve volume of the Golden bough, James G. Frayer advanced another comprehensive proposal extended by his myth-ritual followers, namely that all myths and all folklore stemmed from ancient sacrificial fertility rituals. At one time the myths explained the rituals but with the passing of human and animal sacrifices, the myths went their separate ways and the rites shrank to vestigial harvest customs"[27].

Folk Cultural Method

The experiment based on the folklife is called the Folk Cultural Method. Scholars like Iorworth Peate, Don Yodor showed interest in this method. Don Yodor says:

> "The existing thing about folklife is precisely this, that it covers everything. Every phase of life in traditional or folk society can be studied with the inter-relationships and functions of part to whole. Not only does the researcher study the verbal acts of folk songs, folk tale, riddle, etc., which the folklorist has long ago made his province but also agriculture and agrarian history, settlement patterns, dialectology or folk speech, folk costume, folk religion, folk medicine, folk literature and folkarts and crafts"[28].

Mass Cultural Method

Deep in the 20th century, the battle continues between the urban, technological mass production and mass consumption culture and the rural peasant folk culture. Folk people, leaving their rural areas go to the urban area in want of employment. We can call the 1960s as the renaiscence of the folklore department. Scholars do research, comparing the folk rural culture with the urban culture and found that in the urban culture, the so called dying or fading folk culture is having its impact. Dorson says:

> "We no longer believe that industrialisation necessarily implies the end of a specific folk culture, but rather we attempt to trace the modifications and mutations undergone by folk culture in the industrialised and urbanised world"[29].

Hemispheric Method

This method was formulated by the Folklore scholar Richard M.Dorson. This will suit only the colonial states like United States, Australia, etc. Dorson himself says:

> "The hemispheric theory of folklore which is Dorson's own theory divides the folklore of the old and new worlds for analytical purposes. This theory hinges on the historical fact of colonisation of the American date in recorded history by European maritime powers, notable Spain, France, England and Portugal. The whole sale importation of African Negro slaves by the European colonizers added one more racial element to the population mixture"[30].

Contextual Method

Scholars belonging to social sciences show interest in this method. These ideas unite such Young Turks among the folklorists as Robert George and Kenneth Goldstein. From linguists they have drawn the concept of verbal behaviour, from anthropology of functionalism, from sociology of role playing, from psychology of ego mechanisms and they seek to apply these perspectives to the folklore traditions. Ben Amos emphasises this method, Dorson says:

> "Ben Amos also parts company with the previous scholarship to assert the social interaction of teller and tale, process and product in an artistic form. Folklore actions are distinguished from other modes of social interaction by contextual conventions of time, place and company"[31].

Because of this method, there are ample chances for the growth of field experiments.

Folklore is not static. It has been comparatively stable for thousands of years, because the social class that produced it remained static so long as feudalism lasted. The changes in the social life of the folk has been rapid in the recent past. In the last hundred years, revolutionary changes have taken place in the environment of folks. The mental make-up of the folks has changed considerably. It has not been replacement of old ideas by new, but a modification of the old by new and an unity between the old and the new.

Methodology

Of the methods, the following were used in the inquiry

- — Analytical Method
- — Descriptive Method
- — Interpretative Method
- — Critical Method
- — Historical Method
- — Sociological Method, and
- — Contextual Method

Sources

Bible is the Primary source. Bible related books especially, Commentaries, Dictionaries, Encyclopaedias were used. Scholars and Teachers on Folklore have been contacted.

- The first chapter introduces the theories of folklore, the problem, methodology of study, the sources and the outline of the study.
- The second chapter speaks of people and the Book i.e., The Bible community and the Bible.
- Chapter three deals with folktales in the Bible.
- The Proverbs in the Bible are dealt with in the fourth chapter.
- The fifth chapter attempts an analysis of the Riddles in the Bible.
- Folk Beliefs in the Bible form the content of the sixth chapter.
- Chapter seven engages itself in the study of folkgods in the Bible.
- Folk music and songs are studied in the eighth chapter.
- Nineth chapter deals with the Folk Medicine in the Bible.
- The Folk Games in the Bible are analysed in the tenth chapter.
- Chapter twelve is the conclusion sums up the study.

Conclusion

To conclude A Study of Folk Elements in the Bible by employing different methods reveals a rich repository of folk elements in the Bible. It was comparable to the folklore of Tamil Nadu. Tamil Nadu, both in its language and literature, abounds in folklore. More or less of the same pattern as met with in the Bible. Tamil Nadu has a rich legacy of proverbs, riddles, folk beliefs, tales and songs. There is not much of cultural discripancy in the comparison of the Biblical folklore with Tamil folklore.

The value system adopted by the Bible folklore is the same as that of the Tamil folklore. The moral, ethical and sedimental values find a similar vibration both in the Bible and the Tamil folklore. After all the folklore remains the same although there are different countries involved. It only goes to prove that humanism, universalism and supremacy of God, the creator seem to be the fundamental truth of folklore.

NOTES

1. Don Yodor, "*Folklife" American Folklore*, (Texas; University of Texas 1976) p. 54.
2. James Hastings, *Encyclopaedia of Religion and Ethics*. Vol. 6, (Edinburgh. T&T. Clark. 1967) p. 57.
3. Su. Shanmugasundaram, *Nattupura Iyal* (Chennai: Manivasagar Library 1989) p. 3.
4. Ibid. p. 3.
5. Ibid. p. 3.
6. Ibid. p. 4
7. Shankar Sengupta in the Introduction to the *Studies in Tamil Folk Literature* by N.Vanamamalai. (Chennai NCBH 1969) p. 4.
8. Keval J. Kumar, *Mass Communication in India*, (New Delhi Pusthak Mahal 1989) p. 169.
9. S. Agesthialingam, *Nattupuraviyal*, (Annamalai Nagar Indian Tamil Nattupuravial Kazhagam 1987) p. 7.
10. Lourdu, *Nattar Vazakkatriyal An Introduction*. (Tinnevely: Parivallal Pathipagam 1981) p. 22.
11. S. Sakthivel, *Folklore Literature in India*, (Chidambaram Manivasagar Pathipagam 1983) p. 30.
12. Ibid, p. 31.
13. Ibid. p. 39
14. Richard M. Dorson, (Ed). *Folklore and Traditional History*, (Chicago: The University of Chicago Press 1972) p. 9.
15. Op cit p. 242.
16. P.R. Subramanian, *An Introduction to the study of Indian Folklore* (Tuticorin : Indian Folklore Society. 1972) p. 144.
17. Richard M.Dorson, *Folklore and Folklife—An Introduction*, (Chicago: University of Chicago Press 1972) p. 82
18. Ibid. p. 13.
19. Ibid. p. 14
20. Ibid. p. 17
21. Ibid, p. 21.
22. B. Malinowski, *Myth in Primitive Psychology*, p. 19.
23. Op cit, p. 21.
24. Op cit. p. 19.
25. Ibid. p. 35.
26. S. Sakthivel, *Nattupura Iyal Aaivu* (Chennai Manivasagar Pathipagam 1992) p. 222.
27. Op cit. p. 38
28. Don Yodor, '*Folk Life' American Folklore*, (Texas: University of Texas 1976) p. 54.
29. Richard M.Dorson : Folklore and Folklife an Introduction (Chicago: University of Chicago Press 1972) p. 43
30. Ibid. p. 44.
31. Ibid. p. 47.

2

THE BIBLE AND THE BIBLE COMMUNITY

Introduction

Despite enormous interest in Folklore studies, attempts to make use of the knowledge so gained in the field of the religious literature was at a low ebb. Perhaps the religious books were considered to be too holy to be brought under the category of folk literature. Because folk literature was still considered an erratic expression of sentimental people who wanted to hide themselves under imagery and parabolic statements. But modern research has lifted the folk literature from this morass and as such had gained the status of a credible instrument of analysis of whatever type of people or books. With this an attempt is made here to make a study the Holy Book of the Christians. The Bible in the light of the folklore as depicted by the people of the Book, the Bible Community. Thus the Bible on the one hand, and the people of the Bible on the other form the subject matter of study through the vehicle folklore.

The Bible

Since the title of this book focuses on the Bible, it is important to know about the Bible. For Christians it is the basis of the foundation of their faith. They believe that the Bible is the greatest book ever written. In it God himself speaks to men. It is a book of divine inspiration. It offers comfort in sorrow, guidance in perplexity, advice for our problems rebukes for our sins and daily inspiration for our every need. It is not simply one book. It is an entire library of books covering the whole range of literature. It includes history, poetry, drama, biography, prophecy, philosophy, science and inspirational reading.

The Bible's View of Itself

The Bible is viewed as the word of God and as such should be believed and obeyed. Western civilization is in a severe 'authority crisis' which is not confined solely to the realm of religious faith, nor is it specially or uniquely threatening to Bible believers[1]. Parental authority, Marital authority, Political authority, Academic authority and Ecclesiastical authority are all being deeply questioned. Not only particular authorities—the scripture, the Pope, Political rulers, and so on—but the concept of authority itself is vigorously challenged. Today's crisis of Biblical authority thus reflects the uncertainities of civilizational concerns.

In the Bible, the character and will of God, the meaning of human existence, the nature of the spiritual realm, and the purposes of God for humankind in all ages are stated in propositionally intelligible form that all can understand. The Bible publishes in objective form the criteria by which god judge individuals and nations and the means of moral recovery and restoration to personal fellowship with him.

The Bible is not the only significant reminder that human beings stand daily in responsible relationship to the sovereign God. He reveals his authority in the cosmos, in history, and in inner conscience, a disclosure of the living God that penetrates into the mind of every person[2].

The Bible is considered and believed authoritative because it is divinly authorized; in its own terms "all scripture is God-breathed"[3]. According to this passage the whole Old Testament (or any element of it) is divinly inspired. Extension of the same claim to the New Testament is not expressly stated, though it is more than merely implied. The New Testament contains indications that its content no less authoritative than the Old Testament. The apostle Paul's writtings are catalogued with "other scriptures"[4]. Under the heading of scripture, I.Tim.5:18 cites Lk.10:7 alongside Deut. 25:4. The Book of Revelation, moreover, claims divine origin (Rev.1:1-3) and employs the term "prophecy" in the Old Testament meaning.[5] The apostles did not distinguish their spoken and written teaching but expressly declared their inspired proclamation to be the word of God.[6]

The Composition of the Bible

The Bible is not simply one book. It is an entire library of books covering the whole range of literature. The great theme of the Bible is the Lord Jesus Christ and his work of redemption for mankind. The person and work of Jesus Christ are promised, prophesied and pictured in the types and symbols of the Old Testament. The Bible is divided into two major divisions, namely Old and New Testaments, which simply means 'Covenant'. In Jer.31:31ff., a new covenant is foretold which will supersede that which Yahweh made with Israel in the wilderness[7]. In speaking of a new covenant, he treats the first as obsolete[8]. The New Testament writers see the fulfilment of the prophecy of the new covenant in the new order inaugurated by the work of christ: his own words of institution[9] give the authority for this interpretation.

The Message of the Bible

The Bible's central message is the story of salvation, and throughout both Testament three strands in this unfolding story can be distinguished: the bringer of salvation, the way of salvation and the heirs of salvation. This could be reworded in terms of the covenant idea by saying that the central message of the Bible is God's covenant with man, and that the strands are the mediator of the covenant, the basis of the covenant and the covenant people. God himself is the saviour of his people; it is he who confirms his covenant mercy with them. The bringer of salvation, the mediator of the covenant, is Jesus Christ, the son of God. The way of salvation, the basis of the covenant, is God's grace, calling forth from his people a response of faith and obedience. The heirs of salvation, the covenant people, are the Israel of God, the Church of God.

"The message of the Bible is God's message to man, communicated `in many and various ways' (Heb. 1:1) and finally incarnated in christ. Thus 'the authority of the holy.

> "Scripture, for which it ought to be believed and obeyed, dependeth not upon the testimony of any man or church, but wholly upon god, who is truth itself the author there of; and therefore it is to be received, because it is the word of God"[10].

The Bible is divided into two main divisions namely:

1. The Old Testament—which was written in Hebrew, and contains 39 books.
2. The New Testament—was written in Greek, and Aramaic (Parts of the New Testament were written) language and contains 27 books.

- altogether 66 books.

The Old Testament

The 39 books of the Old Testament are divided under five headings, namely—

1. The Law-Torah
2. History books
3. Wisdom books, or writings or Poetry Books
4. Prophecy
5. Apocalyptic literature

The Law

The first five books are called Pentateuch which simply means five. These books tell the origins of the Jewish race and culture.

Genesis

The book of beginnings describes creation, the first rebellions against God, and God's choosing of Abraham and his offspiring. The important part is God's covenant with Abraham which symbolises the covenant between God and the whole humanity.

Exodus

This book tells about the story of how God rescued the Israelites from slavery in Egypt and led them to the Sinai Desert. The most important part is the Law given by God to Moses to govern the new nation.

Leviticus

God is holy and people are expected to worship him with holiness. This book tells about the laws set by God for the Israelites mostly regarding holiness and worship.

Numbers

This book tells about the wanderings of the Israelites in the wilderness for 40 years due to their rebellion and disobedience.

Deuteronomy

This book tells us the three emotional farewell speeches rendered by Moses, just before his death, recapping history and warning the Israelites against further mistakes.

History Books

The Israelites now moved into the promised land Canaan and established the Kingdom that lasted almost 500 years. The following 12 books continue the history of the people of Israel.

Joshua

After the death of Moses, Joshua commanded the armies that conquered much of the territory in the promised land.

Judges

The history of the Israelites was very much disturbed. The people remain faithful to Lord Yahweh and enjoy a peaceful living. Later they go against to the commands of God and God allows some enemy to take over them. In the oppression they cry to the Lord for help with repentence and God out of compassion raises some saviour who are called judges. This cycle of faithful living, rebellion against God, oppression and deliverance form the main theme in the book of Judges.

Ruth

Ruth is a Moabite woman. Even though she is not an Israelite woman, she found a place in the Bible because of her loyalty and faithfulness. Faithfulness of the covenant in the book of Ruth echoes Israel's covenant with Yahweh.

I & II Samuel

Samuel became a transition leader between the time of the judges and that of the kings. He appointed Israel's first king, Saul, after his own failure, Saul tried violently to prevent God's King-elect David from taking the throne. David, "a man after God's own heart", brought the nation together. But after committing adultery and murder, he was haunted by family and national crisis.

I & II Kings

Solomon succeeded David, with mixed success. At his death, a civil war tore apart the nation, successive Kings were mostly bad, and the prophet Elijah had dramatic confrontations with King Ahab.

II King continues the record of the rulers of the divided kingdom. None of the Northern Kings followed God consistently, and so Israel was finally destroyed by an invader. The South, Judah, lasted much longer, but finally Babylon conquered Judah and deported its citizens.

I & II Chronicles

I. Chronicles opens with the most complete genealogical record in the Bible, then adds much incidents from the life of David (often as same as those in II. Samuel).

II. Chronicles often paralleling the books of Kings, this book records the history of the rulers of Judah, emphasizing the good kings.

Ezra

After being held captive in Babylon for decades the Jews were allowed to return to their homeland. Ezra, a priest, emerged from one of the first waves of refugees.

Nehemiah

Nehemiah returned from the Babylon captivity after the temple had been rebuilt. He concentrated on restoring the protective wall around Jerusalem and joined Ezra in leading a religious revival.

Esther

The story is set among captive Jews in Persia. A courageous Jewish queen foiled a plan to exterminate her people.

Poetical Books or Wisdom Literature

About three-quarters of the 400 occurrences of the word 'wisdom' in the Old Testament appear in just five books, usually classified as wisdom literature. The wisdom literature of the Bible reflects on a wide area of life in order to provide insights into the way things are and the way they should be. The lessons consist of simple observations as well as moral exhortation. Compared with the commandments of the Torah, the teaching deals with the formation of character. Control of the tongue and of all the appetites is the ideal.

Job

The best man of his day suffered the greatest personal tragedy. The entire book deals with the question "WHY?". The main theme is the problem of suffering. Why the just suffer always? This book introduces the adversary of the human race and God, Satan and he is the cause for all the suffering. When man proves that he is just, God blesses him and gives back all the loses abundently. This book is a great piece of philosophy and poetry and gives great hope to the readers.

Psalms

The book of Psalms is the hymn book and prayer book of the Bible. Composed by different authors over a long period of time. These hymns and prayers were collected and used by the people of Israel in their worship, and eventually this was included in their scriptures.

These religious poems are of many kinds: there are hymns of praise and worship of God; prayers for help, protection and salvation, pleas for forgiveness; songs of thanks giving for God's blessings; and petitions for the punishment of enemies. These prayers are both personal and national; some portray the most intimate feelings of one person, while others represent the needs and feelings of all the people of God.

The Psalms were used by Jesus, quoted by the writers of the New Testament, and became the treasured book of worship of the Christian church from its beginning.

Proverbs

The book of Proverbs is a collection of moral and religious teachings in the form of sayings and proverbs. Much of it has to do with practical, everyday concerns. It begins with the reminder that "to have knowledge, you must first have reverence for the Lord", and then goes on to deal with matters not only of religious morality, but also of common sense and good manners. Its many short sayings reveal the insights of ancient Israelite teachers about what a wise person will do in certain situations. Some of these concern family relations, others business dealings. Some deal with matters of etiquette in social relationships, and others with the need for self-control. Much is said about such qualities as humility, patience, respect for the poor and loyalty to friends.

Ecclesiastes

The book of Ecclesiastes contains the thoughts of 'the philospher', a man who reflected deeply on how short and contradictory human life is, with its mysterious injustices and frustrations, and concluded that "life is useless". He could not understand the ways of God, who controls human destiny. Yet, in spite of this he advised people to work hard, and to enjoy the gifts of God as much and as long as they could.

Song of Songs (Songs of Solomon)

The Song of Songs is a collection of love poems, for the most part in the form of songs addressed by a man to a woman, and by the woman to the man. In some translations, the book is called the 'Song of Solomon', because it is attributed to Solomon in the Hebrew title.

These songs have often been interpreted by Jews as a picture of the relationship between God and his people, and by Christians as a picture of the relationship between Christ and the church.

Prophetical Books

Although Israelite prophecy was something special, we must recognize that it was part of a wider human culture. It is not the nature of Biblical prophecy to see the future like a photograph. Prediction was, indeed often part of the prophetic message, but prediction was permitted to the prophet always in terms of what he knew and what would be understood by his heavens. Isaiah's prophecy of Sena-cherib's invasion[11] is a classical example : the prophecy was fulfilled, but under circumstances not expected by the prophet. The means of prophetic communication were dreams, visions, ecstatic or mystical experiences, and various divinatory practices. The oracles of Balaam in Numbers[12] were regarded as true prophecies from Yahweh, although Biblical traditions classified Balaam with the enemies of God and his people[13]. The same person might prophecy both truth and false hood, depending on whether or not he had been touched by the Spirit of God.

Isaiah

The most eloquent of the prophets, Isaiah analyzed the failures of all the nations around him and pointed to a future Messiah who would bring peace.

Jeremiah

Jeremiah led an emotionally tortured life, yet held to his stern message. He spoke to Judah in the last decades before Babylon destroyed the nation.

Lamentations

All Jeremiah's warnings about Jerusalem came true, and Lamentations records five poems of sorrow for the fallen city.

Ezekiel

Ezekiel spoke to the Jews who were captive in Babylon. He often used dramatic stories and 'enacted parables' to make his points.

Hosea

By marrying a loose—living wife, Hosea lived out his message : that Israel had committed spiritual adultery against God.

Joel

Beginning with a recent catastrophe in Judah (a locust plague), Joel foretold God's judgement on Judah.

Amos

A country shepherd, Amos preached to Israel at the height of its prosperity. His grim warnings focused on materialism.

Obediah

Obediah warned Edom, a nation bordering Judah.

Jonah

Jonah reluctantly went to Nineveh and found Israel's enemies responsive to God's message. The love of God and the statement 'God hates sin but loves the sinners is proved here in this book.

Micah

Micah exposed corruption in every level of society, but closed with a promise of forgiveness and restoration.

Nahum

Long after Jonah had stirred Nineveh to repentence, Nahum foretold the mighty city's total destruction.

Habakkuk

Habakkuk addressed his book to God, not people. In a frank dialogue with god, he discussed problems of suffering and justice.

Zephaniah

Zephaniah focused on the coming day of the Lord, which would purge Judah, resulting in a remnant used to bless the entire world.

Haggai

After returning from the Babylonian captivity, the Jews began rebuilding the temple of God. But before long they set aside that task to work on their own homes. Haggai reminded them to put God first.

Zechariah

Writing around the same time as Haggai, Zechariah also urged the Jews to work on the temple. He used a more uplifting approach, describing how the world point to the coming Messiah.

Malachi

The last Old Testament prophet, Malachi faced a nation that had grown indifferent. He sought to stir them from apathy.

Apocalyptic Literature—Daniel

Apocalypsis means some message is given for a particular audience in the guise of some thing else. Normally, it is given in the form of visions and dreams.

The book of Daniel was written during a time when the Jews were suffering greatly under the persecution and oppression of a pagan King. Using stories and accounts of visions, the writer encourages the people of his time with the hope that God will bring the tyrant down and restore sovereignty to God's people.

The book has two main parts:

(1) Stories about Daniel and some of his fellow exiles, who through their faith in God and obedience to him triumph

over their enemies. These stories are set in the time of the Babylonian and Persian Empires.

(2) A series of visions seen by Daniel, which in the form of symbols present the successive rise and fall of several empires, beginning with Babylonia, and predict the down fall of the pagan oppressor and the victory of God's people.

The New Testament

The New Testament is really the volume Two of the story of salvation which is the theme of the whole Bible. If Vol.I, begins with the creation and the Fall of Adam (which is Hebrew for man) Vol. II, records how:

> "A second Adam to the fight
> And to the rescue came" [14]

It tells how, ('when the time had fully come') God fulfilled the promises made through his prophets to Israel by sending his son Jesus to be his people's Messiah or Deliverer; and how, when they rejected him, the new people of God went forth to proclaim the salvation he had brought to the wider world.

The New Testament comprises twenty-seven books; but some are very short; and altogether, the New Testament is only about a third of the length of the Old Testament. These twenty- seven books, we may classify as follows.

First we have four documents called 'Gospels' which at first look like biographics of Jesus but which, on closer study, hardly answer to our modern ideas of biographical writing. These Gospels are namely Matthew, Mark, Luke and John named after their writers.

Next comes a volume of history, the Acts of the Apostles, which, as its preface shows (Acts 1:1), is really a sequel to the third Gospel namely St.Luke.

Then follow twenty-one documents which we know as Epistles, (means letters). The term is very elastic, because it covers many literary types, from a massive theological treatise (Romans) to a charming little private letter (Philemon), and includes a highly rhetorical homily (Hebrews) and an ethical scrap book (James); and the whole is rounded off with a book of apocalyptic visions known as the Revelation of St. John. So the two Testaments form two volumes of one work. The first is incomplete with out the second, and the second cannot be understood without the first. Together, they are God's revelation to people of the provision he has made for their salvation.

Folklore Studies and the Old Testament

It has been a premise of Old Testament scholarship that behind much of the Biblical material lies an oral literature. Many of the major attempts to reconstruct Israel's pre-history have relied upon the assumption that behind the patriarchal narratives lies material which was originally oral transmitted by word of mouth over an extended period of time. Therefore, it is hardly surprising that Old Testament scholars have turned to the findings of folklore studies in order to understand the nature of oral literature, its composition and transmission.

It is almost a century since the pioneers of such an interdisciplinary approach began their work. Since that time neither Biblical nor folklore scholarship has stood still. Many of the conclusions previously arrived at by folklorists have now been either abandoned or considerably modified. It is, therefore, imperative that Biblical scholars should not only be assure of contemporary folklore research, but also, in the light of its findings, revise their own theories concerning the possibility of recovering a presumed original oral form of the Biblical text:

> "The extent to which Old Testament scholars are indebted to many of the presuppositions and conclusions of Folklore studies is well-known. In the past century it has frequently been the case that the questions and debates with in one discipline have been paralleled in the other. The reason for this is quite straight forward, namely, both disciplines

were concerned with the sociological and historical environment in which various oral and written traditions had been composed and transmitted"[15].

It is not surprising to find, therefore, that in their attempts to write the history of ancient Israel, Old Testament scholars frequently turned to the methods of contemporary folklorists to aid them in their reconstructions. It was J.G. Frazer's 'Folklore in the Old Testament', published in 1918, which was the first study to acknowledge the relationship between these two disciplines. It was also the first attempt to assess the extent to which the Old Testament contained elements of folklore. Frazer's methods were largely comparative, and where as his work has received criticism for its evolutionary view of human societies it is nonetheless a veritable mine of folklore material[16].

The scope of the work was determined in large part by the all inclusive definition of folklore which Frazer accepted:

> "long after the majority of men in a community have ceased to think and act like savages, not a few traces of the old ruder modes of life and thought service in the habits and institutions of the people. Such survivals are included under the head of folklore which in the broadest sense of the word may be said to embrace the whole body of a people's traditionaly beliefs and customs so far as these appear to be due to the collective action of the multitude and cannot be traced to the individual influence of great men"[17].

By adopting a comparative approach, Frazer isolated a number of beliefs and customs in the Old Testament which he argued were vestiges of more ancient practices. Frazer's essential presupposition was that each culture under want the same process of evolution, albeit at different rates culture from anywhere in the world would thus react in the same way and would produce similar literature and other art forms, which could be compared. In this way Frazer was able to accumulate comparative material with which to prove the antiquity of various customs described in the Old Testament, and went on to argue that certain of these customs had been observed during a patriarchal age.

Thus the authors of the patriarchal narratives were either describing what they themselves had witnessed or were writing down customs which had been preserved by oral tradition.

Folklore Research on Old Testament Studies

There have been three main areas of folklore studies which have influenced approaches to Old Testament studies. The first, as it is already mentioned, was that area of folklore studies which could be identified with the cultural anthropological approach of J.G. Frazer; secondly the generic approach as practised by the brothers Grimm and then adapted by Biblical literary critics; and thirdly and closely allied to the second, theories relating to oral composition and transmission most clearly outlined[18].

The influence of folklore studies on theories relating to oral composition and transmission of Biblical narrative has not always been openly acknowledged. More often than not scholars in the past have given scant recognition to a discipline which undoubtedly informed many of their presuppositions and provided them with a methodology with which to interpret the Biblical text. Research has shown the influence the brothers Grimm had on 20th century German Biblical scholarship[19].

Wellhausen, a German Biblical scholar has formed a hypothesis regarding the authorship of the Pentateuch, that the sources, to have been written by separate authors and then combined by different redactors, he did suggest that atleast some of the material reflected much earlier period than that of its composition. On the one hand he stated.

> "We attain to no historical knowledge of the patriarchs but only of the time when the stories about them arose in the Israelite people; this later age is here consciously projected in its inner and outward features into hoar antiquity and is reflected there like a glorified mirage"[20].

He also conceded that however much the source betrayed a later age, some of them had their beginnings in a much earlier period of Israel's history. Oral transmission of these stories had played a part, but the history of that transmission was now lost. He has also come to the conclusion that from the mouth of the people there comes nothing but the detached narratives which may or may not happen to have some bearing on each other, to weave them together in a connected whole is the work of the poetical or literary artist.

Wellhausen came to the conclusion that the Pentateuch was compiled from four separate sources called Jehovaist, Elohist, Deutronomic and Priestly (JEDP) writtings. Although he acknowledged and made reference to 'Oral folklore' he went to great lengths to argue against such remnants existing in any intelligible form in genesis. Indeed where he does discuss ideas of oral folklore or oral traditions it is with reference to the "P" i.e., Priestly source, which he denies betrays any suggestion of having been orally transmitted. The extent of oral tradition is limited to speculation about numbers:

> "Oral folklore can very well contain round numbers, such as the twelve sons and the seventy souls of the family of Jacob, the twelve wells and the seventy palm trees at Ehin ..., but a chronological system, whole lists of exact and considerable numbers, bare catalogues of personal names, none of them having any significance, date and measurements such as those in the account of the flood in the Priestly code, require writing even to originater, not to speak of transmitting them"[21].

It is clear then, that apart from a general idea that there is such a thing as oral folklore and that it was probably responsible for the legends of the patriarchs, Wellhausen does not elaborate upon the subject of oral composition and transmission. He is definite that the period reflected in the patriarchal narratives is that of the period of Israel's monarchy.

Apart from Frazer, Wellhausen, scholars like Hermann Gunkel, G.VonRad and M.Noth have contributed much to the study of folklore study of the Old Testament.

Bible Community—A Folk Community

The Book, the Bible has played a main role in the life of the Israelites and it is the foundation of not only their faith but social life. What is Israel and who are the Israelites, and what sort of speciality is there that they claim that they are the chosen race of God among all the people on the earth? are some of the questions need to be answered.

Israel, is the collective name of the twelve tribes descended from Jacob, whose name was also 'Isarel'.[22] In the Bible the people are called "the children of Israel or the people of Israel", or simply "Israel". According to Biblical tradition "Israel" was the name of the ancestor of the people as well as the people themselves.

The new name given to Jacob after his night of wrestling at Penuel: Your name, said his supernatural antagonist, snall no more be called Jacob, but Israel, for you have striven with God and with men, and have prevailed", (Gen. 32:28). And there is another account of Jacob's renaming in Gen.35:10. The ancestor of the Israelites, therefore, was known by two names, a fact that suggest to many scholars that too partiarchs lie behind the figure of Jacob-Israel.

"The earliest occurrence of the name outside the Bible is in a hymn celebrating the victories of the Egyptian King Merneptah, composed about 1230 B.C. The poem which lists numerous enemies defeated in Palestine, contains the boast that "Israel has perished: its seed is no more". In the Egyptian text 'Israel' is marked with the hieroglyphic determinative signifying 'foreign people', not 'foreign land'. This is usually taken to mean that a group called Israel was present in Palestine at this time, but that they had not yet settled in the land and claimed territory for themselves"[23].

The whole Israel nation, after its conquest of the Promised land Canaan, was divided in to Twelve Provinces, based on their Twelve Tribes. De Geus—a historian and anthropologist makes the following points on this regard:

(1) "The Israelites did not have a pre-Palestinian existence as flock herding nomads. Pastoral nomadism is in reality a specialised off shoot of agriculture and not a way of life that always or usually preceed an agrarian, sedentary life-style".

(2) Tribal organisation can not longer be regarded as a necessary preliminary stage along the road to the formation of a state. On the contrary, it is a considerable obstacle along such a road, and De Geus quotes the anthropologist M.H.Fried to the effect that tribalism is an evolutionary cul-de-sac.

(3) Genealogists have only a slight historical value and serve simply to express the living continuity inhereat in a unilateral and unilineal Kinship system [24].

When did this tribal society emerge from? "It was, says Lemche", the result of a movement which owed its origins to the choices made by individual persons, families and lineages with respect to their way of life. In other words, the parties involved had said good bye to their previous existence, which had been made miserable by the poor social conditions which were all the Canaanite states had to offer in the Late Bronze Age" [25].

Occupation

The occupation of the Israelites prove them as a folk community. Cattle rearing and agriculture are the main occupation of the Israelites. We are not able to locate the real date of first II chapters of Genesis. Abraham is the first historical person, and his date is put around 2000-1825 B.C. But we read about the punishment given by God to Adam to labour hard on the soil and eat the products from that. God said to Adam:

> "You will have to work hard and sweat to make the soil produce anything, until you go back to the soil from which you were formed"[26].

This gives us a picture that agriculture seems to be the first occupation of man kind. But, the human history proves that agriculture became man's occupation very late. When human beings were leading a life of nomads—the first occupation could have been hunting.

Hunting

Gen. 10:9, introduces a man called NIMROD. He is said to be the first on earth to become a mighty warrior and a mighty hunter before the Lord[27]. Anthropologists have found evidences about the early man's hunting processes of "australopithencines" with primitive weapons like stones etc.[28]

Agriculture

Both agriculture and cattle rearing went together. The first children of Adam and Eve. Cain and Abel were of typical example. Cain became a tiller of the soil and Abel a keeper of the cattle. The story in Gen. 4th chapter tells how Cain's offering to God was rejected and Abel's was accepted and subsequently. Abel was killed by Cain and Cain was punished by God and the punishment from his kindred to a nomad. When the population got increased density have been accomplished through more intensive exploitation of choice areas. Such areas are usually those endowed with fertile soil temperate climates, adequate rainfall and accessibility, often by water routes. People began to concentrate in such desirable areas when it was found that steady and reliable food supply could be assured through the cultivation of plants and the domestication of animals[29].

Shepherd or Herdsman

The patriarchal period was largely a time of nomadism for God's chosen remnant. It is uncertain whether Abraham was actually living a sedentary life with in the city of Ur when he was called by God. He is later called 'the Hebrew' (Gen. 14:13), and this may indicate that he was one of the Hebiru (Hebrews) living out side the city in perhaps a client status[30]. Abraham's occupation was largely of sheep and goats, and included asses[31], so that some world class him as a semi nomad or an 'ass-nomad'.

The life of a shepherd is a nomadic life. He must find grass and water in a dry and story land[32] protect his charges from weather and from fiercer creatures (Amos. 3:12), and retrieve any strayed animal (Ezk. 34:8; Mt.18:12). When his duties carried him far from human hunts, a bag held him immediate necessities (I.Sam. 17:40, 49), and a tent might be his dwelling. He might use dogs to assist him, like his modern counterpart (Job. 30:1).

Other Trades

Carpenter

A worker in wood; a builder Joseph, the legal or foster father of Jesus, was a carpenter[33]; so also was Jesus[34]. The work of carpenters is often mentioned in the Bible[35]. David employed Phonenician carpenters in building his palace[36]. Some of the tools used by the people were the adze, saw, square, awl, hammer and gluepot[37]. The adze was their favourite implement. In ripping a board with the saw, the carpenter sat on the board and sawed away from himself[38]. In its broadest sense, carpentry included crafting in stone and metal, as well as in wood[39]. Occupations of the folk artisans like Masonry[40], Pottery[41], Smith[42], a workman in stone, wood or metal, spinner[43], Tanner of the skin of animals[44] are also mentioned in the Bible. All the above occupations belong to the folk community i.e., the Israelite folk community.

Worship

Israelite community is noted for its monotheistic ideology. But till the dawn of the prophetic period, people were involved in the worship of their God Yahweh as per the practices of their neighbours—mainly Canaan. There are ample evidences for their idol worship, which was later banished. The Teraphim which was stolen by Rachael from her father (Gen. 31:19) is an idol of their family - god. Jacob's pillars[45] are the same as the idolatrous stones with which Canaan was familiar. Later it was prohibited. *Ancestor Worship* was also in practice. Deut.26:14 suggest that it was necessary to prohibit offerings to dead, which proves the worship of the dead.

There are records of animism and nature worship in the Bible, which are discussed in detail in the chapter "Folk Gods in the Bible".

Sacrifices

Folk religious practices and worship pattern has the sacrifices esp. of live animals and birds as an important factor. The Bible has important sacrifices as rituals in their worshipping pattern. The types of offerings are as follows—the burnt offering, meal offering both meat the cereal, guilt offering, sin offering. In all these, the animal is cut and burnt as offerings to God. Human sacrifice was also common and in Gen. 22, God reveals to Abraham that he does not desire human sacrifices.

Music

Israelite community was rich in music abilities. Their musical instruments were also very special and show their folk music ability. Their instruments like pipe, trumpet, flute, harp, kinnor, tambourine were all made by them mainly for their amusement later were used in their worship. For trumpets and pipes they used the rams horns. A detailed study can be found in the chapter on Folk music and songs in the Bible.

The Proverbs and Riddles were widely used. Especially the Proverbs shows the life pattern and the Wisdom of the Hebrews. The use of folk medicine and games and the references regarding are also found in the Bible scatteredly.

All the above things prove the Israel community as a folk community.

Conclusion

Although the Bible consists of many different books written over a long period of time by a great variety of writers, most of whom did not know one another, it has an organic unity that can be explained only by assuming, as the book itself claims, that its writers were inspired by the Holy spirit to give God's message to man. The theme of this message is the same in both Testaments, the redemption of man.

NOTES

1. Walter A. Elwell (Ed), *Baker Encyclopedia of the Bible*. (Michigan: Baker Book House. 1995) p. 296.
2. Rom. 1:28-20; 2:12-15.
3. 2. Tim. 3:16
4. 2. Pet. 3:15,16
5. Rev. 22:9,10,18
6. I.Cor. 4:1; 2.Cor. 5:20; I.Thess. 2:13
7. Exo. 24:7f
8. Heb. 8:13
9. I.cor. 11:25
10. J.D.Douglus, *New Bible Dictionary* (Leicester: Inter versity Press. 1986) p. 140.
11. Isa. 10:27-34
12. Num. 22-24
13. Num.31:8; Jos.13:22; 2.Pet.2:15; Jude.11; Rev.2:14
14. A.M.Hunter, *Introducing the New Testament* (Gateshead Britain. S.C.M. Press Ltd., 1972) p. 17.
15. Patricia G. Kirkpatrick, *The Old Testament and Folklore Study* [Sheffield (UK): Sheffield Academic Press Ltd. 1988] p. 13.
16. S.Thompson, *The Sociological Study of Religion* (London: Robertson and smith.1974) p. 382.
17. J.G. Frazer, *Folklore in the Old Testament*. (London: Appollodorus.1918) p. 7.
18. Patricia G.Kirkpatrick: "The Old Testament and Folklore Study [Sheffield (UK): Sheffield Academic Press. 1988] p. 18.
19. W. Klatt, "Hermann Gunkel" (Gottingeu: Frlant.100. 1969) p. 129-144.
20. J. Wellhausen, '*History of Israel*' (Geschichte Israel, Berlin. 1878) p. 366.
21. Ibid. p. 327
22. Gen. 32:28; 35:10
23. Paul J.Achtemeier, *Harper's Bible Dictionary*: (Bangalore. Theological Publications in India. 1990) p. 434.
24. R.E.Clements, *The world of Ancient Israel* (Cambridge: Cambridge University Press. 1989) p. 98.
25. N.P. Lemche, *Early Israel. Anthropological and Historical Studies on the Israelite Society before the Monarchy* (Leiden. E.J.Brill. 1985). p. 431.

26. Gen. 3:19.
27. Gen. 10:8,9
28. Davydd J. Green Wood, *Nature, Culture and human History A Biocultural Introduction to Anthropology*. (London; Harper & Row Publishers. 1977) p. 66.
29. Ibid. p. 77.
30. J.D.Douglas, *The New Bible Dictionary* (Leicester. Inter Versity Press. 1986) p. 839.
31. Gen. 22:3
32. Ps. 23:2
33. Matt. 13:55
34. MK. 6:3
35. Gen. 6:14; Exo. 37; Isa.44:13
36. 2.Sam. 5:11; I.Chro.14:1
37. Exo. 21:6; Jer.10:14
38. Isa. 44:13
39. Marrill C. Tenney, *The New International Dictionary of the Bible* (Grand Rapids USA. Zondervan Publishing House. 1984) p. 718.
40. 2. Kings. 12:12; 22:6; I.Chro.22:15; II.Chro.24:12; Ezra.3:7.
41. Jer. 18:2-4; I.Chro. 4:23;
42. Gen. 4:22; Isa.44:12; 54:16; Jer.24:1
43. Pro. 31:19; Matt.6:28
44. Acts. 9:43; 10:6,32
45. Gen. 28:18; 31:13,45; 35:14,20.

3

FOLK TALES IN THE BIBLE

Introduction

The genesis of the tales cannot be fixed. The impulse to tell a story and the need to listen to it, have made narrative the natural companion of man through out the history of civilization. Tales are able to adapt themselves to any local and social climate.

Because of their oral existence, folktales float in an unlimited number of variants around a limited number of plots. Hence a perfect classification based on form, content and function would hardly be possible. All categories have them to remain abstractions from real life, for the convenience of scholarly study.

"The folktale embodies the highly polished, artistic story generes that have a relatively consistent finished form. Their origin, goals and themes on the other hand are diverse"[1].

Like novels and short stories, their sophisticated counterparts, folktales are told primarily for entertainment although they may have secondary purposes. They are believed to be fictitious and are cited as lies by story tellers and commentators, who mean that tales are the creation of human fantasy.

Classifications of Folktales

The *Encyclopaedia Britanica* divides it into three categories:

(i) Myth
(ii) Legend
(iii) Popular tale[2]

S.Saktivel divides them into six categories.

(i) Human tales
(ii) Animal tales
(iii) Magic tales
(iv) Deities tales
(v) Myths and Legends
(vi) Miscellaneous stories[3]

The Bible and Folktales

What has the Bible to do with folktales? Is it not an attack on the prestige of the holy book to seek in it products of the imagination? And how can the lofty religion of Israel—to say nothing of the New Testament—contain material filled with what may be creative, yet nevertheless entirely subordinate, belief? These questions must be answered, first by saying that the Bible hardly contains a folktale anywhere. The elevated and rigorous spirit of Biblical religion tolerated the folktale as such at almost no point and this near total eradication from the holy tradition is one of the great acts of Biblical religion.

An ancient people without folktales seems hardly credible to us—an observation that supports answering this question positively, especially since folktales were cultivated by the Egyptians, apparently with particular affection and skill, and since they are also obvious in the Babylonian Gilgamesh Epic.

"The relationship of a few Biblical stories to folktales have already struck the folklorists, even though, of course, scholars of "Biblical knowledge nowadays is insufficiently comprehensive for them to have been able to view properly the whole subject"[4].

The proof that some Old Testament material belongs to the world of folktale can be demonstrated in two ways: either parallels from undoubtedly folktale stock can be cited in other literatures, or its folktale quality is patently manifest from the nature of the material itself.

Hermann Gunkel calls the Biblical Tales as Poetical stories. He says: "Poetical stories, however have a far less serious and strict purpose: they want not so much to inform people about reality as to tell the kind of story people enjoy hearing; they are there to make people happy or sad, to fill them with enthusiasm and to entertain them"[5].

The poetical stories of the Old Testament belong to the most beautiful, sublime and charming stories in the whole of world literature; they are in fact what we loved most in the Old Testament. For e.g.

— Samson—whose strength is supposed to have been in his hair.
— Jonah—who was swallowed by a large fish and was regurgitated alive after three days.
— Baalam's—talking donkey.

The poetical stories are of extraordinarily varied kinds. Thus the scholar entering this colourful world needs some clear basic concepts if he or she is to cope with them. It is far less a question of precisely contoured definitions than of quite simple explanations which are easy to apply in each individual case, and these are all the more necessary as there is by no means unanimity on the main terms, myth, saga, legend and folktale :

by *'Myth'*—we understand a story in which the high figures of the great gods play the main role.

by *'Saga'*—a story where historical persons - or characters thought to be historical are the effective participants in the action;

by *'Legend'*—a story with a characteristically spiritual tone and

by *'Folktales'*—the stories of less sophisticated peoples and circles, and the fairytales of our children.

Tales in the Bible

Mythical Tales

Myth is a narrative literary game which appears in one form or another in all the religions outside the Judaeo-Christian tradition.

H.Gunkel defines Myth 'as the story that accompanies ritual. It has been defined as a narrative about gods[6].
The first Eleven chapters of the first book, Genesis are called Myth—Raymont E.Brown calls them as the story of the Nations. This passage has the main stories like the creation of the world[7], creation of man and woman[8], marriage of Divine Beings with women of the earth[9], and the flood[10].

Story of Creation

Genesis tells that God created the whole world and universe in six days.

First Day : Heaven and earth, light and darkness are created.

Second Day : God separates water and sky.

Third Day : God separates water from earth—the waters he called seas and the dry land earth. He created vegetation of all kinds in the dry land.

Fourth Day : God created sun to give light during day time and moon and stars for night.

Fifth Day : God created living creatures, and birds from the sea, and also ordered for pro-creation.

Sixth Day : God ordered the earth to produce living creatures, live-stock, wild animals. At last God created human beings in his own image and gave him power to domain over all the creation.

Seventh Day : On the seventh day, after creating all the things in six days god rested on the seventh day and made it holy.

Creation of Man and Women

The second chapter of genesis gives a different account regarding the creation of man. God made an image out of earth and breathed into his nostrils the breath of life. Seeing that man is alone, he wanted to give him a companion. He made him to sleep, and took a rib from his side and made it a woman and brought to him. The man was called Adam and Adam called the woman as Eve[11].

It is quite interesting to see that the same kind of myths are prevalent in other countries also.

Babylonian myth portray Marduk their god as the creator of this universe. The existence of water in the beginning and separating of waters[12] are all go in parallel with the Bible Gen. 1:1,2. Later god Marduk created the cosmic.

We have similar stories of creation of the universe, man and woman in countries like India, Japanese, Northern Europe, China, Nigeria, Peru, Gutemala and Mexico.

Flood Story

The second great Myth is the *Flood Story.*

By seeing the sinful life of man, God felt sorry that he had created man, and decided to destroy the world and all the living creatures including man. But, Noah, who was sincere in the sight of God, found favour from God. He was ordered to make a huge ship, and took all the living creatures in pairs. He did every thing by the instructions of God himself. Heavy rain was pourd for 150 days destroyed the whole world, and Noah with his family and animals got saved. God made a covenant with him by putting his bow on the sky—i.e. the rainbow[13].

Similar kind of story is found in the Babylonian Myth, Gilgamesh the sincere man in the sight of gods[14].

Hero Stories

The heroes in the Bible are all men of God, Chosen by him for a specific purpose. They were anointed by God with special gifts and powers and did great wonders sometimes super natural. They are:

The Patriarchs Called Abraham, Isaac and Jacob

Abraham is called the father of the faithful. The whole Israel was brought in to a covenant with God through him. He is the first of the Patriarchs, with Isaac, his son and Jacob, his grand son considered to be the Patriarchs of the Israelite community. The God of Israel was not known to the public with a particular name first, and he was called as the God of Abraham, Isaac and Jacob.

His obedience to God is shown with his attempt to offer his only son Isaac to God and won the test of faith. So he is called the father of the faithful. Isaac is respected as a Patriarch because of his obedience in submitting himself to be sacrificed, and Jacob, for his desire to receive the blessings. He is portrayed as a deceiver first later became a changed person and possessed the status as a Patriarch.

Moses

Moses, the law giver to Israelites was called by God to liberate his people from the Egyptian bondage. When the King of Egypt hardened his heart, Moses by the power given by God brought ten plagues on the Egyptians. Then later on, their way to the promised land Canaan, did lot of miracles. Greater among them was the separating of the Red sea which enabled the Israelites to walk across the sea safely and drowned all the Egyptian army when they attempted to cross the sea. So he has become an important person in the life of the Isralites to the extent of participating in the Transfiguration event of Jesus representing the Law.

The first five books of the Bible namely, Genesis, Exodus, Leviticus, Numbers and the Deuteronomy were said to be written by Moses by some traditions.

Samson

Samson, the strong man was one of the Judges, God appointed over the Israelites. His main duty was to liberate them from the bondage of the Philistines.

His strength is unimaginable. The secret of it is given in the Bible. One is—when ever the spirit of the Lord came upon him, he had some kind of supernatural power and did an extraordinary thing. The second one is—his strength was lying in his hair. Samson was a Nazarite. In Israel, the Nazarite was one who got separated himself from others by consecration to Yahweh with a special vow. The Nazarite had to abstain the integrity and holiness of a Nazarite from possession by a spirit other than that of Yahweh. He must not cut his hair during the time of consecration. He must not go near a dead body, even that of his nearest relation, a prohibition applied also in the case of the high priest.

Numbers 6th chapter provide the fullest and most convenient basis for discussion.

Killing of A Lion

First story is about his victory over a young lion. When he saw a young lion charging him, the spirit of the Lord came upon him, and he killed that lion barehanded[15].

Destroying the Crops

Second story is—Samson wanted to take vengeance on the Philistines. So he caught three hundred foxes and tied them tail to tail in pairs. He then fastened a torch to every pair of tails, lit the torches and let the foxes loose in the standing grain of the Philistines. He burned up the stocks and standing grain to gether with the vineyards and olive groves[16].

Thousand men killed by a jawbone of an ass

The Philistines wanted to punish Samson for what he had done to their crops. So they bound him with new ropes. When the spirit of the Lord came upon him in power, the ropes on his arms became like charred flax, and the bindings dripped from his hands. Finding a fresh jawbone of an ass, he grabbed it and struck down a thousand men[17]

The final triumph

The Philistines persuaded the woman of Samson, Delilah to find the secret of his strength and tell them. She managed to get the real secret of his strength, and informed the Philistines. Since she herself is a Philistine, she made him to sleep on her lap, she called a man to shave his head. After that, Samson's strength left him. The Philistines gouged out his eyes and tied him and took him to

Gaza, a Philistine city. By that time his hair began to grow again in his shaved head. Samson was brought to their temple of Dagon, and was asked to entertain them. He cried to the Lord for help to take revenge for his eyes and the insults inflicted on him, reached towards the two central pillars on which the temple stood. Bracing himself against them, pushed them with all his might, and down came the temple on the rulers and all the people in it[18].

David

King David is one of the great heroes in the Israelite folk heroes with Elijah and Moses. He was an ordinary shepherd and was chosen by God to replace the King Saul when Saul disobeyed the Lord.

David and Goliath

Before David became the King, he went to see his brothers who were fighting against the Philistines with the army of Saul. Goliath, who was a Philistine soldier, a giant was insulting not only the Israelites, but also their God. David came forward to fight this giant. He went before him, armed with his sling and five smooth stones and his staff. He struck the giant on his forehead and Goliath the giant fell dead[19].

Solomon

King Solomon is the son of King David, the wisest man ever born in this world[20]. There is a story how he got the wisdom.

Wisdon of Solomon

When Solomon was at a place called Gibeon, the Lord God appeared to him in a dream and said "Ask for whatever you want me to give you". Solomon answered that he is grateful to God for all his kindness and riches to him. And, he said "Now, O Lord my God, you have made your servant King in place of my father David. But I am only a little child and do not know how to carry out my duties. Your servant is here among the people you have chosen, a great people, too numerous to count or number. So give your servant a discerning heart to govern your people and to distinguish between right and wrong". The Lord was pleased that Solomon had asked for wisdom and granted his wish. Thus Solomon became a great wise man among all the people of this world[21].

There is another story to prove his wisdom.

Once two prostitutes came with a case to King Solomon both were living in a same house. Both of them had one child each - and now, there is only one baby live and the other is dead. Both of them put the claim for that baby. Every body in the court were puzzled. And King Solomon, very wisely did one thing. He asked for a sword and ordered the baby to be cut in to two pieces and be given each one a part. The woman whose child was alive was filled with compassion for her baby and said to the King, "Please, my Lord, give her the living baby! Do not kill it!" But the other said, "Neither I, nor you shall have it. Cut it in two!" Then the king gave his ruling: "Give the living baby to the first woman. Do not kill it, she is the mother".

When all Israel heard the verdict the King had given, they held the king in awe, because they said that he had wisdom from God to administer justice[22].

Elijah

Elijah was one of the great and important prophets in Israel. There are lot of stories about him.

Elijah and the widow of Zarephath

Once there was a great famine in Israel. Because of the sins of the King and the people, God had stopped the rain for some years. God ordered his servant Elijah to go to a near by village called Zarephath. He went there and as per the guidance of the Lord he found a widow who was gathering sticks. Elijah first asked for some water and some piece of bread. She replied him—"I don't have any bread-only a handful of flour in a jar and a little oil in a jug. I am gathering a few sticks to take home and make a meal for myself and my son, that we may eat it - and die", Elijah told her, "Don't be afraid, go home and do as you have said. But first make a small cake of bread for me from what you have and bring it to me, and then make something for yourself and your son. For this is what the Lord, the God of Israel, says: "The jar of flour will not be used up, and the jug of oil will not run dry until the day the Lord gives rain on the land". It happened[23].

Dead son of the widow brought back to life

Some time later, the son of that woman became sick and grew worse and breathed last. She cried to Elijah, and he took him to his room and cried to the Lord, God to give back his life. Then he stretched himself out on the boy three times and cried to the Lord, "O Lord my God, let the boy's life return to him!" The Lord heard Elijah's cry, and the boy's life returned to him, and he lived. Elijah picked up the child and carried him down from the room in to the house. He gave him to his mother[24].

Elijah on Mount Carmel

At that time Baal's, (a canaanite God) worship was at peak. Elijah threw a challenge to the King to prove the reality of God. So they chose the Mount carmel. An alter was built. Elijah stood alone for the God of Israel and there were four hundred and fifty prophets of Baal were standing before him. Elijah said—"Get two bulls for us. Let them choose one for themselves, and let them cut it into pieces and put it on the wood but not set fire to it. I will prepare the other bull and put it on the wood but not set fire to it. Then you call on the name of your god, and I will call on the name of the Lord. The God who answers by fire—he is God".

The challenge was accepted. It was the turn of the prophets of Baal. They called on the name of Baal from morning till noon. But, there was no response, and they danced around the alter. They shouted louder and slashed themselves with swords and spears, as was their custom, until the blood flowed. But, every thing went waste.

Then Elijah took twelve stones and built an alter in the name of the Lord, and he dug a trench around it large enough to held about two seah's (15 litres) of seed. He arranged the wood, cut the bull in to pieces and land them on the wood. He asked the people to pour four large jars of water on the offering and on the wood. He ordered them to do it again and they did it. Then he prayed to the Lord.

Then the fire of the Lord fell and burned up the sacrifice, the wood, the stones and the soil, and also licked up the water in the trench. When all the people saw this, they fell prostrate and cried "the Lord—he is God! The Lord—he is God".

Thus Elijah proved the Lord as the real God[25].

Elisha

The call of Elisha itself is a fascinating story. The purpose of Elisha's call is given in I.Kings. 19:17. He was called to be a zealous servant of God. Elijah was given instruction by god to call and appoint Elisha as his assistant.

When Elijah saw Elisha, he was ploughing with twelve yoke of oxen, and he himself was driving the twelth pair. Elijah went up to him and threw his cloak around him. Elisha then left his oxen and ran after Elijah. Then he asked permission from Elijah to bid farewell to his parents and others. When the permission was granted he went and killed the oxen and cooked them with the yoke as firewood and made a feast to the people, and came and became a real servant of God under Elijah[26].

Elisha-healing of the water

The men of Jericho city said to Elisha, that even though the city is well situated, the water is bad and the land is unproductive. Then Elisha asked for a new bowl and told them to put salt in it. Then he went to the spring and threw the salt into it, saying, "This is what the Lord says: "I have healed this water. Never again will it cause death or make the land unproductive." And the water has remained wholesome all the days, according to the word Elisha had spoken[27].

Elisha is jeered

Once Elisha was walking in the streets of Bethel. Some youths came out of the town and jeered at him by saying, 'Go on up you bald head!' Elisha turned around and called down a curse on them in the name of the Lord. Then two bears came out of the woods and mauled forty two of the youths[28].

Elisha and the widow's oil

A man who was in the company of Elisha died. His wife came to Elisha for help. She said that the creditors are coming to take her two boys as their slaves for the money they lent to her dead husband. When Elisha asked about her belongings, she said only a little oil. Then he told her to collect empty jars from her neighbours as much as she can. He instructed her to pour the oil in to all the jars, and as each is filled, put it to one side. She did as Elisha told her, and got lot of jars filled with oil. Then Elisha told her to sell the oil and pay the debts[29].

Dead boy is raised

One Elisha went to a place called Shunem. There he was hosted by a rich woman. She was barren with out a child, and her husband was an old man. Then Elisha told her she will be having a son next year. It happened. Some years later, once when the boy was out to field with his father, suddenly took ill and collapsed, and he died. The woman carried the boy to Elisha. Elisha went to the boy's room, laid down on the boy. As he lay stretched out over the boy, the boy's body started to get warm. Elisha got up walked around the room, and went back again and did as he did earlier. The boy sneezed seven times and then opened his eyes. Thus the dead boy came alive[30].

Food multiplied

A man came from Baal Shalishah, bringing Elisha twenty loaves of bread made from the first barley harvested that year, and some fresh-cut heads of grain. Elisha told his servant to feed the group of prophets with this, but he answered, "Do you think this is enough for a hundred men?" Elisha replied, "give it to them to eat, because the Lord says that they will eat and still have some left over". So the servant set the food before them, and as the Lord had said, they all ate, and there was still some left over[31].

Naaman—the leper healed

Naaman was the commander of the Syrian army, a well respected, great soldier. But he was suffering from a dreaded skin disease. He had a small Israelite maid servant. Once she told to her mistress the wife of Naaman, that the prophet Elisha in her country can help her master to get rid of the disease. Persuaded by his wife Naaman went to see Elisha. Elisha didn't see him but gave the instructions to Naaman through his servant and asked Naaman to go and wash in the river Jordan for seven times. Naaman did as per the instructions and got cured[32].

All the heroes were men of God with great power, which they exercised to prove God's power. They acknowledged that the power is a divine power not human.

Tales About Children

The Bible considers children as the gift of God. The Psalmist says:

> "Sons are a heritage from the Lord, Children a reward from him"[33].

The Bible illustrates some fabulous stories about children.

Isaac

Birth of Issac

Isaac is the son of Abraham. His birth was foretold by three men of God. At that time Abraham and his wife Sarah were already old, and well advanced in years, and Sarah passed the age of child bearing. The men of God told him, that they will have a son, and also said—"Is anything too hard for the Lord?". After this Sarah got conceived and bore a son to Abraham in his old age. When the child was born, Abraham gave the name Isaac. Abraham was a hundred years old when Isaac was born to him[34].

Test of Faith

Some time later when Isaac was a grown up boy, God said to Abraham, to take his only son Isaac, to the region of Moriah, and sacrifice him to God as a burnt offering. Abraham obeyed the command of God and took his only beloved son to be sacrificed to the Lord, and the angel of the Lord called Abraham, and commanded him to stop the sacrifice. Because of this obedience, Abraham was called the "father of the faithful", and Isaac was counted as one among the Patriarchs of Israel[35].

Moses

Moses, the Law Giver, is an important person in the religious history of the Israelites. The story of his birth is very interesting.

At that time, the Israelites were slaves to the Egyptians. Since, they were growing enormously in their numbers, an order was given to the midwifes to kill all the male child as soon as they were born. When Moses was born to his parents, his mother hid him for three months, and when she could not hide him for anymore time, she got a papyrus basket, and coated it with tar and pitch, put the boy Moses in it an put the basket among the reeds along the banks of river Nile. His sister stood at a distance to see what would happen to him.

The Pharaoh's daughter came there to bathe found the boy and wanted to take him to her place. It so happened she engaged the mother of Moses (unknowingly) to nurse the baby, and he became the son of Pharaoh's daughter. She named him Moses saying, "I drew him out of water". Moses was grown in the place later, was chosen by God to liberate his people, the Israelites from bondage[36].

Birth of Jesus

Jesus, the Saviour of this world's birth was not an accident. It was foretold by the prophets several centuries ago. Prophet Isaiah said:

> "Hear now, you house of David! Is it now enough to try the patience of men? Will you try the patience of my God also? Therefore the Lord himself will give you a sign: The virgin will be with child and will give birth to a son, and will call him Immanuel"[37].

Jesus was born to Virgin Mary. Mary and her husband Joseph could not find a place to babe the child, finally got settled in a cattle shed and put the baby Jesus in a manger. His birth was announced to Mary first by the Angel Gabriel. When the angel appeared to Mary, and announced that she would have a son she was disturbed because she was not yet married and she was only a Virgin. Then the angel said: "The Holy Spirit will come upon you, and the power of the Most High will overshadow you. So the holy one to be born will be the son of God"[38]. The birth of Jesus was announced to the shepherds who were in the fields, they came and worshipped the baby[39]. Three wise men from East came, enquiring about Jesus. They said that they were guided by a new star. They found the baby, worshipped him and put offerings of Gold, in cense and myrrh[40].

King Herod wanted to kill boy Jesus, because he feared him as a threat to his office. So Mary and Joseph (Mary's husband) were warned by the Angel of the Lord, and ordered to take the baby to Egypt and they remained in Egypt till the death of King Herod [41].

Birth of John the Baptist

When the angel of the Lord, Gabriel announced the birth of Jesus of Mary, he said that her relative Elizabeth will also have a child in her old age, who was said to be barren, is in her sixth month.

Before this the Angel of the Lord, Gabriel appeared to Zachariah who was a priest offering prayers to the Lord in the temple and announced that his wife Elizabeth would have a son and they should name him "John". But Zachariah doubted the words of the Angel Gabriel, because both he and his wife Elizabeth were already very old. The angel said that since Zachariah did not believe the words of the Lord, he would be mute till these things came true. From that day he became dumb. When the child was born. People asked him what should be the name for the boy. Then Zachariah got a writing tablet and wrote "His name is John". Immediately his mouth was opened and his tongue was loosed, and he began to speak, praising god. This John the Baptist was considered to be the forerunner of Jesus, who came to prepare the way for Jesus[42].

Animal Stories

Animals have a story link in the human history. The Bible has few stories on the animals—All of them were depicted in a special manner and ability.

Speaking Serpent

The first animal we are introduced in the Bible is the serpent. It was more crafty than any other animal created. Here he tempted Eve first, through her tempted Adam which made them to fall short of the glory. We do not know what kind of enmity was there in between the serpent and God. Most of the christians believe this serpent was Satan in disguise.

It spoke to Eve and tempted her and made her to eat the forbidden fruit. Because of this act, the fall happened, and the serpent was cursed by god, and the enmity between serpent and man happened till date[43].

Baalam's Donkey

Baalam was a prophet of God. He was summoned by the King of Moab, Balak to go and curse the people of Israel who were very powerful. Baalam was warned by god in the dream and instructed to do what the Lord tells. Baalam saddled his donkey and went and on the way it saw the Angel of the Lord with a drawn sword. When the donkey refused to go further, it was beaten up by Baalam. Then it opened its mouth and started speaking by asking him ... "Am I not your own donkey, which you have always ridden, to this day? Have I been in the habit of doing this to you?" Then his eyes were opened and he saw the angel of the Lord[44].

Tales of Two Cows

In a war the Philistines defeated the Israelites and took the 'Ark of the Lord' with them, symbolizing that they have taken the God of Israel as captive. This thing kindled the furry of the God of Israel, and he sent some pestilance on the Philistines. So they were adviced by the Priests and diviners to send back the 'Ark' to the Israelites. As per their instructions they brought a new cart, and put two cows that have calved and have never been yoked. Those cows with out any one on the driver's seat went straight to Beth Shemesh, which was the territory of the Israelites. Thus these two cows were used by God to accomplish his will[45].

Jonah's Fish

The story of the Jonah's fish is very interesting. Jonah a prophet of God was summoned by God to go to Nineveh to warn the people about the judgement of God on them because of their sin. But Jonah was not willing to go to Nineveh, but went to the shipyard and paid money to go to Tarshish. In the sea, God sent a great wind, and such a violent storm arose that the ship threatened to break up. When all the people were praying to their gods, Jonah was sleeping deeply. Then the sailors said to one another that the lots can be put to find out who is responsible for this calamity and the lot fell on Jonah. They enquired and knew that he was fleeing from the Lord. Then Jonah told them, to pick him up and throw in to the sea. And the raging sea grew calm. The Lord commanded a great fish, it went and swallowed Jonah unhurt, and Jonah was inside the fish for three days. From there he prayed to God for mercy, and the Lord commanded the fish again, and it vomited Jonah on to dry land. Again the word of the Lord came to Jonah to go to Nineveh and preach. This time Jonah obeyed and went[46].

Daniel and the Lions

Daniel was a very sincere servant of God. When the king Darius passed an order on the instigating of some people that if any man who prays to any god or man during the next thirty days except the king, will be thrown in to the den of lions. On the contrary, Daniel being an officer put in to authority could not follow this command, and he continued to pray to the Lord of Israel as he was doing earlier. This matter was brought to the notice of the King and he ordered Daniel to be thrown in to the lion's den. To the surprise of all, the lions did not do any harm to Daniel because the Lord had already sent an angel and shut the mouths of the lions[47]. Thus Daniel was saved from the lions.

Elijah and Ravens

After the episode at Mount Carmel, Elijah was ordered by God to hide himself in the Kerith Ravine, east of the Jordan. And the Lord said that he had ordered the revens to feed him and he can drink from the brook. So he did what the Lord had told him. He went to the Kerith Ravine and stayed there. The revens brought him bread and meat in the morning and in the evening, and he drank from the brook[48].

All the above stories involved animals, birds and fishes, prove that they are controlled by god and the Israelites use them to prove the power of God.

Tales on Spirits, Demons

Jesus had some encounter with the Devils and Demons.

In Matthew's Gospel we read about the Temptations of Jesus by Devil. The devil tempted Jesus thrice, first with his hunger. Jesus took fasting for forth days and after that when he was feeling hungry, the devil came and asked him to use his divine power and change the stones in to bread and eat for which Jesus refused. The second one is the devil took Jesus to the top of the temple and asked him to throw himself down to prove his divine power. For this also Jesus refused. The last one is, the devil took him to a very high place and showed him all the kingdoms and told him that if he fell at his feet and worshipped him, he would give everything to him. Now Jesus rebuked devil and he left him[49].

Demoniac in the Synagogue

Once Jesus was teaching in a synagogue, the worshipping place of the Jews. In that place, there came a man who was possessed with an evil spirit. It started crying said: "What do you want with us, Jesus of Nazareth? Have you come to destroy us? I know that who you are—the Holy one of God !" "Be quiet"! said Jesus sternly, "come out of him!" The evil spirit shook the man violently and came out of him with a shriek[50].

Jesus and the Two Demon Possessed Men

When Jesus was arrived at the other side in the region of the Gadarenes, two demon possessed men coming from the tombs met him. They were so violent that no one could pass that way. "What do you want with us, Son of God?" they shouted. "Have you come here to trouble us before the appointed time?"

Some distance from them a large herd of pigs were feeding. The demons begged Jesus, 'If you drive us out send us in to the herd of pigs". He said to them 'Go! So they came out and went in to the pigs, and the whole herd rushed down the steep bank in to the lake and died in the water[51].

Legion

There are same kind of stories in the other gospels. Here it is a single man. When Jesus ordered the demon possessed man to tell his name - he said. "My name is Legion, for we are many". So Jesus ordered the evil spirits to come out, and they requested permission to go in to the herd of pigs and the pigs ran down and got drowned and died. Nearly two thousand pigs died due to this[52].

War Between the Devil and God's Army

The Book of Revelations is a book of Apocalypse. The whole book is written about the dream of John one of the disciples of Jesus. Here he explains the events of the last days. The Devil alias Satan the enemy to God and his subjects goes to war with God and his armies. At the end he is defeated, and thrown in to the fiery lake of burning sulfur. All the other supporters of him are killed and became the feast for the birds of the sky and animals of the land[53].

Tales of Giants

There are some stories of giants in the Bible. Goliath is one such.

Goliath

Goliath is a Philistine warrior. He stood against the Israelites and fought. His structure is given. He was over nine feet tall. He had a bronze helmet on his head and wore a coat of scale armour of bronze weighing five thousand shekels, on his legs he wore bronze greaves, and a bronze javelin was slung on his back. His spear shaft was like a weaver's rod, and its iron point weighed six hundred shekels. His shield bearer went ahead of him.

He was insulting the God of Israel. David, the shepherd boy went to war with him and killed him with a stone and sling. After killing him, he drew his sword and cut off his head[54].

Samson

Even though Samson is not called a giant in the Bible, his enormous strength shows him only as a giant.

(i) Samson kills a young lion bare handedly—he tore the lion apart with his bare hands as he might tore a young goat.

(ii) Samson was bound by the Philistines with new ropes once. The ropes on his arms became like charred flax, and the bindings dropped from his hands. He found the jaw bone of a donkey and with that killed a thousand men.

(iii) Samson had a woman called Delilah, and through her the Philistines learned the secret of Samson. So, they shaved his head and Samson became weak and could not do any thing. He became a prisoner. They blinded him. When the hair started grow, they took him to the temple of their god and wanted him to entertain them. He pulled down the whole building, by pulling down the center pillars - and died with them[55].

Tales of Magic

Magic and Sorcery were prohibited in the religion of the Hebrews. In the Old Testament we find that the kings had their court magicians. Pharaoh, the king of Egypt had his court magicians. When Moses and Aaron wanted him to relieve the Israelites from their bondage, he refused. In order to prove the power of God—Aaron threw his staff which became a snake. The court magicians threw their staffs down they also became snakes. But Aaron's snake swallowed up their staffs[56].

Power in objects

The body of the men of God like Elijah was filled with power. It can also be appreciated that the hairy cloak which Elijah wears is filled with power. When the prophet strikes the river Jordan with his cloak, the water divides[57]. He catches Elisha his disciple by throwing the cloak over him without uttering any word[58].

The staff of Moses—

— Changed in to a snake.
— When he beats with it the river Nile, the river changes in to blood[59].

— When he stretches it over the waters, frogs emerge and cover the land of Egypt[60].
— With the staff, he strikes the dust of the ground, and, as it whirls up, it changes into mosquitos[61].
— When Moses raises it against the Red sea, the sea splits in to two so that they can walk through on dry ground[62].
— And when he strikes the rock with it, water gushes forth[63].

With this "wand of God" lifted high, he conjures away all possibility of victory over the Israelite hosts; but as soon as he allows it to sink through fatigue, the Amalekites win the upper hand, until finally his arms are supported left and right by two companions[64].

Other magical like powerful objects or devices are also available to the men of God. Elisha makes an unclean source of water whole some by throwing salt[65], and a poisonous meal is made edible by mixing flour meal with it[66]. Moses makes bitter water sweet by using some wood[67].

The Powers of the Men of God in Israel

We can now ask ourselves what such men of God in Israel are capable of. They have power over the sun and moon:

— Joshua forced the sun to stand still in the sky[68].
— Isaiah made the shadow on the sun dial go backwards[69].

They hold Sway over the elements : Seas and rivers give way when they order it walking over or through water is also one of the commonest miracles elsewhere. Illnesses, even the most terrible like leprosy, come and go on their word[70]. At their wish iron loses its heaviness and is made to float on water[71]. They decide on life and dead : in Hosea, Yahwah says of the prophets:

"Therefore I have shattered by means of the prophets, have murdered them by words of my mouth"[72].

There is thus nothing in heaven or on earth to which their divine force cannot give effect.

The Spoken Word

Among such powerful magic like devices belongs also the spoken word, the efficacy of which was a matter of strongly based belief in ancient Israel. Some times such a powerful divine word accompanies the magical act e.g., the Elisha saga, which accomplishes victories over Aram by both word and action. Similarly, in the Balaam saga where a heathen magician's behaviour is clearly depicted: first, he entices the deity by means of sacrifices; then he approaches the deity and receives from it the magic word[73]. In other cases, the divine word is totally independent. Examples are as follows. Elijah closes the skies so that no rain can be sent down 'except on his word'[74]; similarly he miraculously fills the oil pitcher of the widow through his word[75], and he even calls down fire from heaven[76].

The Book of Genesis is full of such stories of spells: Noah, for example. 'blesses' his sons Japhet and Shem, but 'curses' canaan[77]. Old Isaac only had a single 'blessing', which he wanted to leave to his favourite son on his death bed, but because of Jacob's deception he could not do other than pronounce the blessing over his son with on possibility of neversing it, however much he might have wished to[78]. An interesting assumption in this case is that the blessing is pronounced 'in front of' the deity and that the person blessing must have eaten well in order to imbue this action with strength. Always, however there is the basic idea that such divine sayings are not dissipated in the air like normal human speech, but they are a vital force, effective and productive.

Jesus did great miracles by his word.

Creation: Jn.1:1-3
Leperhealed : Matt.8:3; Mk.1:41; Lk.5:13
Invalid healed : Jn. 5:5
Centurian's servant healed : Matt.8:5; Lk.7:2.
Raising of widow's son : Lk.7:11.
Tempest stilled : Matt. 8:26; Mk.4:39; Lk.8:24.
Raising of Jairus' daughter : Matt.9:18; Mk.5:42; Lk.8:41.
Bleeding healed : Matt. 9:20; Mk.5:25; Lk.8:43.

Blind men : Matt. 9:27.
Daughter of a Canaanite woman healed : Matt. 5:22; Mk.7:25.
Deaf and dumb healed : Mk.7:23.
Ten lepers healed : Lk.17:12.
Lazarus raised : Jn.11.

All the deliverance from the demons stories, the spoken word of jesus played an important role.

Humans Changed into other Forms

What is widespread throughout the whole world is the asserting that certain human like stone formations are really human petrified by magic, it is most frequently local sagas that contain this feature. Ancient Israel also interpreted a pillar of salt standing on the Dead Sea as Lot's wife changed to stone[79]. The sin which she is supposed to have committed is looking back contrary to the injunction to flee, that turning around is forbidden occurs frequently in folktales.

Every reader of folktales is familiar with the motif of humans being changed into animals through magic. We can find something similar in the legend of Nebuchadnezzar in the book of Daniel. Because he behaved arrogantly on seeing the magnificance of Babylon 'he was given the mind of an animal'[80] and 'made to live among the animals of field'[81].

"He was driven from men,
He ate grass like the oxen,
His body was drenched by the sky's dew,
until his hair grew like eagle's feathers
and his nails like bird's claws".

This story does not really mean that Nebuchadnezzar was changed into an animal, but rather that his mind was transformed so that he thought of himself as an animal and behaved thus. This motif arose through observing mental illnesses where people are struck with the ideas of having become animals: observations which also live on elsewhere in folktales and sagas.

Folktales with Primitive Beliefs about the Soul

Following on from the preceding discussion, we can now add the different kinds of motifs or narratives arising from primitive conceptions of the mind and soul.

The Secret Place of Soul

According to very ancient belief, the soul of a person can be in some place other than its normal one, so that only someone aware of this secret can master the person, who otherwise remains out of every one else's reach. Folktales then go on to relate how, despite this, the person can still be overcome; blindly unsuspecting, he himself reveals the secret information to the woman for whom his heart has fallen, and she betrays the secret to his enemies, so bringing his down fall.

This motif is applied to Samson in the Old Testament. His secret is that his mighty strength is contained in his hair—he is strong as long as he has his locks of hair, if they are cut off, he will be 'like any other man'. Cunning Delilah, however, whom he loves too well, is successful in enticing the secret from him and in robbing him off his strength by cutting his hair, with the result that he can be overcome by his enemies, the Philistines[82].

The Soul's Location

That the human soul has its proper seat in the blood, is a primitive belief which is particularly typical of ancient Israel[83]. It is, therefore, hardly surprising that blood can speak an idea for which there is also occasional further evidence in the folktale. This was the way in which the ancients used to explain to themselves the weighty problem of the deity avenging murder: blood spilt in violence cries to heaven for vengeance. And so Yahweh says to the murderer Cain : 'the blood of your brother cries to me from the field'[84]. That this concept was originally more than just a poetic, an image is demonstrated by the fact that it was thought that the cry could be silenced if the spilt blood were covered over with earth[85].

In the same way, the human soul can even be situated outside the body; we are thinking of the words in the description of God's chariot in the book of Ezekiel; "the spirit of the animals were in the wheels"[86].

Having been freed by the power of the angel from prison, Peter knocks at Mary's house in the night. When the maid answers the door, those inside will not believe that it is actually he who is standing outside but say: "It will be his angel"[87]. This is based on the belief that every one has a guardian angel who looks like him or her, or at least, who can take on their appearance. We might regard this as a progression in the older belief in the ghostly double of a person.

Dreams and the Future

In the life of primitive people's a major role is played by the belief in dreams fore shadowing the future. This belief, which has still not totally vanished is our own times, also held sway over Israel in ancient times.

Such oracle dreams are very common in the narratives of the book of Genesis. At the very mention of the subject, what Bible reader does not think immediately of Joseph's and Pharaoh's dream visions, both of which were fulfilled? Such oracles are considered particularly significant, if they happen twice-both Joseph and Pharaoh had double dreams-or when they are granted to several people at the same time-thus both Peter and the Captain, Cornelious, though living in separate localities, receive revelations corresponding with one another[88]. This kind of dream, which two different persons have at the same time, occurs in folktales.

Joseph has seen his future elevation over his brothers predicted in his dreams; they then get rid of the dreamer 'in order to see what will become of his dreams'[89]. However, that is the very cause of the dream's fulfilment: in Egypt, where he is delivered by the Ishmaelites, he becomes the second in the kingdom, and when the brothers, driven by starvation, go there to fetch grain, they must prostrate themselves before him: "Then Joseph could no other than recall the dream which he had dreamt about them"[90]. Another example of an attempt to escape from an oracle is given in I. Kings 22:30.

Aetiological Motifs

People have often been intriqued by conspicuous characteristics of animals and they have tried to explain these by means of short stories. So there are, for example, stories about why the pigeon grieves, why the cuckoo cries 'cuckoo', why the crow caws and why the magpie is so curious, and many more. The explanations are, for example, that the tortoise was flown high in to the sky by the eagle and fell down, and that is how it got its split back, or that the raven was cursed because of its talkativeness, and that is why it is now black, and so on[91].

Curse on the Serpent

Such an aetiological folktale motif is provided in the Old Testament by the story of the cursing of the serpent at the end of the paradise narrative[92]. The considerations leading to this curse are roughly as follows : People observed the strange manner of movement which is peculiar to the snake amongst wild animals : all others use legs, it alone crawls on its belly. Also odd was its miserable food: for people thought that they saw it nourishing itself from the dust. However the speculations of the ancients were particularly concerned with the awful battle which had been waged eternally between snakes and humankind. No animal is as hateful to humans as this one: whenever they see one they try to crush its head with their feet. The snake, however is able to revenge itself in its own way : as soon as it sees any one it darts at their heels. What—the ancients ask themselves—might be the cause of this horrible fate of the snake of all animals. The answer : that God himself had cursed this beast in former times; and therefore—they reasoned - it must once have committed a sin. This was located through the insertion of the motif in to the paradise narrative : it was because this demonic animal had lead the then still innocent humans astray that it was cursed by God in this dreadful way. Of course it is well known that more profound truths were then discovered, long ago, in this simple passage and it was applied to the struggle of christ against the devil; so that even today it is difficult for many Biblical scholars not to regard this historical explanation as trivial.

Cain and Abel

Cain and Abel, the first children of the first human beings, Adam and Eve represents the two basic community based on their profession namely Pastoral and Agriculture. Cain represented the agricultural community—a settled life of the human beings and Abel the Pastoral community a nomadic. The story goes like this. Both of them bring their offerings to God. God accepts the offerings of Abel and subsequently rejects both cain and his offerings. Cain became furious and slained his brother Abel[93]. The following motifs can be brought in based on this story:

(i) Why there is oppression in the settled community? The answer can be, in the hierarchical set up of the settled community—under the system of the ownership and labourer systems the haves oppress the have nots.

(ii) What is the reason for the struggle and enmity between the people?

The answer is prejudice.

(iii) Does God take a side when two persons involve in a struggle?

The answer is yes. Because God takes the side of the oppressed— He acts as an advocate he condemns Cain for what he has done for his brother Abel.

The Tower of Babel

When the human race is created by God through Adam and Eve, how lot of languages and cultures emerge? The answer for this question is revealed through the Tower of Babel story.

> "Now the whole world had one language and a common speech. As men moved eastward, they found a plain in Shinar and settled there. They said to one another, "Come let's make bricks and bake them thoroughly". They used brick instead of stone, and bitumen for mortar. Then they said, "come, let us build ourselves a city, with a tower that reaches to the heavens, so that we may make a name for ourselves and not be scattered over the face of the whole earth". But the Lord came down to see the city and the tower that the men were building. The Lord said, 'If as one people speaking the same language they have began to do this, then nothing they plan to do will be impossible for them. Come, let us go down and confuse their language so they will not understand each other". So the Lord scattered them from there over all the earth, and they stopped building the city. That is why it was called Babel—bacause there the Lord confused the language of the whole world. From there the Lord scattered them over the fact of the whole earth"[94].

Conclusion

It is self evident that the folktale material which we have collected from the Old Testament, and which stretches over a period of almost a thousand years, did not all come in to existence in the living folk tradition at the same time. It will have been just the same in Israel as every where else—folk narratives are popular for a certain time and flourish, then they are forgotten and make way for new compositions. In any case, we should be careful not to fix the history of these changes simply according to the period in which this material is attested. More or less by chance, in the Bible; such folktales ignored by literature, can live on among the people for hundreds of years.

NOTES

1. G.Santhi : *Folklore Survey of Thanjavur District*. (Thanjavur: Tamil University. 1994) p. 80.
2. *Encyclopaedia Brittanica*. vol.9, p. 519.
3. S. Saktivel, *Nattupura Iyal Aaivu* (Chennai. Manivasagar Pathipagam. 1992) p. 66
4. Hermann Gunkel, *The Folktale in the Old Testament*. (Sheffield. England: Almond Press. 1987) p. 34.
5. Ibid. p. 22.
6. Raymond E.Brown , *The New Jerome Biblical Commentary*. (Bangalore: Theological Publication in India.1992) p. 6.
7. Gen. 1:1-2:3
8. Gen. 2:4-4:26
9. Gen. 6:9-9:17
10. Gen. 6:9-9:17
11. Gen. 2:4-24.
12. Namiharan Mittal, *World Famous Mythologies* (N. Delhi: Family Books Pvt. Ltd., 1990), p. 13.
13. Gen. 6-9th chapters.
14. Donna Rosenberg, '*World Mythology*'. (Illinois. USA., National Text Book Company. 1987) p. 181
15. Jud. 14:5-6
16. Jud. 15:3-5
17. Jud. 15:9-17
18. Jud. 16:18-30.
19. I. Sam. 17th. Chapter.
20. I. Kings. 4:29-34.
21. I. Kings. 3:5-15.
22. I. Kings. 3: 16-28.
23. I. Kings 17: 7-16.
24. I. Kings. 17:17-24.
25. I. Kings. 18:16-39.
26. I. Kings. 19:19-21.
27. I. Kings. 2:19-22.
28. II. Kings 2:23-25.
29. II. Kings 4:1-7.
30. II. Kings. 4:8-37.
31. II. Kings. 4:42-44.
32. II. Kings. 5:1-14.
33. Ps. 127:3
34. Gen. 18:1-14, 21:1-5.
35. Gen. 22:1-19.
36. Exo. 2:1-10.

37. Isa. 7:13-14.
38. St. Luke. 1:26-38.
39. St. Luke. 2:8-20.
40. St. Matt. 2:1-12.
41. St. Matt. 2:13-15
42. St Luke. 1:36, 57-66
43. Gen. 3:1-15.
44. Num. 22:21-33.
45. I. Sam. 6: 7-12.
46. Jonah. 1:1-2:10.
47. Dan. 6:1-22.
48. I. Kings. 17:1-6.
49. Matt. 4:1-11.
50. Mk. 1:2-26; Lk.4:31-35.
51. Matt. 8:28-32.
52. Mk. 5:1-13, Lk. 8:26-33.
53. Rev. 19:17-21.
54. I. sam. 17:1-51.
55. Judges. 15th, 16th chapters.
56. Exo. 7:8-12.
57. 2. Kings. 2:8.
58. I. Kings. 19:19ff.
59. Exo. 7:14ff
60. Exo. 7:26ff
61. Exo. 8:13.
62. Exo. 14:16.
63. Exo. 17:5ff.
64. Hermann Gunkel, *The folktale in the Old Testament* (Sheffield: The Almond Press. 1987) p. 114.
65. 2. Kings. 2:19ff.
66. 2. Kings. 4:38ff.
67. Exo. 15:23.
68. Josh. 10:12f.
69. Isa. 38:7ff.
70. 2 Kings. 5:1ff.
71. 2 Kings. 6:1ff.
72. Hosea : 6:5.
73. Num. 28:1ff
74. I. Kings. 17:1
75. I. Kings. 17:14
76. II. Kings. 1:10
77. Gen. 9:20ff.
78. Gen : 27.
79. Gen. 19:26
80. Dan. 5:21

81. Dan. 4:22,29
82. Jud. 16:4ff.
83. Lev. 17:11, 14, Deut. 12:23.
84. Gen. 4:10.
85. Job.16:18; Eze.24:7f; Isa.26:21.
86. Eze. 5th chapter.
87. Acts. 12:15.
88. Acts.10.
89. Gen. 37:20.
90. Gen. 42:9.
91. Hermann Gunkel, *The Folktale in the Old Testament*. (Sheffield (UK): The Almond Press. 1987) p. 57.
92. Gen. 3:14ff.
93. Gen. 4:1ff.
94. Gen. 11: 1-9.

4

PROVERBS IN THE BIBLE

Introduction

As manifested in the folklore of many other lands, the Hebrew folklore, as revealed in the Old and New Testaments of the Holy Bible contain their wisdom in the form of proverbs. The wisest King Solomon has collected all these Pithy sayings into a book. Apart from this source, we have proverbs found scattered in the Holy Bible. Other writers seem to have interested themselves in collecting these proverbs.

Proverb-Definition

"A proverb is the child of experience" says an English Proverb.

Ralph Waldo Emerson says:

> "Proverbs are the sanctuary of the institutions. A proverb is a pithy sentence which tells an unpalatable truth in a condensed way. The statement of the truth however is incomplete, it: is exaggerated and expressed metaphorically"[1]
>
> "Proverbs are one of the most easily observed and collected games of traditional expression, yet one of the least understood"[2].

Maria Leach defines proberbs as:

> "Proverb is one of the ancient and significant games of oral folklore. Proverbs reflect wisdom of a community. It

> reveals experienced fact. Proverb is a short sentence based on a long experience. A proverb is what men think. Proverbs are daughters of daily experience. They are index of folk mind and they provide valuable record of the vocabulary and language of common people. Proverbs are words of ancient or saying of the community. The wisdom of many and the wit of one. Proverbs may be said to be the abridgement of wisdom"[3].

Proverbs are short and witty traditional expression that arise as part of every day discourse as well as in the more highly structured situation of education and judicial proceedings. Roger D.Abraham sees each proverb as a full statement of an approach to a recurrent problem. It presents a point of view and a strategy that is self-sufficient, needing nothing more than an event of communications to bring it in to a play. Proverbs are nearly always stated in the form of a single sentence. They are among the shortest forms of traditional expressions that call attentions to themselves as formal artistic entities:

> "A proverb is a description made up of two or more elements, and these elements often confirm to the two parts of the balanced structure. These two or three elements are usually tied together either by a verb of equivalance or a verb of causation"[4].

Alexander H. Krappe Says:

> "A proverb represents in its essential form, some homely truth expressed in a concise manner so as to recommend itself to a more or less extended circle. It may express the general truth literally, by a mere statement of fact"[5].

Proverbs also reflect the deep knowledge of folk people. It has the quality of mingling in each and every aspect of the life of folk people. Proverbs are as old as human beings. They are not only old, but soft and natural. With the help of proverbs, one can easily understand the cultural and traditional aspect of folk people.

Thus proverbs can be generally defined as the literature of the people, by the people and for the people. Number of essential characters of proverbs can be traced, but it is not a 'must' to be applicable to all proverbs.

Characteristics of the Proverbs

(i) Should contain meaning.
(ii) Short in size
(iii) Must be alterative, having rhyme
(iv) Easy to remember.
(v) Must be pin pointedly sharp in wording.
(vi) Must be founded on universal truth.
(vii) Must be appealing and alterative style.
(viii) Very popular among the people.
(ix) Effective in language.
(x) Have moral value.
(xi) Must be metaphorical in nature.
(xii) Reflect the culture of the people.
(xiii) Based on experience.
(xiv) Must be anonymous.
(xv) Must have popular acceptance[6].

Classifications of Proverbs

Robert D.Abraham classifies the proverbs in to four categories:

(i) Positive equivalance.
(ii) Negative equivalance.
(iii) Positive causational.
(iv) Negative causational.

B. Browne classifies proverbs in to two categories as:

(i) Literary
(ii) Non-literary

S. Sakthivel divides the Tamil proverbs in to five categories.

(i) Size basis.
(ii) Subject basis.
(iii) Alphabet basis.
(iv) Structural basis.
(v) Functional basis.

Stylistic Study of Proverbs

S. Sakthivel divides the stylistic study of proverbs into the following categories.

(i) Echo word.
(ii) Parallelism.
(iii) Coupling.
(iv) Onomatopoeie.
(v) Epistrophe.
(vi) Anadiplosis.
(vii) Epanalepsis.

The Structural Study of Proverbs

Can be divided in to three categories. They are:

(i) Oppositional Proverb.
(ii) Non-Oppositional Proverb.
(iii) Oppositional and Non-oppositional Proverb.

Non-oppositional Proverbs can be divided in to sub-clauses as follows:

(i) Equational Proverbs.
(ii) Causal Equational Proverbs.

Oppositional Proverbs can be divided as follows:

(i) Better than Proverbs.
(ii) 'A' becomes 'C" instead of 'C'
(iii) Antithetical Contradictions[7].

Hebrew Wisdom

In the Near Eastern countries of the past, Hebrew wisdom was much respected. The proverbs and riddles come under the wisdom literature of the Bible.

In its present form, it is certainly post-exilic, though it doubtless rests on more ancient materials.

> "Many of the individual sayings must be ancient, and we have evidence elsewhere in the Bible that the Hebrews, like others, could coin pithy sayings to embody the lessons of experience. The 'wise' were found in every age, and collections of wise sayings were probably made at various times"[8].

Wisdom represents a distinct category in Israel's legacy, comparable to prophecy, law, history and Psalmody. Book of Job, Proverbs and Ecclesiastes are the wisdom books in the Biblical canon.

Besides alluding to the wise in Israel, the Old Testament also gives evidence that ancient Israel was aware of the existence among other nations of leaders called 'wise' or 'wise men' in Egypt (Gen. 41:8,39; Exo.7:11; Isa. 19:11f), in Canaan (Jud. 5:29) in Phoenicia (Eza. 28:26; Zach 9:2), in Edom (Obe. 1:8), in Babylon (Jer. 50:35; 51:57; Dan. 2:12ff; 4:6,18; 5:8,15) and, in deed, among the Hebrews (Jer. 10:7). These sages are the aides and counsellors of kings, intimates of the court who were often equated with magicians, astrologers, sorcerers and other purveyors of oracles.

Literary Types of Wisdom

The Mashal

The basic literary unit in Old Testament wisdom is the Mashal, usually translated 'Proverb', though used in numerous senses. While the original meaning of the word is not certainly known, atleast two attempts to trace its etymology deserve attention. Some believe that it is derived from a verb meaning 'rule', so that the 'mashal' was originally 'a ruling saying'—an authoritative word. This seems appropriate in that, it is often a statement which conveys the wisdom of the ages in capsule form and as such commands assert.

A more widely held view is that Mashal derives from a verb meaning 'be like', and thus originally meant a 'likeness' or 'comparison'. This verb occurs several times in the Old Testament.

"Like mother like daughter"—Eze. 16:44.

"Like vinegar to the teeth, and smoke to the eyes, so is the sluggard to those who send him"—Pro. 10:26.

Such proverbs explicitly convey the notion of comparison.

Often the Mashal is a short popular saying. These are widely scattered through out the Old Testament. In addition to those quoted above, often well re-organized examples are:

> "The fathers have eaten sour grapes, and the children's teeth are set an edge".
>
> —*Eze. 18:2; Jer. 31:29.*

> "Out of the wicked comes for the wickedness".
>
> —*I. Sam. 24:13.*

In Luke. 4:23, Jesus refers to the familiar proverb "Physician heal yourself".

Sometimes the Mashal is a taunt or taunt song—a word of mocking, scornful derision directed against those who have justly received punishment from Yahweh (Isa. 14:4-20; Mich. 2:4; Heb. 2:6-8)[9].

Concept of Old Testament Wisdom

The concept of Old Testament wisdom is elusive because it is exceedingly complex. Wisdom can stand for the skill of a craftsman, such as that possessed by those Aaron's vestments (Exo. 28:3) or by the carpenters who constructed the Mosaic Tabernacle (Exo. 31:3-5; 36:1). It denotes the ability of a professional mourner (Jer. 9:17) or a sailor (Ps. 107:27). The sage is an adviser to Kings (Jer. 50:35; Pro.31:1) but is also an aslute (shrewed) old woman (II. sam. 20:16). It also has an intensely religious aspect fear of the Lord (Pro. 1:7). Wisdom is somehow divine. (Pro.8)[10]. These many faces of wisdom cannot be captured in any logical outline. Here we can only give some—indication of the variety of its uses and implications with in the wisdom literature itself.

The rewards promised to those who acquire wisdom are expressed in the concept of life: "A path to life is his who heeds admonition" (Pro. 12:28). The attainment of wisdom and virtue is associated with the "tree of life" (Pro 11:30; 13:12; 15:4), Path of life (Pro. 6:23; 15:24), and `fountain for life' (Pro.10:11; 16:22). Under this broad concept were subsumed many values: mere length of days (Pro. 10:27), but also the goods of this life, such as riches, a large family, success and prestige. It is not likely that any notion of personal immortality after death is involved in this notion. However the very concept of life is one that is capable of development.

Wisdom and God

In early thought of the Hebrews, wisdom belongs to the herman, given by God. Yahweh 'makes wise' or 'gives wisdom' much as he 'makes riches' or 'gives riches'. Eventually wisdom is predicated of God (Job. 12:13; Dan. 2:20), and it is a characteristic of his creative activity (Ps. 104:24; Job. 38:37; Pro. 3:19).

Wisdom is remote, the season for wisdom's remoteness is that she is divine 'poured forth' (Pro. 8:23); 'from the mouth of the most High', 'a púre effusion of the glory of the Almighty'. Wisdom is represented not only as originating from God, but as being active as craftsman in creation (Pro. 8:30; 3:19). These descriptions have given rise to the problem of wisdom as a person. She seems to be no more than a personification, just as other aspects of God are personified in the Old Testament.

> "The theme of wisdom as a divine communication is an important theological development. It is a more fruitful insight than is the mere personification of wisdom. Some theologians have seized upon the personification, as pointing to the christian mystery of the persons of God"[11].

Proverbs in the Bible

The proverbs in the Bible can be divided in the various categories.

Occupation

One of the main blessings in the Bible is—

> "You shall eat the fruit of the labour of your hands; You shall be happy, and it shall go well with you".
>
> —*Ps. 128:2*

God wants every one to work and earn their food. When the origin of the human kind is recorded in the Bible, the first man Adam was summoned to work hard in the field. When the first generation comes Cain and Abel, Cain was made as a farmer, who worked on the field and Abel became a shepherd.

Hunting is used as a word to convey different meanings related to human life for e.g.

> "A slothful man will not catch his prey".
>
> —*Pro. 12:27*

In this group of proverbs classified under the title occupation, one can find them in an order as seen in the human history of occupation. They are: Hunting, Agriculture, Shepherd, Pottery, Trade and Business.

These proverbs are very much ethical in their form. They teach that God expects sincerity and faithfulness in business, and he hates bribery false balance etc. The proverbs on occupation follows.

The Bible mentions some occupations like Hunting, Agriculture, Shepherd, Pottery, Trade and Business.

Hunting

(1) "Can you hunt the prey for the lion, and satisfy the appetite of the young lions".

Job. 38:39.

(2) Let not the slanderer be established in the land let evil hunt down the violent man speedily.

Ps. 140:11

(3) "A slothful man will not catch his prey".

Pro. 12:27.

Agriculture

Tilling the Land

(1) He who tills his land will have plenty of land

Pro.12:11; 28:19

(2) Those who plough iniquity and sow trouble reap the same.

Job. 4:8

(3) Does he who ploughs for sowing plough continually.

Isa. 28:24

(4) No one, having put his land to the plough and looking back, is not fit for the kingdom of God.

Luke. 9:62

Sowing and Reaping

(1) A son who gathers in summer is prudent, but a son who sleeps in harvest brings shame.

Pro. 10:5

(2) May those who sow in tears reap with shouts of joy.

Ps. 126:5

(3) One who sows righteousness get a sure reward

Pro. 11:18

(4) He who sows injustice will reap calamity.

Pro. 22:8

(5) A time to plant, and a time to pluck up what is planted.

Eccl. 3:2

(6) In the morning sow your seed and at evening with hold not your hand.

Eccl. 11:6

(7) Happy are you who sow beside all waters.

Isa. 32:20

(8) Sow not among thorns.

Jer. 4:3

(9) They sow the wind and they shall reap the whirl wind.

Hos. 8:7

(10) Sow for yourselves righteousness reap the fruit of steadfast love.

Hos. 10:12

(11) He who reaps receives wages.

John.. 4:3

(12) One sows and another reaps.

John. 4:37

(13) What you sow does not come to life unless it dies.

I. Cor. 15:36

(14) (with the resurrection of the dead) What is sown is perishable, what is raised is imperishable?

II. Cor. 15:42

(15) He who sows sparingly, will also reap sparingly, and he who sows bountifully will also reap bountifully.

II. Cor.9:6

(16) Whatever a man sows, that he will also reap

Gal. 6:7

Shepherds

(1) Be not as sheep which have no shepherd

Num. 27:17

(2) The Lord is my shepherd

Ps. 23:1

(3) The good shepherd lay down his life for the sheep

John. 10:11

Potter

(1) (O.Lord, thou art our Father) We are the clay, and you are our Potter.

Isa. 64:8

(2) (God says to Israel) Behold, like the clay in the potter's hand, so are you in my hand.

Jer. 18:6

Trade or Business

(1) A false balance is an abomination to the Lord. But a just weight is his delight.

Pro. 11:1

(2) Better is a little with righteousness than great revenues with injustice.

Pro. 16:8

(3) A just balance and scales are the Lord's; all the weights in the bag are his work.

Pro. 16:11

(4) Bribe corrupts the mind.

Eccl. 7:7

Investment in Business

(1) Cast your bread upon the waters, for you will find it after many days.

Eccl. 11:1

Ornaments

Gold, silver and precious metals have played their own role in the lives of the Hebrews. They love to have them. When they came out of Egypt, out of their slavary in to freedom, they collected the gold and silver from the Egyptians[12]. At the same time greediness or over desire for the ornaments is condemned in the Bible. And also those who forget God because of their desire for ornaments, they are compared to a bridal maiden who forgets her ornaments and dresses. The Proverbs on ornaments are as follows.

The dresses and ornaments have their own role play in the life and culture of the Israelites. In the Bible, the over desire for dress and ornaments than God is condemned.

> "Like Gold ring or an ornament of gold is a wise reprover to a listening ear."

Pro. 25:12

God's Complaint on His People

> "Can a maiden forget her ornaments or a bride her attire? Yet my people have forgotten me days without number".

Jer. 2:32

Nature

According to the beliefs of the Israelites, God is the source of nature. He has created the sun, moon and stars mainly with the purpose to give light on the fourth day of the creation[13]. The Psalmist say that the sun, moon and all the objects of nature praise God. These natural objects will not be bright and blessing for a sinful man[14]. These objects are also used as the symbols of blessings on the ones loved by God. Proverbs on Nature, such as Sun, Moon, Stars, Wind, Cloud and Rain are as follows.

Sun, Moon and Stars

> "How then can man be righteous before God? How can he who is born of woman be clean?
> Behold, even the moon is not bright and the stars are not clean in his sight".
>
> *Job. 25:4-5*

Blessing is Bestowed on the Dynasty of David

> Like the moon it shall be established forever.
>
> *Ps. 89:37*

General Blessing

> "Your sun shall no more go down, nor your moon withdraw itself".
>
> *Isa. 60:20*

Reference to the Beauty of a Woman

> "Who is this that appears like the dawn, fair as the moon, bright as the sun, majestic as the stars in procession?"
>
> *Song of Solomon 6:10*

Wind, Cloud and Rain

> Like clouds and wind without rain is a man who boasts of gifts he does not give.
>
> *Pro. 25:14*

> He who observes the wind will not sow; and he who regards the clouds will not reap.
>
> *Eccl. 11:4*

Birth, Life and Death

There are but three general events which happen to mankind; birth, life and death. For the Israelites God is the source of birth, life and death.

Bhagavad Gita says :

> "For that which is born death is certain and for the dead, birth is certain".

So death is a biological necessity. The Hebrews, like all the other primitive people, did not regard death as utter non-existence; death—'being gathered to one's father's—meant joining the departed souls in the underworld (Sheol), a dreary, meaningless existence where one was cut off from 'the land of the living' and from the presence of Jehovah[15]. It is clear from a perusal of the Psalter that the distress which the approach of death caused to the genuinely religious consciousness of the men of the Old Testament resulted not from the fear of extinction; but from the expectation that all intercourse with God would be at an end. God is the source of Birth, Life and Death for the Israelites. The proverbs on birth, life and death are as follows :

Birth

> "A stillborn child is better off than he".
>
> *Eccl. 6:3*

Life

(1) Our days on earth are like a shadow we are aliens and strangers.

I.Chro. 29:15

(2) Our days on earth are a shadow.

Job. 8:9

(3) Each man's life is but a breath.

Ps. 39:5

(4) To live is christ and to die is gain.

Phil. 1:21

(5) Keep your heart with all vigilance for from it flows the springs of life.

Pro. 4:23

(6) (Wisdom says) "He who finds me (wisdom) finds life and obtains favour from the Lord".

Pro. 8:35

(7) The mouth of the righteous is a fountain of life.

Pro. 10:11

(8) The wages of the righteous leads to life.

Pro. 10:16

(9) In the path of righteousness is life.

Pro. 12:28

(10) A desire fulfilled is a tree of life.

Pro. 13:12

(11) The fear of the Lord is the fountain of life.

Pro. 14:27

(12) A tranquil mind gives life to the flesh.

Pro. 14:30

(13) A gentle tongue is a tree of life.

Pro. 15:4

(14) He who is greedy for unjust gain makes trouble for his house hold. But he who hates bribes will live.

Pro. 15:27

(15) Death and life are in the power of the tongue.

Pro. 18:21

(16) The fear of the Lord leads to life.

Pro. 19:23

(17) He who pursues righteousness and kindness will find life and honour.

Pro. 21:21

Following are the Proverbs on Death :

(1) Precious in the sight of the Lord is the death of his saints.

Ps. 116:115

(2) Man born of a woman is of few days and full of trouble. He springs up like a flower and withers away; like a fleeting shadow, he does not endure.

Job. 14:1-2

(3) My days are like an evening shadow, I wither away like grass.

Ps.102:11

(4) Man passes like a shadow.

Eccl. 6:12

(5) (our) Days are swifter than a weavers shuttle.

Job. 7:6

(6) My (our) days are swifter than a runner.

Job. 9:25

(7) Each man's life is but a breath.

Ps. 39:5

(8) You (we) are a mist that appears for a little while and then vanishes.

James. 4:14

(9) Like a water spilled on the ground which cannot be recovered, so we must die.

2. Sam.14:14

(10) No man has power over the wind to contain it. So no one has power over the day of his death.

Ecl. 8:8

(11) The wages of sin is death.

Rom. 6:23

(12) A mind of sinful man is death.

Rom. 8:6

(13) A good name is better than precious ointment and the day of death, than the day of birth.

Eccl. 7:1

(14) You are dust and to dust you shall return.

Gen. 3:19

(15) Thou (God) sweep people away they are like a dream, Like grass which is renewed in the morning; In the morning it flourishes and is renewed, In the evening it fades and withers:

Ps. 90:5,6

(16) Who long for death, but it comes not.

Job. 3:21

(17) For in death there is no remembrance of God.

Ps. 6:5

(18) Her house (loose woman's) sinks down to death.

Pro. 2:18

(19) Her (loose woman's) bed got down to death. His steps follow the path of death to Sheol.

Pro. 5:5

(20) The lips of the righteous feed many but fools die for lack of sense.

Pro. 10:21

(21) There is a way which seems right to man, But it's end is the way to death.

Pro. 14:12

(22) He who keeps the commandment keeps his life. He who despises the word will die.

Pro. 19:16

(23) The desire of the sluggard kills him, for his hands refuse to labour.

Pro. 21:25

Marriage/Women

Marriage is regarded as normal, and there is no word for 'bachelor' in the Old Testament. The record of the creation of Eve[16] indicates the unique relationship between husband and wife, and serves as a picture of the relationship between God and His people[17]. In the Book of Revelation of the Bible, Christ in figured as the bride groom and the church as the bride. The belief of the Bible is that marriage is God ordained and so marriage is holy.

Woman, with man was 'made in the image of God' male and female he created them[18]. She is considered to be man's better half, a companion [19]. In Hebrew society the family is central, and its character and maintenance is determined by marriage.

Here are the Proverbs on Marriage and Women

(1) He who finds a wife finds a good thing and obtains favour from the Lord.

Pro. 18:22

(2) A quarrel some wife is like a constant dripping.

Pro. 19:14

(3) Better to live on a corner of the roof than share a house with a quarrelsome wife.

Pro. 21:9

(4) Better to live in a desent than with a quarrelsome and ill-tempered wife.

Pro. 21:19

(5) A quarrelsome wife is like a constant dripping on a rainy day; restraining her is like restraining the wind or grasping oil with the hand.

Pro. 27:15,16

(The wife of Noble Character)

(6) A wife of noble character who can find? She is worth for more than rubies.

Pro. 31:10

(7) Charm is deceptive, and beauty is fleeting; but a woman who fears the Lord is to be praised.

Pro. 31:30

Adultery/Prostitution/Sexual Sins

In the Old Testament, adultery had a percise and limited definitions: Sexual relations between a married woman and any man other than her husband[20]. It was considered a most grievous transgression, to be punished by the death of both parties.

In the New Testament period, it appears that the definitions of adultery was extended in its scope. In the Sermon on the Mount, Jesus tells that whoever sees a woman with lust, he has already committed adultery[21]. Adultery was forbidden by various New Testament writers[22]. It was sometimes used as a symbol of the unfaithfulness of the people toward God[23].

Prostitutes in the Hebrew society were considered very mean. Priests could not marry harlots[24]. Israelites should not make their daughters harlots[25] and a priest's daughter who become a harlot should be burned[26]. The payment a prostitute received was considered like the price of a dog: neither could be used to fulfil vows[27]. Like the death of the children in battle, the turning of wives into harlots was considered a tragedy of destruction[28].

The Proverbs on Adultery and Prostitution

(1) The lips of a loose woman drip honey, and her speech is smooth than oil.

(2) But in the end she is bitter as worm wood, sharp as a two edged sword.

Pro. 5:3,4

(3) Can a man carry fire in this bosom and his clothes not be burned?

(4) Or can one walk upon hot coals and his beet not be scorched?

(5) So is he who goes into his neighbour's wife none who touches her will go unpunished.

Pro. 6:27-29

(6) He who commits adultery has no sense; he who does it destroys himself.

(7) Wounds and dishonour will he get and his disgrace will not be wiped away.

Pro. 6:32-33

(8) With much seductive speech she persuades him, with her smooth talk she compels him.

(9) All at once follows her, as an ox goes to the slaughter or as a stag is caught fest.

(10) Till an arrow pierces in to entrails; as a bird rushes into a snare. He does not know that it will cost him his life.

Pro. 7:21-23

(11) For a prostitute is a deep pit and a way ward wife is a narrow well.

(12) Like a bandit she lies in wait, and multiplies the unfaithful among men.

Pro. 23:27,28

(13) The prostitute reduces you to a loaf of bread.

Pro. 6:26

Good Government

In the early history of Israel, the early nomadic tribes were ruled by the Patriarchs. During the Exodus from Egypt rule was exercised by Moses, succeeded by Joshua, in what was a virtual theocracy, with the non-hereditary leader elected by divine call and acknowledged by the people. Till the time of Samuel, people were having an idea that God is their king, leading them victorious in the wars. But during the time of Samuel they wanted to have a king, and Samuel explained them the otherside of the kingship. When the people pestered him, he consults God and the painful words of God comes that the people of Israel did not reject Samuel, but God himself and allowed Samuel to give a king for them[29].

The Book of Proverbs list three Kings in its credits: Solomon, Hezekiah and Samuel. So naturally, it shows concure for what makes good government. The qualities needed in a king still apply to governmental heads today. Proverbs does not mention political philosophy or administrative efficiency. Justice and fairness matter most. The proverbs on good Government are as follows:

(1) Kings are pleased with competent officials but they punish those who fail them.

Pro. 14:35

(2) Inspired decisions are in the lips of a King; his mouth does not sin in judgement.

Pro. 16:10

(3) It is an abomination to Kings to do evil.
(4) The those is established by righteousness.
(5) Righteous lips are the delight of a king.

Pro. 16:12,13

(6) A wise King wins the wicked.

Pro. 20:26

(7) He who loves purity of heart, and whose speech is gracious, will have the King as his friend.

Pro. 22:11

(8) Take away the wicked from the presence of the King and his throne will be established in righteousness.

Pro. 25:5

(9) By justice a King gives stability to the land but one who exacts gifts ruins it.

Pro. 29:4

(10) If a King judges the poor with equity his throne will be established forever.

Pro. 29:14

(11) Give not strength to women your ways to those who destroy Kings.
(12) It is not for Kings, It is not for Kings to drink wine, or for rules to. desire strong drink.
(13) Lest they drink and forget what has been decreed and prevent the rights of all the afflicted.

Pro. 31:3-5

(14) A ruler who lacks understanding is a cruel oppressor.

Pro. 28:16

(15) Like a roaring lion, or a charging bear is a wicked ruler over a poor people.

Pro. 28:15

(16) If a King judges the poor with equity his throne will be established for ever.

Pro. 29:17

Relationship

God values the human relationships. In the Ten commandments, a way is given for the long life—i.e. honouring the parents[30]. We find lot of proverbs answer some of the basic questions like 'How to be a good friend?' Can good parents produce bad children? and 'How to raise children?' Family members should be allies, not adversaries says the Bible.

God values friendship more than any other form of relationship. It is said that 'the Lord would speak to Moses face to face, as a man speaks with his friend'[31]. Jesus defines the power and the model of friendship like this:

> "Greater love has no one than this, that he lay down his life for his friends"[32].
> He calls his disciples as friends. He says "You are my friends, if you do what I command"[33].

Lot of questions regarding relationships are raised—like what is more effective way in raising children: Punishment, and discipline, or verbal instructions and encouragement?

Parent-Child Relationship

(1) My son, do not despise the Lord's discipline, and do not resent his rebuke

(2) Because the Lord disciplines those he love, as a father, the son he delights in.

Pro. 3:11,12

(3) A wise son brings joy to his father, but a foolish son, grief to his mother.

Pro. 10:1

(4) He who gathers crops in summer is a wise son but, he who sleeps during harvest is a disgraceful son.

Pro. 10:5

(5) A wise son heeds his father's instructions, but a mocker does not listen to rebuke.

Pro. 13:1

(6) He who spares the rod hates his son, but he who loves him is careful to discipline him.

Pro. 13:24

(7) He who fears the Lord has a secure fortress, and for his children it will be a refuge.

Pro. 14:26

(8) Children's children are a crown to the aged, and parents are the pride of their children.

Pro. 17:6

(9) To have a fool for a son brings grief, there is no joy for the father of a fool.

Pro. 17:21

(10) Discipline your son, for in that there is hope; do not be a willing party to his death.

Pro.19:18

(11) He who robs his father and drives out his mother is a son who brings shame and disgrace.

Pro. 19:26

(12) If a man curses his father or mother, his lamp will be suffered out in pitch darkness.

Pro. 20:20

(13) Folly is bound up in the heart of a child, but the rod of discipline will drive it far from him.

Pro. 22:15

(14) Do not withhold discipline from a child; if you punish him with the rod, he will not die.

Pro. 23:13

(15) Punish him (son) with the rod and save his soul from death.

Pro. 23:14

(16) The rod of corrections imparts wisdom, but a child left to himself disgraces his mother.

Pro.29:15

(17) Discipline your son, and he will give you rest, he will give delight to your heart.

Pro. 29:17

Here are the Proverbs on Friendship

Friendship and Neighbourhood

(1) Do not with hold good from those who deserve it. When it is in your power to act.

Pro. 3:27.

(2) He who be littles his neighbour lacks sense but a man of understanding remain silent.

Pro. 11:12

(3) A righteous man is cautious in friendship.

Pro. 12:26

(4) He who covers over an offense promotes love, but who ever repeats the matter separates close friends.

Pro. 17:9

(5) A friend loves at all times, and a brother is form for adversity.

Pro. 17:17

(6) A man of many companions may come to ruin, but there is a friend who sticks closer than a brother.

Pro. 18:24

(7) Do not make friends with a hot tempered man do not associate with one easily angered.

Pro. 22:24

(8) Let your foot be seldom in your neighbour's house lest he become weary of you and hate you.

(9) A man who bears false witness against his neighbour, is like a war club, or a sword or a sharp arrow.

(10) Trust in a faithless man in time of trouble, is like a bad tooth or a foot that slips.

(11) He who sings songs to a heavy heart, is like one who takes off a garment on a cold day and like vinegar on a wound.

Pro. 25:17-20

(12) Like a mad man shooting fire brands or deadly arrows, is a man who deceives his neighbour and says I was only joking.

Pro. 26:18-19

(13) Wounds from a friend can be trusted but an enemy multiplies kisses.

Pro. 27:6

(14) Like a bird that strays from its nest is a man who strays from his home.

Pro. 27:8

(15) Perfume and incense bring joy to the heart, and the pleasantness of one's friend springs from his earnest counsel.

Pro. 27:9

(16) Better neighbour nearby than a brother far away.

Pro. 27:10

(17) If a man loudly blesses his neighbour early in the morning it will be taken as a curse.

Pro. 27:14

(18) As iron sharpens iron, so one man sharpens another.

Pro. 27:17

(19) Who ever flatters a neighbour is spreading a net for his feet.

Pro. 29:5

Liquor (on Dangers of Wine)

"Naturally in a land and climate particularly suited to the cultivation of the vine, one can find that wine was often associated with grain, and together they stand for a full and adequate supply of food and of the good gifts of life. They can be promised therefore as the tokens of the blessing of God[34].

Wine, with bread often together as main food and drink[35] in the Old Testament. But dangers of abuse recognized[36]. Priests are forbidden to drink wine during their period of service[37]. A Nazarite was forbidden to drink wine during his period of vow[38]. Even though drinking wine is accepted, becoming drunk is prohibited in the Bible.

(1) Wine is a mocker, strong drink a brawler; and whoever is led astray by it, is not wise.

Pro. 20:1

(2) He who loves wine and oil will not be rich.

Pro. 21:11

(3) Do not join those who drink too much wine or gorge themselves on meat.

(4) For drunkards and gluttons become poor, and drowsiness clothes them in rags.

Pro. 23:20,21

(5) Do not gaze at wine when it is red, when it sparkles in the cup, when it goes down smoothly....!

(6) In the end it bites like a snake and poisons like a viper.

Pro. 23:31-32

(7) It is not for Kings to drink wine, or for rulers to desire strong drink.

(8) Lest they drink and forget what the law decrees, and deprive all the oppressed of their rights.

(9) Give beer to those who are perishing, wine to those who are in anguish.

(10) Let them drink and forget their poverty and remember their misery no more.

Pro. 31:4-7

Economy (Money)

The Bible does not teach that the possession of wealth is evil in itself, but that capacity, greed and the desire to become rich are sources of spiritual danger and of social misery. "The love of money is the root of all kinds of evil" says the Bible[39]. Rich men are almost always bad men; so the prophets had discovered "The wealth of the rich is their fortified city, but poverty is the ruin of the poor"[40]. Poor people are lazy says one person, some one else claims the opposite. They are poor because the rich control the system. People tend to over simplicity, when they discuss wealth and poverty. Curiously, both sides may quote proverbs to prove their point. The Book of Proverbs says that people are poor for various reasons. Because of laziness and drunkeness, they are poor. There is also another reason—i.e. the oppression by the rich. This is also a reality. People get rich for various reasons too: because of hard work, Lord's blessings, etc. The worse part of the reason is the exploitation. The rich become richer by exploiting the poor.

Proverbs gives an even handed view of what money does for people. Wealth brings benefits, including eager friends, but it also brings worries and troubles. Proverbs strongly urges the rich and powerful to be generous and fair to poor people. It remains remarkably clear-eyed about the tangled causes of poverty and about the dangers and benefits of wealth.

Here are the proverbs on Economy/Money : Proverbs on Money:

(1) A slack hand causes poverty, but the hand of the diligent makes rich.

Pro. 10:4

(2) A rich man's wealth is his strong city, the poverty of the poor is their ruin.

Pro. 10:15

(3) The blessing of the Lord makes rich.

Pro. 10:22

(4) Riches do not profit in the day of wrath, but righteousness delivers from death.

Pro. 11:4

(5) He who trusts in his riches will wither.

Pro. 11:28

(6) Poverty and disgrace come to him who ignores instruction.

Pro. 13:18

(7) A goodman leaves an inheritance to his children's children: but the sinners wealth is laid up for the righteous.

Pro. 13:32

(8) The poor is disliked even by his neighbour but the rich has many friends.

Pro.14:20

(9) He who oppresses a poor man insults his maker but he who is kind to needy honours him.

Pro. 14:31

(10) In all toil there is profit.

Pro. 14:23

(11) Better is a little with the fear of the Lord than great treasure and trouble with it.

Pro. 15:16

(12) Wealth brings many new friends, but a poor man is deserted by his friend.

Pro. 19:4

(13) He who is kind to the poor lands to the Lord, and he will repay him for his deed.

Pro. 19:17

(14) Love not sleep, lest you will come to poverty.

Pro. 20:13

(15) The plans of the diligent lead surely to abundance but every one who is hasty comes only to want.

Pro. 21:5

(16) He who loves pleasure will be a poor man; He who loves wine and oil will not be rich.

Pro. 21:17

(17) A goodman is to be chosen rather than great riches, and favour is better than silver or gold.

Pro. 22:1

(18) The reward for humility and fear of the Lord, is riches and honour and life.

Pro. 22:4

(19) The rich rules over the poor, and the borrower is the slave of the lender.

Pro. 22:7

(20) He who has bountiful eye will be blessed, for he shares his bread with the poor.

Pro. 22:9

(21) A poor man who oppresses the poor is a beating rain that leaves no food.

Pro. 28:3

(22) He who gives to the poor will not want, but he who hides his eyes will get many curses.

Pro. 28:27

(23) A righteous man knows the rights of the poor, A wicked man does not understand such knowledge.

Pro. 29:7

(24) Treasures gained by wickedness do not profit.

Pro. 10:2

(25) He who loves money will not be satisfied with money; nor he who loves wealth, with gain.

Eccl. 5:10

(26) The love of money is the root of all evil.

I. Tim. 6:10.

Language

"A perverse man stirs up dissension, and a gossip separates close friends"[41]. What could be wrong with just talking as long as you don't actually lie? Proverbs see plenty of danger. Words are like dynamite; they can even destroy people. They should be carefully weighed before they are spoken. Even truthful words can damage. Yet they can also save a friend from going wrong. Proverbs speak strongly about both the danger of gossip and the good done when some one justly rebukes his friend.

"The tongue has the power of life and death, and those who love it will eat its fruit"[42]. Proverbs teach us the skill of speaking so as to give life.

Proverbs on language and speak are classified as the Right way to speak, the wrong way to speak, On changes of words, on importance of words:

Right Way to Speak

(1) Wise man lay up knowledge, but the babbling of a fool brings ruin near.

Pro. 10:14

(2) The lips of the righteous feed many.

Pro. 10:21

(3) The lips of the righteous knows what is acceptable, but the mouth of the wicked, what is perverse.

Pro. 10:32

(4) A gentle answer turns away wrath, but a harsh word stirs up anger.

Pro. 15:1

(5) To make an apt answer is a joy to a man.

Pro. 15:23

(6) The mind of the righteous ponders how to answer, but the mouth of wicked pours out evil things.

Pro. 15:28

(7) Righteous lips are the delight of a King, and he loves him who speaks what is right.

Pro. 16:13

(8) The mind of the wise makes his speech judicious, and adds persuasiveness to his lips.

Pro. 16:23

(9) Pleasant words are like a honey comb, sweetness to the soul and health to the body.

Pro. 16:24

(10) He who restrainds his words has knowledge.

Pro. 17:27

(11) A soft tongue will break a bone.

Pro. 25:15

(12) Better is open rebuke, than hidden love.

Pro. 27:5

Wrong way to Speak

(1) With his mouth the godless man would destroy his neighbour, but by knowledge, the righteous are delivered.

Pro. 11:6

(2) A man who be littles his neighbour lacks sense, but a man of understanding remains silent.

Pro. 11:12

(3) A gossip betrays a confidence, but a trust worthy man keeps a secret.

Pro. 11:13

(4) Reckless words pierce like a sword.

Pro. 12:18

(5) He who speaks rashly will come to ruin.

Pro. 13:3

(6) A worthless man plots evil, and his speech is like a scorching fire.

Pro.16:27

(7) A hot tempered man stirs up dissension.

Pro. 15:18

(8) A fool's lips bring him strife, and his mouth invites a beating.

Pro. 18:6

(9) A fool's mouth is his undoing, and his lips are a snare to his soul.

Pro. 18:7

(10) He who answers before listening, that is his folly and his shame.

Pro. 18:13

(11) Like a coating of glaze over earthenware are fervent lips with an evil heart.

Pro. 26:23

(12) A lying tongue hates those it hurts.

Pro. 26:28

(13) Whoever flatters his neighbour is spreading a net for his feet.

Pro. 29:5

On Changes of Words

(1) When words are many, transgression is not lacking, but he who restrains his lips is prudent.

Pro. 10:19

(2) In all toil there is profit, but mere talk tends only to want.

Pro. 14:23

On Importance of Words

(1) The mouth of the righteous is a fountain of life,

Pro. 10:11

(2) The tongue of the righteous is choice silver.

Pro. 10:20

(3) The lips of the righteous nourish many.

Pro. 10:21

(4) From the fruit of his lips a man is filled with good things, as surely as the work of his hands rewards him.

Pro. 12:14

(5) The tongue that brings healing is a tree of life.

Pro. 15:4

(6) A rebuke impresses a man of discernment more than a hundred lashes a fool.

Pro. 17:10

(7) The tongue has the power of life and death, and those who love it will eat its fruit.

Pro. 18:21

(8) A word aptly spoken is like apples of gold in settings of silver.

Pro. 25:11

God

'God is' and 'he may be known'[43]. These two affirmations form the foundation and inspiration of all religion. The first in an affirmation of faith, the second of experience. Since, the existence of God is not subject to scientific proof, it must be a postulate of faith; and since God transcends all his creation, he can be known only in his self-revelation.

God, in his being, is self-existing. He not only has life, but he is life to his universe, and has the source of that life with in himself. In his nature, God is pure spirit. In his character, God is personal. In his will, God is sovereign. He is a God of Love, Mercy, Grace, Justice and Almighty. He is a God, who is active in history [44].

He is a God of forgiveness, hates sin but loves the sinner. He blesses those who believe him, fear him and walk according to his law. He is a compassionate God, who takes the side of the oppressed and do justice by saving them from the hands of their enemies.

Here are the Proverbs on God

(1) The blessing of the Lord makes rich and he adds no sorrow with it.

Pro. 10:22

(2) The fear of the Lord prolongs life.

Pro. 10:27

(3) The Lord is a stronghold to him whose way is upright.

Pro. 10:20

(4) Better is a little with the fear of the Lord than great treasure and trouble with it.

Pro. 15:16

(5) Every word of God proves true.
(6) He is a shield to those who take refuge in him.

Pro. 30:5

(7) The fear of the Lord is the beginning of wisdom.

Pro. 1:7

Person

Man is the master piece of God's creations. The Bible says that God created man in his own image and he created them as man and woman and gave them to domain over all the creations. Man lost his status because of his sin.

The Proverbs on persons are classified under the subheadings as wise person, Foolish person and Lazy person.

Wise Person

> "He who walks with the wise grows wise, but a companion of fools suffers harm"[45].

'Proverbs judges every thought or action by one standard:" Is this wise?" The word wisdom brings up pictures of grey haired old men muttering obscure philosophic maxims. But that is almost the opposite of what Proverbs mean by the word. Wisdom is above all practical and down to earth. Wisdom teaches us how to live. It combines understanding with discipline, the kind of discipline an athelet needs in training. It also adds a healthy doings of good common sense—except that common sense is not, and never has been, common.

Proverbs on Wise Person

(1) For the Lord gives wisdom; from his mouth come knowledge and understanding.

Pro. 2:6

(2) Whoever corrects a mocker invites insult; whoever rebukes a wicked man incense abuse

Pro. 9:7

(3) A wise son makes a glad father.

Pro. 10:1

(4) A son who gathers in summer is prudent.

Pro. 10:5

(5) The memory of the righteous is a blessing.

Pro. 10:7

(6) The wise of heart will heed commandment.

Pro. 10:8

(7) Wise men lay up knowledge.

Pro. 10:4

(8) The tongue of the wise brings healing.

Pro. 12:18

(9) The wisdom of a prudent man is to discern his way.

Pro. 14:8

(10) The lips of the wise spread knowledge.

Pro. 15:7

(11) The fear of the Lord teaches a man wisdom, and humility comes before honour.

Pro. 15:33

(12) A wise man's heart guides his mouth, and his lips promote instruction.

Pro. 16.:23

(13) Pleasant words are a honey comb, sweet to the soul and healing to the bones.

Pro. 16:24

(14) A discerning man keeps wisdom in view.

Pro. 17:24

(15) The heart of the discerning acquires knowledge the ears of the wise seek it out.

Pro. 18:15

(16) A man's wisdom gives him patience.

Pro. 19:11

(17) When a wise man is instructed, he gets knowledge.

Pro. 21:11

(18) Mockers stir up a city, but wise men turn away anger.

Pro.29:8

(19) A wise man keeps himself under control.

Pro.29:11

Foolish Person

"As a dog return to its vomit, so a fool repeats his folly"[46].

Pro.26:11

Fools, in modern English, are people who lack brain. But the word has a different meaning in the Bible. Fools may have high

IQs. People may admire their reputation for success. Yet a wise person views them as a disaster.

One of the Bible's worst insults is "You Fool !" People become fools by ignoring the wisdom, God offers them. Preferring to follow the crowd or their own conceited opinions. They may think themselves very clever, but their cleverness will land them in trouble. Proverbs aim its sharpest warnings, not against acting immoraly, but against becoming a fool. It one develops such a character, no set of rules can keep him/her out of trouble. A wise person ought to learn to recognize a fool from far away, and stay out of his/her path.

Poignant Proverbs on Foolishness

(1) Fools despise wisdom and instructions.

Pro. 1:7

(2) A chattering fool comes to ruin.

Pro 10:8

(3) The way of a fool is right in his own eyes.

Pro. 12:15

(4) A fool shows his annoyance at once.

Pro. 12:16

(5) The heart of fools blurts out folly.

Pro. 12:23

(6) The folly of fools is deception.

Pro. 14:8

(7) The folly of fools yields folly.

Pro. 14:24

(8) A rebuke impresses a man of discernment more than a hundred lashes a fool.

Pro. 17:10

(9) Better to meet a bear robbed of her cubs than a fool in his folly.

Pro. 17:12

(10) A fool finds no pleasure in understanding but delights in aiming his own opinions.

Pro. 18:2

(11) A fool's lips bring him strife, and his mouth invites a beating.

Pro. 18:6

(12) It is to a man's honour to avoid strife, but every fool is quick to quarrel.

Pro. 20:3

(14) A whip for the horse, a halter for the donkey, and a rod for the backs of fools!

Pro. 26:3

(14) As a dog returns to its vomit, so a fool repeats his folly.

Pro. 26:11

(15) Though you grind a fool in a mortar, grinding him like grain with a pestle, you will not remove his folly from him.

Pro. 27:22

(16) He who trusts in his own mind is a fool.

Pro. 28:26

(17) A fool gives full vent to his anger, but a wise man quietly holds it back.

Pro. 29:11

Lazy Person

The sluggard is a very lazy person. His only exercise is turning on his bed; Proverbs say, 'he is hinged to it'. Any far fetched excuse—

'there is a lion in the street'—will keep him from going to work. Proverbs laughs at the sluggard a little, but uses him to teach serious lessons. One can be like him very easily; for it doesn't require much: 'a little sheep, a little slumber, a little folding of the hands, to rest'. Putting things of making excuses, sleeping in: who doesn't some times fall victim to these tendencies?

The result of such a life? Poverty, frustration, broken relationships. The sluggard still wants the luxuries hard work earns, but he never gets them.

Proverbs on Laziness

(1) Lazy hands make a man poor.

Pro. 10:4

(2) As vinegar to the teeth and smoke to the eyes, so is a sluggard to those who send him.

Pro. 10:26

(3) Laziness ends in slave labour.

Pro. 12:24

(4) A slothful man will not catch his prey.

Pro. 12:27

(5) The way of the sluggard is blocked with thorns.

Pro. 15:19

(6) Laziness brings on deep sleep, and the shiftless man goes hungry.

Pro. 19:15

(7) The sluggard buries his hands in the dish; he will not even bring it back to his mouth !

Pro. 19:24

(8) A sluggard does not plow in season; so at harvest time he looks but finds nothing.

Pro. 20:4

(9) The sluggard's craving will be the death of him, because his hands refuse to work.

Pro. 21:25

Conclusion

Many of the classified proverbs reflect the life and faith of the folks of a particular clime and customs. Some of the Proverbs are difficult to understand as a lot of cultural and social change has taken place. To understand, one has to delve deep into the times and language of Hebrew folks. However, it is a tout that Proverbs summarize cultural and social history of the Hebrew folks much more pithily than any voluminous history book could portray.

NOTES

1. Durga Bhagwat, "*Proverbs and Idioms"— an out line of Indian Folklore* (Bombay Popular Book Depot. 1958 p. 46
2. Richard M.Dorson, *Folklore and Folklife - An Introductions.* (Chicago. The University of Chicago Press. 1972) p. 117.
3. Maria Leach, *Standard dictionary of folklore, Mythology and Legend.* (New York: Funk and Wagnalls. 1949) p. 902
4. Op cit. p. 120
5. Alexander H. Krappe, *The Science of Folklore* (New York. W.W. Norton & Company INC 1964) p. 143.
6. G. Shanthi, '*Folklore Survey of Thanjavur District*'. (Thanjavur. Tamil University Publications. 1994) p. 211.
7. S. Sakthivel, *Nattupura Iyal Aaivu* (Chennai - Manivasagar Pathipagam. 1992) pp. 102,111,115.
8. H.H. Rowley, *The Literature of the Old Testament—Peakes Commentary* (Ed) Mathew Black (London: Thomas Nelson Printers Ltd. 1967) p. 70.
9. Charles H.Laymon (Ed), *The Interpreters one volume commentary on the Bible* (New York. Abington Press. 1971) p. 1102.
10. Raymond E. Brown, *The Jerome Biblical Commentary* (Bangalore. Theological Publications in India. 1972) p. 492.
11. Ibid. p. 494.
12. Exo. 12:35, 36.
13. Gen. 1:14-16.
14. 14 Job. 25:4-5.
15. Ps. 88:10-12.

16. Gen. 2:18-24
17. Jer. 3; Eze. 10; Hosea. 1:3
18. Gen. 1:27
19. Gen. 2:20
20. Exo. 20:14; Deut. 5:18; Lev.20:10.
21. Matt. 5:28
22. Matt. 5:32; Mark. 10:11; Luke. 16:18
23. Hos. 9:1; Matt. 12:39
24. Lev. 21:7
25. Lev. 19:29
26. Lev. 21:7
27. Deut. 23:18
28. Amos. 7:17
29. I. Sam. 8:4-22
30. Exo. 20:12
31. Exo. 33:11
32. John. 15:13
33. John. 15:14
34. J.D.Douglas, '*New Bible dictionary*' (England. Leicester. Inter versity Press. 1986) p. 1254.
35. Gen. 14:18; Jud. 19:19; Neh. 5:15.
36. Gen. 9:21; Pro.20:1; 23:30; 31:4; Isa.5:11; 28:7.
37. Lev. 10:9, Eze. 44:21
38. Jud. 6:3; Jud. 13th chapter full and Amos.2:12
39. I.Tim. 6:10
40. Pro. 10:15
41. Pro. 16:28
42. Pro.18:21.
43. J.D. Douglus, '*New Bible Dictionary*' (Leicester, England, Inter versity Press. 1986) p. 427.
44. Josh. 3:10, Hos. 1:10; I.Tim. 3:15; Heb. 9:14; 10:31.
45. Pro. 13:20

5

RIDDLES IN THE BIBLE

Introduction

Riddle is a branch of folklore, and it has an important place in folklore because of its structural pattern, easy understanding. Contrary to the common assumption that they are mere word puzzles proposed by punsters at evening parties, riddles rank with myths, tables, folktales and proverbs as one of the earliest and most widespread types of formulated thought. A good case could probably be made for their priority to all other forms of literature or even to all other oral lore, for riddies are essentially metaphors, and metaphors are the result of the primary mental processes of association, comparison, and the perception of likenesses and differences. It is a literary form involving a matching of wits: the challenger hints at a concealed meaning which the contestant is to discover.

Riddle-Definition

"A riddle is a question, direct or indirect, complete or incomplete, in traditional form where by the questioner challenges a listener to recognize and identify the accuracy, the unity, the truth in a statement that usually seems implansible, or self contradictory, but that is in its own peculiar light always true. The riddle is universal, as every folklore collector who has ever tried to collect riddles has discovered—once he has also discovered the proper local term by which his informants identify the riddle concept"[1].

Contrary to the common assumption that they are mere word puzzles proposed by punsters at evening parties, riddles rank with myths, fables, folktales and proverbs as one of the earliest and most widespread types of formulated thought. A good case could probably be made for their priority to all other forms of literature or even to all other oral lore, for riddles one essentially metaphors and metaphors are the result of the primary mental processes of association, comparison, and the perception of likenesses and differences.

"Although Aristotle several times pointed out the close relation between metaphor and the riddle, the fact and its significance seem not to have been often or sufficiently noticed by anthropologists, philologists, psychologists or students of folklore"[2].

Again Maria Leach says that folklore is the lore or learning or common sense or mother wit of the people as passed down from parent or grand parent to child or grand child, and that folk knowledge must be packaged and capsuled for easier transmission down through the generations. This is where the proverbs and especially the riddle come in.

L.W.Chappell says - "Riddles, perhaps even more than most types of traditional lore have a way of `staying put'. Their vigorous compactness of form seems to give them a peculiar hold on the popular imagination and in many cases to insure their preservation for centuries"[3].

Forms and types of Riddles

Riddles are questions that are framed with the purpose of confusing or testing the wits of those who do not know the answer. Abrahams in his paper 'Riddles' demonstrates that opposition is only the most salient form techniques by which the image gestalt presented in the riddle question is impaired and therefore is, in most cases, indecipherable. These techniques are:

— opposition—gestalt is impaired because the component parts of the presented image do not harmonize.
— incomplete detail—not enough information is given for proper gestalt to be made (i.e., for the parts to fit together).
— too much detail—the important traits are buried in the midst of inconsequential detail, thus 'scrambling', 'Gestalt'.

— false—gestalt-details are provided that lead to an ability to discern a reference and thus call for an answer, but the answer is wrong. This answer is often an embarrassing, obscene reference. This technique is most common in catch riddles.[4]

James Hastings defines riddles as :

"Riddle is a comprehensive term for a puzzling question or an ambiguous proposition which is intended to be solved by conjucture. Obscure terms are employed on purpose, in order to conceal the meaning, and there by to stimulate the intellect and imagination of the reader or listener"[5].

From one point of view, the riddle is a product of humour, from another it is the result of man's ability to perceive analogies in nature; its capacity to puzzle is due very largely to analogies which are unconsciously stored up in metaporical speech. While a genuine riddle possess the quality of obscurity—the more obscure the better —yet at the same time it must be a perfectly true description. Every term ought to be as accurate and exact as in a logical definition, but put in a form to babble and puzzle.

The power of a riddle to arrest the attention and make truth impressive is largely due to an element of incongruity which is usually present, the irreconcilable and incompatible being associated together.

Types of Riddles

The general term 'riddle' covers several different types of enigmatical questions and sayings.

Logogriph

The difficulty may be concentrated in a single word, when the puzzle lies in the double sense which the word bears. This type of riddle may be spontaneous and natural, or, with the development of the literary art, it may be worked out artificially until thelogogriph is developed. Strictly speaking, the logogriph covers a class of riddles in which the puzzle is based upon the addition, subtraction, or transposition of letters.

The ancient Hebrews, in disguising a word or name by substituting the last letter of the alphabet for the first, the next last for the second, and so for the, formed what may not in aptly be termed an anagram[6].

Enigma

This type of riddle is very closely allied to both the allegory and the parable. The Greeks would have regarded Nathan's famous parable (2.Sam. 12), and Isaiah's song of the Vineyard (Isa. 5) as riddles. The prophet Ezekiel (ch.17) works out an allegory in which the monarchs of Babylon and Egypt are described as Eagles. The prophet himself designates his allegory a riddle as well as a parable, and the art revealed in his working out of the imagery indicates that Hebrew writers were masters of the symbolical riddle. The conversation of Jesus with Nicodemus is an example of an enigmatical discourse employed for the purpose of making profound religious truth impressive (Jn.3).

Rebus

The rebus is a third type. Originally it was a riddle put in the form of a picture of things in words or syllables.

Another type of the rebus was put in the form of an object lesson.

Charade

The charade is a later development of riddle making, a product of literary activity rather than of primitive efforts at poetry or rhetoric, and thus is essentially artificial. The charade usually turns upon letters or syllables composing a word, sometimes on words composing a phrase. It has not in aptly been termed a 'syllable - riddle'.

Epigram

According to the Greek view, the epigram, in its original sense of a poetical inscription on votive offerings or grave stones, was closely related to the riddle. In many instances the resemblance would have been complete if the epigram had suggested a challenge to solution.

Arithmetical Riddle

The arithmetical riddle or numerical riddle is next to be noted. Many of these are very trivial and as based upon the form of the numeral. A serious form of arithmetical riddle was developed, especially by the Jews, through the numerical value of the letters of the alphabet. Instead of the intended word, its numerical value was produced by permutation of the letters, in course of time this developed into the Kabbalistic method of interpreting Old Testament Scripture.

One numerical riddle appears in the pages of New Testament; it is the number of the beast, 666. (Rev.13:18).

Another form of the arithmetical riddle is found in the Old Testament, and was much cultivated by the Jews of post - Biblical days. A typical example occurs in Pro. 30:15-16.

Durga Bhagawat classified riddles into seven as—

(i) The riddle story
(ii) The riddles of death.
(iii) The recreative riddle.
(iv) Riddle poetry.
(v) The questionless riddles.
(vi) The name riddle, and
(vii) The marriage riddle.

The above classifications are mainly based on the content, situation in which the riddles are put.

Shanthi classified riddle in to five classes. They are:

(i) Descriptive riddles
(ii) Question riddles.
(iiii) Rhyming riddles
(iv) Fun riddles and
(v) Riddles in which similies, comparisons are used[7].

Descriptive riddles are those in which the riddles describes the thing in a common, peculiar manner, in which clue can be found for the answer from the description itself.

In question riddles, the riddles form the question and mostly this type of riddles are within one or two lines. These riddles consists of the question words like what? who? etc.

Rhyming riddles consists of rhyming words. In this type of riddle, the riddles uses rhyming words automatically without the riddler's knowledge.

In fun riddles, things are described in funny way.

In some riddles comparison, similies etc are used to give clue to the things described.

Encyclopeadia Britanica classifies the riddles in to two types:

(i) Descriptive riddles.
(ii) Witty questions.

S.V.Subramanian divides riddles in to two based on its nature:

(i) Folk riddles.
(ii) Literary riddles.

He also divides them in to four types based as the usage:

(i) Descriptive riddles.
(ii) Witty question riddles.
(iii) Ritualistic riddles.
(iv) Recreative riddles[8].

Biblical Riddles

Riddle in the Bible is a literary form involving a matching of wits: the challenger hints at a concealed meaning which the contestant is to discover. The propounder of a riddle is sly. He has observed an amusing analogy, and he is both revealing and keeping it for himself as one who peeps at a treasure held between cupped hands. The riddle is a form of humour and akin to the figures: table, allegory, parable, simile. The numerical proverb, which has a Canaaite (Ugartic) ancestry, may be a derivative of the still more ancient riddle form[9].

But the riddle was not merely a game. It was a test of wisdom. Solomon's renown rested largely on his skill at solving riddles: "when the queen of Sheba heard of the fame of Solomon... she came to test him with hard questions (lit. riddles). And Solomon answered all her questions[10].

Another great King who shall arise "at the latter end of the indignation", is characterized as a "King of bold countenance, one who understands riddles.[11] It is the wise who deal in riddles, and skill in understanding them is wisdom[12]. Riddles were, moreover, a deposit of tradition and lore, "dark sayings from of old, ... that our fathers have told us ... the glorious deeds of the Lord".[13] And the riddle was a literary form employed for communication even by the prophets. Prophet Ezekial called his song of eagles and a cedar tree a "riddle and... an allegory"[14].

Many prophetic utterances which are not thus specifically designated riddle have the same form and probably developed from the riddle type of literary expression. Isaiah's song of the vineyard is a good example—the riddle propounded in detail in Isa. 5:1-6 solved in verse 7.

In fact, the riddle was one of the media by which God was thought to reveal himself. Of Daniel it was said: "An excellent spirit, knowledge, and understanding in interpreting dreams, explain riddles, and solve problems were found in this Daniel"[15] and so endowed, he interpreted the Egyptic revelation written on the wall. Tradition distinguished Moses as one prophet with whom God communicated directly, "mouth to mouth, clearly, and not in dark speeches".[16] That this was Moses, distinctiveness implies the normality of divine communication through 'dark speech'. There was probably more to the riddle than appears as the surface. It seems to be a heritage from the age of mythology, when men sought to get power over gods and nature by uncovering this carefully guarded secrets.

Riddle of Samson

The classic Biblical example of the riddle is Samson's in Jud.14, and the setting may be typical. At his wedding feast, as a game with takes Samson proposes his riddle.

He has already killed a lion and some days after he saw the honey comb in the corpse of the lion. He eats it. He narrates it in the form of a riddle. He puts a bet also i.e. thirty festal garments. This is the riddle :

"Out of the eater came some thing to eat
Out of the strong came something sweet".

Jud. 14:14.

His friends were not able find the answer for this riddle since it was not a common one but coined by Samson based on his experience. So they pestered the woman who was friendly to Samson and got the answer revealed. The answer is also in the form of a question.

"With in the Samson narrative the riddle alludes to the honey which Samson had found in the carcass of the lion. So exceptional was his finding of honey thus, that his guests were at a disadvantage and had to be told. It was Samson's wife who gave them the answer"[17].

"What is sweeter than honey? what is stronger than a lion?"

Jud. 14:18.

Now it is quite possible that both the riddle and what here passes for its answer are really older than the Samson narrative and themselves prompted the story of the slain lion and the swarm of bees, rather than the reverse. Actually the answer, in question form, is itself a riddle the solution of which is not hard to find: it is love which is "sweeter than honey" and "stronger than lion". It this is correct, than Samson's riddle must have had another answer, and this, too, can be found out. One may eat too much at a celebrations and overly indulge in sweet wine, and the results may be drastic, so that from the eater his food may come forth and from even the strong the sweet. This uncommon experience may have been the original solution to Samson's riddle, and both riddles may well have been old folk sayings before they were woven into the Samson narrative, sayings quite appropriate at a wedding feast.[18]

Jotham's Fable[19]

Jotham is the son of Jerub Baal, who is the son of Gideon who saved the Israel from the hands of Midianites. Abimelech wicked son of Jerub Baal wanted to usurp his father's Kingdom dared not to kill his seventy brothers on a single stone and came to power. Jotham the youngest son of Jerub Baal escaped by hidding. Mean while the people at Shechem which is a great city gathered and crowned Abimelech the King over them. Jotham climbed on a mountain and shouts at the people of Shechem the reality of the things in the form of a table - which is in the form of a riddle. He said that:

"One day the trees want out to a anoint a king for themselves. They requested the olive tree. It refused their offer and said that it cannot leave its precious oil, by which both gods and men are honoured.

Then all the trees approached the fig tree and requested it to be their King. It also turned down their request by saying that it cannot leave its fruits so good and sweet and become their King.

Then the trees approached the Vine - and the Vine answered that it cannot leave its wine, which cheers both god and men and be their King.

Finally the thornbush was approached. Then the thornbush agreed by saying - "If your really want to anoint me King over you, come and take refuge in my shade: but if not then let fire come out of the thornbush and consume the cedars of Lebanon!"[20].

The fable ends here—but the personification is Abimelech is compared to the thornbush. In Jud. 9:16-20, Jotham explains how the people in Shechem are going to suffer in the hands of Abimelech- and it happened.

Even though it doesn't sound like a riddle, Harper's Bible Dictionary says:

"The element of 'hiddenness' implied in the riddle allowed the term riddle to be used...."[21] .

Ezekiel's Riddle

Eze. 17th chapter opens like this:

> "Son of man, pose a riddle, and speak a parable to the house of Israel"[22].

A riddle—the Hebrew term so translated is also rendered 'dark speech' and 'dark saying' (Num. 12:8; Ps.78:2). This allegory is in the nature of a riddle because the correspondance between metaphor and reality is not as obvious as in the parable of the adulterous wife in Eze. 16th Chapter[23].

The whole 17th chapter of Ezekiel talks about two eagles and the twig from a cedar tree and planted in a vineyard-later got whithered. Since it is in the form of an allegory, the question is not asked. The whole thing is narrated in Eze. 17:1-10. And the answer is given in the rest of the chapter 11-24.

Since the allegorical identifications are clear to us, the 'riddle' is how God will bring about the promise in vv.22-24. The cast of characters is as follows:

The first great 'eagle' is Nebuchadnezar, King of Babylon. (Eze.17:3); 'Lebanon' is an image for Israel and, more particularly, Jerusalem (Jer. 22:6; Zech. 11:1-3; Isa. 10:34). the topmost twig (v.4) is Jehoiachin, taken into exile in 598 BC (2.Kings. 24:8-15). The 'land of traders is Babylon, and the 'seed of the land' (V.5). Zedekiah, Jehoiachin's uncle, who was named in his place (2.Kings 24:17-18). It became a 'vine' like a 'willow' (vv.5-6) in that it grew extremely quickly and luxuriantly.

The second 'great eagle (in v.7) is the Pharoah of Egypt, with whom Zedekiah had made a treaty to help lift the Babylonian attack on Jerusalem in 588 BC (Jer. 37:4-11). Finally the 'east wind' is the desert sirocco that belows during certain times of the year, withering up all in its searing heat, withering up all in its searing heat and providing a metaphor for God's anger (Exo. 10:13; 14:21; Ps. 78:26).

Vv. 22-24. The imagery returns to the fable of vv.1-10. The new twig from the top of the cedar represents a future King from the house of David (2.sam. 7:13). If the cedar is the King of Judah, then the trees are the kings of the surrounding nations. They will know that God humbles the mighty and raises up new power from nothing. The lesson is repeated in chap. 31 in which Pharaoh is humbled. Here God brings new King of Israel to glory from the lowly state of purnishment to which Judah has fallen in vv.1-21.

Isalah's Song of Vineyard: Isa 5:1-6,7

The whole riddle is in the form of a song. Isa. 5:1-6 is the song with a hidden meaning and v.7 is the answer.

"The song itself is in three parts. Vs. 1-2 are introduction which catches the attention of the audience and sets the scene; in Vs. 3-4 the Lord himself speaks and asks the audience for a verdict; in Vs.5-6 the Lord, as owner of the vineyard, announces his own decision, and finally, in Vs.7, the Prophet again speaks in his own voice and makes a specific application to Israel"[24].

This song is about a land owner who puts the vine seeds and carefully nursing it with an expectation for good grapes. Inspite of all the patient care he has lavished upon it, it has produced only worthless "Wild grapes". So the master became angry and remove its protective wall and abandon it.

Now the explanation of the hidden meaning is given in Isa.5:7.

> "The Vineyard of the Lord is the house of Israel. The men of Judah are the garden of his delight"[25].

Visions with Hidden Meaning—Riddles

The Bible records some incidents with hidden meaning revealed to his servants. The famous visions are of Joseph and Daniel.

Vision of Joseph

Joseph's father Jacob had twelve sons and Joseph is the eleventh one and he was loved by his father very much which ended in the envy by his brothers. The two dreams with a hidden meaning - i.e. both the dreams had same meaning.

The first dream is recorded in Gen. 37:5-7,8.

"Joseph had a dream, and when he told it to his brothers, they hated him all the more. He said to them, `Listen to this dream I had: we were binding sheaves of grain out in the field, when suddenly my sheaf rose and stood upright, while your sheaves gathered around mine and bowed down to it".

The hidden meaning is revealed and his brothers found it... in v.8.

"His brother said to him. Do you intend to reign over us? will you actually rule us? And they hated him all the more..."

The second dream is recorded in Gen.37:9-10.

"Then he had another dream, and he told it to his brothers. 'Listen', he said, I had another dream, and this time the sun and moon and eleven stars were bowing down to me".

The meaning is revealed V.10 and his father Jacob himself is annoyed.

"When he told his father as well as his brothers, his father rebuked him and said, what is this dream you had? will your mother and I and your brothers actually come and bow down to the ground before you? His brothers were jealous of him, but his father kept the matter in mind".

Actually, the dreams are foretold the real things that are going to happen in future which happened truly[26].

Joseph had a gift of revealing the hidden meaning of dreams. He reveals the meaning of the cupbearers dreams. (Gen. 40.8 - 22). It is recorded that the Israel's wise men will have the wisdom to solve riddles and interpret dreams[27].

Dream of the Cupbearer : (Gen.40:9-15)

The chief cupbearer and the chief baker offended their master, the King of Egypt and were imprisoned with Joseph who was put into prison on false charges. On a day's morning, both of them had long faces and the reason is their dreams and Joseph reveals them.

The cupbearer's dream in his own words:

"In my dream, I saw a vine in front of me, and on the vine were three branches. As soon as it budded, it blossomed, and its clusters ripened into grapes. Pharaoh's (King of Egypt) cup was in my hand, and I took the grapes, squeezed them in to Pharaoh's cup and put the cup in his hand".

Joseph reveals the meaning of it—

"This is what it means", Joseph said to him. "The three branches are three days. With in three days Pharaoh will lift up your head and restore you to your position, and you will put Pharaoh's cup in his hand, just as you used to do when you were his cupbearer[28].

It came true. (Gen. 40:21).

This was the dream of the chief Baker. In his own words:

"When the chief baker saw that Joseph had given a favourable interpretation, he said to Joseph, I too had a dream: on my head were three baskets of bread. In the top basket were all kinds of baked goods for Pharaoh, but the birds were eating them out of the basket on my head".

Joseph explains the hidden meaning of it:

"This is what it means", Joseph said. "The three baskets are three days. With in three days Pharaoh will lift off your head and hang you on a tree. And the birds will eat away your flesh"[29].

It came true. (Gen. 40:22).

Pharaoh's Dreams

Gen. 21st chapter records two dreams of Pharaoh the King of Egypt. The dreams were so horrible and he could not even sleep. Joseph, by the help of his God Yahweh, reveals the meaning of them.

The first dream was about seven sleek and fat cows, grazing among the reeds. After them, seven other cows, ugly and gaunt, came out the river Nile and stood beside those on the river bank. And the cows that were ugly and gaunt ate up the seven sleek, fat cows[30].

The second dream was, about seven heads of grain, healthy and good, were growing on a single stalk. After them, seven other heads of grain sprouted-thin and scorched by the East wind. The thin heads of grain swallowed up the seven healthy, full heads[31].

In the morning the King was disturbed and seeked the help of wisemen and magicians of his court and none could help him. Then he was informed about Joseph and on the request of the King he reveals the meaning of the dreams. Even though the whole episode is not put in the form of a question—the meaning is hidden, and the hidden meaning is revealed. Joseph's interpretation was like this - and the answer was—

"Then Joseph said to Pharaoh, 'the dreams of Pharaoh are one and the same. God has revealed to Pharaoh what he is about to do. The seven good cows are seven years, and the seven good heads of grain are seven years, it is one and the same dream. The seven lean, ugly cows that came up afterward are seven years, and so are the seven worthless heads of grain scorched by the east wind : They are the seven years of famine"[32].

Joseph said to Pharaoh that God had revealed the coming of the horrible famine for seven years, and the advice was to take necessary steps to meet the situation by saving the extra food grains of the bumper harvest they are going to have in the first seven years. Then the Pharaoh made Joseph as the person in charge of Egypt, and he saved the food grains in the first seven years and meets the situation of the next seven years.

Hard sayings of Jesus

Not all the sayings of Jesus were simple and plain. Sometimes he spoke with hidden meaning. This led to a hard situation and many of his followers deserted him.

> "On hearing it, many of his disciples said, 'This is a hard teaching. Who can accept it?'"
>
> *John 6:60*

In the parables of Jesus, some of the parables are stories with a lesson can be called as riddles. The meaning of the word PARABLE is 'putting things side by side'[33].

The open Bible calls Parable as the earthly story with a heavenly meaning. Jesus used Forty Parables to teach various lessons to his diciples and the public. If we want to understand them we have to know the back ground of them. Among those Forty Parables only two parables have the resemblance of the riddle. Jesus tells them a story and at the end he asks a question. When the disciples are not able to answer him he tells them the answer.

The following Parables are similar to the riddle.

(i) Parable of the sower[34].
(ii) Parable of the Good samaritan[35].

Parable of the Sower

The purpose of this parable is Jesus wants to tell the people that like the land is made ready for the sowing, our hearts too need to be made ready to receive the word of God.

A sower goes out to his field and sows the seeds. Some of the seeds fell along the path, and the birds came and ate them up. some fell on rocky places, where it did not have much soil. It sprang up quickly, because the soil was shallow. But when the sun came up, the plants were scorched and spoiled. Some fell among thorns, and the plants were chocked by the thorns. Some seeds fell on good soil, where it produced a good crop which led to a bumper harvest.

The disciples with the people did not understand the meaning of it. When they ask the meaning for it Jesus asks them: "Don't you understand this parable?[36]

Then Jesus gives answer:

The sower sows the word of God.

'when anyone hears the message about the Kingdom and does not understand it, the evil one comes and snatches away what was sown in his heart. This is the seed sown along the path.

The one who received the seed that fell on rocky places is the man who hears the word and at once receives it with joy. But since he has no root, he lasts only a short time. When trouble or persecution comes because of the word, he quickly falls away.

The one who received the seed that fall among the thorns is the man who hears the word, but the worries of this life and the deceitfulness of wealth choke it; making it unfruitful.

But the one who received the seed that fell an good soil is the man who hears the word and understands it. He produces crop, yielding heavily.

This one is different from other riddles, because it is not small as all the others are. But the story has a hidden meaning which is not easily understandable by others and Jesus himself has to unveil the answer.

The Parable of the Good Samaritan[37]

Once an expert in the law of Jesus came to Jesus and wanted to justify himself by asking a question—who is my neighbour'? In order to teach him a truth Jesus tells a story. The story ends with a question and the people around answers it.

A man has travelling down from Jerusalem to Jericho. On the way he was attacked by some robbers who robbed everything he had and left him wounded. Two people, who are the religious leaders, but they did not help him. A third person comes—he is a Samaritan, who was an outcaste for the Jews. He helps this wounded man and took him to a near by resting place and took care of him. after this story Jesus asks a question among these three who was his neighbour. The answer came—'the one who had mercy on him'[38].

Here the meaning is hidden in the story. Like the riddle, the question is asked after the story; virtually the expert in law responded correctly. He gave the correct answer and Jesus gave him a good lesson—"go and do like wise".

The parables of Jesus on the Kingdom of God too have the meaning hidden. But here they do not have a question and answer type.

Conclusion

Riddles normally act as a communication channel in the sense the words items, of culture, the signals of various images act as carriers of a message from the central nervous system of the questioner or encoder to the central nervous system of the decoder, where the decoder interprets the chosen items of the code. Riddles help to sharpen the thinking power of both the riddler and the solver of the riddle.

The riddles in the Bible so employed helps us to understand the people and their life in the distant past. To a large extent, riddles enable us to get a portrait of the social and economic life of the people of those days.

NOTES

1. William Hugh Jansen, *American Folklore* (Washington D.C. voice of American Lectures. 1974) p. 231.
2. Maria Leach, *Standard Dictionary of Folklore, Mythology and Legend.* New York Funk & Wagnalls. 1972 (p. 938).
3. B.A. Botkin(Ed), *Folksay.* (NewYork. Funk & Wagualls. 1930) p. 227
4. G. Shanthi, *Folklore Survey of Thanjavur District.* (Thanjavur Tamil University. 1994). p. 152.
5. James Hastings, *Encyclopedia of Religion and Ethics.* Vol.10. (Edinburgh. T&T. Clerk 1971) p. 765.
6. Ibid. p. 766.
7. G. Shanthi, *Folklore Survey of Thanjavur District.* (Thanjavur, Tamil University 1994) p. 152
8. S. Sakthivel, *Nattupura lyal Aayvu* (Chennai. Manivasagar Pathipagam. 1992) p. 122.
9. George Arthur Buttrick (Ed), *Interpretars Dictionary of the Bible.* Vol. IV. (New York. Abington Press. 1962) p. 79.
10. I. Kings. 10:1-5, II.Chro. 9:1-4.
11. Dan. 8:19;23.
12. Pro. 1:5-6; Ps.49:1-4.
13. Ps. 78:1-4.
14. Eze. 17:2; 20:49.
15. Dani. 5:12.
16. Num. 12:8; Jer. 23:28.
17. George Arthen Buttrick, *Interpreter's dictionary of the Bible.* Vol.IV. (New York, Abington Press 1962) p. 79.

18. Ibid. p. 79.
19. Judges. 9: 7-20.
20. Judges. 9:7-15.
21. Paul J.Achtemeier, *Harper's Bible Dictionary* (Bangalore Theological Publications in India. 1990) p. 871.
22. Eze 17:2.
23. Walter R.Roechrs, *Concordia Self-study Commentary* (Missouri. Concordia Publishing House. 1979) p. 547.
24. Barry Webb, *The Message of Isaiah.* (Leicester, England. Inter Versity Press. 1997) P.55.
25. Isa. 5:1-7.
26. Gen. 42,43 chapters.
27. Ps. 49:4; Pro.1:6.
28. Gen. 40:12,13.
29. Gen. 40:16-19.
30. Gen. 41: 1-4.
31. Gen. 41: 5-7.
32. Gen. 41:25-27.
33. J.D.Douglus, *New Bible Dictionary* (Leicestar. Inter versity Press. 1986) p. 877.
34. Matt. 13:1-23; MK. 4:1-20; LK.8:4-15.
35. Lk. 10:30-37.
36. Mk. 4:13.
37. Luke. 10:30-37.
38. Luke. 10:37.

6

FOLK BELIEFS IN THE BIBLE

Introduction

The only information we have about the earliest stages of religion comes from archeological material, which is quite scarce. Wayland D.Hard says:

> "The relentless climb of man from the primitive state to a life of increasing knowledge and culture has been marked by the retention of age-old folk beliefs".[1]

Beliefs are formed by people and preserved by their society. Religion consists of beliefs and practices. Anthroplogists have always agreed on the importance of the practices but their treatment of the beliefs has been very different at different times. Lucy Mair says:

> "In the nineteenth century, the beliefs were thought to have existed first as naive interpretations of experience, and the religion to have been built on them. Then came a phase in which practices were treated as all important, and beliefs were held to have arisen to justify practice"[2]

The purpose of this chapter is to find out the beliefs of the people of the book, i.e. the Bible. Judaism the religion of the Jews was filled with various beliefs. O' Dea defines religion as way that man has paved to have contact with the non-empirical world to the non-rational world.[3]

Mircea Eliade, a religious historian says:

> "... every manifestation of the sacred is important: every rite, every myth, every belief, or divine figure reflects the experience of the sacred and hence implies the notions of being, of meaning, and of truth".[4]

Emile Durkheim says that the religious cults and rites are based on beliefs. He says:

> "In principal, the cult is derived from the beliefs, yet it reacts upon them, the myth is frequentyly modelled after the life inorder to account for it, especially when its sense is no longer apparent".[5]

Religion forms an important element in the life of any community in the ancient Near East—as in corporate societies of other cultural groups and periods. It is not primarily a matter for the individual, but for the community as a whole, so that its practice is one of the most important features of life.

God

At the outset it is essential to realize that according to the Bible the knowledge of God is not reached by abstract speculations, as in Greek philosophy, but in the actual every day business of living, social relationships and of current historical events. God is known not by thinking out ideas about him, But by seeking and doing his will as made known to us by prophetic men and by our consciousness of right and wrong. (e.g. John. 7:17; James 1:27, I.John 4:76). No passage in the Bible expresses this truth better than Jer. 22:15, 16.

> "Did now thy father do judgement and justice? then it was well with him. He judged the cause of the poor and needy; then it was well was not this to know me? said the Lord".
>
> *—Jeremiah. 22:15,16*

The Bible presents men, with a fourfold revelation of God.

In nature	—	a God above him
In Providence	—	a God beyond him
In law	—	a God against his sin
In grace	—	a God for him and in him.[6]

In the Old Testament, we don't find any definition of God (Such as 'God is Love' or 'God is spirit are found in the New Testament'). Passages like Isa. 31:3; Num. 23:19, and Malachi 3:6, refer God as an Unchanging one.

The Bible teaches monotheism. The God of the Bible, is living and true God and Declared to be:

> "Greater than all gods" (Exo. 15:11, 18:11). "God of gods, and Lord of lords" (Deut. 10:14-17). "To be feared above all gods" (I.Chro. 16:25). "King above all gods"
>
> *(Ps. 95:3;97:9)*

In the law given to the people by God, the conditions are very clear:

- No other gods to take God's place (Deut. 5:7, Exo.20:3)
- No images were to be made of heathen gods (Exo.20:4,23, 34:17; Lev. 19:4).
- No mention was to be made of other gods (Exo. 23:13; Josh.23:7).
- These gods were to be destroyed, not worshipped (Exo. 23:27).

As the people of the law, the Israelites simply believed their God as the most supreme one, uncomparable with any other God. God is not a God of fate, a machine God, an indifferent God, a revengeful but a loving God and the pitying father to all those who trust him.[7]

The Israelites believed God as a pure spirit of infinite perfections "God is spirit" says John.4:24, Deut.4:15,16,19, Psalms.147:5 and

Isa. 40:25,26. Spirit is the highest form of being, and God is essentially and eternally "spirit". This means that he is not confined to the limitations of matter, and does not posses a human body in any way visible to the physical eye.

They believed, although God, without a body, or person, has yet personality. He is addressed as a person, and possesses all the attributes of personality such as life, intelligence with self consciousness, self, determination.

God's Moral Attributes

We can summarize all of the moral traits under two divisions, namely Holiness and Love. 'God is love' and 'God is light', and in these pregnant sentences we have a comprehensive definition of the divine character.

Holiness

God is absolutely holy. God is free from evil and hates and abhors sin[8]. He is glorious in holiness. (Exo.15:11) holiness being the most sparkling jewel in his crown. As his power makes him mighty, so his holiness makes him glorious.

Love

Holiness presents God as the moral governor of the universe. As light he dispels all darkness. 'God is Light', Love declares him to be the gracious father of all who trust and obey him. As love, he diffuse all grace "God is Love". In his care in providing for the wants; cares habits and instincts of every living thing. God's love is also evident in the bestowed upon man of that superb adoptation of the other works of his hand for their benefit. The manifold gifts of life, health comforts, friends and money, they all speak of his love [9].

Justice

Although God is absolutely holy and unfailing in his love, yet, in his dealings with rational creatures, He is perfectly just and righteous. He acts fairly and rightly with all men[10].

Divine holiness and love reveal themselves in the administration of divine justice and righteousness with the end of maintaining moral order among intelligent creatures. The justice of God is that attribute leading. Him always to do right. "Justice is to give every man his due", and divine justice is the rectitude of God's holy loving nature whereby he is prompted to the accomplishment of that which is right and equal.

Mercy

God's goodness or mercy is the result of his greatness. As a merciful God, he is full of pity, slow to punish and ready to pardon. It was because of his mercy that we come to know how he regards in pity the sinful and the suffering.

It was his mercy that prompted God the son to undertake the plan of atonement, and for God the Father to accept that plan on our behalf.

It is mercy prompting God the spirit to strive with sinners, enlightening them as to the nature and consequences of their sin.

It was mercy that inspired the promises of scripture for the relief of the sorrowing and afflicted among the saints.

Mercy is free from God-even though no one deserves it[11]. Because God is great, every virtue he possesses bears the imprint of his greatness and his mercy is eternal.[12]

Truth

A being of perfect holiness, as God is, he must possess essential truthfulness. The Bible declares him to be, 'A God of truth and without iniquity, just and right is he and he is faithful'[13].

God cannot lie nor suffer his faithful to fail (Ps.89:37). He is "plenteous in truth" (Ps. 86:15), a being upon whom we can rely without fear.

Providence

The Bible makes it clear that providence is God's wise and benevolent care of his creatures and creation. "The Lord will provide" (Gen. 22:8). God is good to all and "His tender mercies are over all his works (Ps.145:a). W.J.Townsend explains providence as:

> "That unceasing and efficient government which is carried on by the divine being through out the universe, by which the creatures are preserved, their wants supplied, and the purposes of the vast creation are accomplished. This active, all pervading providence is a prominent doctrine of scripture"[14]

The Wrath of God

The permanent attitude of the holy and just God, when confronted by sin and evil is designated his "WRATH". It is in adequate to regard this term merely as a description is `the inevitable process of cause and effect in a moral universe', or as another way of speaking of the results of sin. It is rather a personal quality, without which God would cease to be fully righteous and his love would regenerate in to sentimentality. His wrath, however, eventhough like his love it has to be described in human language, is not way ward, fitful, or spasmodic, as human anger always is. It is as permanent and as consistent, an element in his nature as is his love.

The injustice and impiety of men, for which they have no excuse, must be followed by manifestations of the divine wrath in the lives both of individuals and of nations[15].

The Old Testament contains numerous illustrations like this, such as the destruction of Sodom and Gomorrah and the downfall of Ninerah[16].

In their unredeemed state of man's rebellion against God is, infact, so persistent that they are inevitably the objects of his wrath, and "Vessels of wrath bitted to destruction"[17].

It is a fact that God reacts in anger. Isaiah, the prophet collects all sorts of inspired images by which God's wrath is expressed [18].

This wrath brings as its result death and all that goes with death. David must choose between famine, flight or pestilence. It is recorded in 2. Sam. 24, King David disobeyed the command of the Lord. God ordered him to take a census of Israel and Judah. (V.I.). But David ordered to take the counting of the able bodied fighting men. In punishment God sent a plague on Israel and 70,000 of the people from Dan to Beersheeba died. In Exo.1 also we read the wrath of God results in plague. Since the King of Egypt refused to send the Israelites out from bondage, God has sent ten plagues which ended in the plague on the first born in Egypt.

Wrath of God Brings Disease

In Numbers 12 we read about the rebellion of Aaron and Miriam (the brother and sister of Moses) against Moses[19] and they were punished by leprosy.

The Bible portrays examples of "Holy Anger" which give visible expression of God's reaction to Man's rebellion. Thus Moses rages against the Israelites for their lack of faith (Exo. 16:20), for the apostasy at Horeb (Exo. 32:19,22), the neglect of the liturgy (Lev.10:16), and for their failure to observe the stipulation against booty (Num. 31:14).

Elijah, who massacred false prophets (I Kings. 18:40) and brought fire from heaven on the delegates of the King (2. Kings. 1:10,12). Finally we have Paul's animus at Athenian idolatry (Acts. 17:16). These men of God were like Jeremiah 'filled with God's wrath in the face of idols and sin'[20].

The wrath of God is God's Holy Anger on the wicked. In God the emotions of anger and mercy strain against each other (Isa. 54:8bt; Ps.30:6). But both express God's ardent attachment to man, each in its own way.

Anthropomorphism

God is, and he may be known. These two affirmations from the foundation and inspiration of all religion. The first is an affirmation of faith, the second of experience. Since the existence of God is not subject to scientific proof, it must be a postulate of faith, and since God transcends all his creations, he can be known only in his self revelation[21].

The Bible, esp., the Old Testament makes confession of God as effective power, it understands God through his relationship to man and to the world. Only in statements about God which directly or indirectly include man and the world can this nature of God be recognized and expressed. The anthropomorphisms of the Old Testament make it possible to speak of God in connection with man, and so to conceive of the reality of God in connection with time, while it is said of the ineffective idols that 'they speak not, they see not, they hear not', that is, they cannot enter into particular events. So the anthropomorphisms are not only intend to confirm that God encounters men personally; they make it possible to understand God's existence as a historical one[22].

There is no ultimate limit for the God of the Old Testament either. He can loose the bond to his own place, and breakup the link to his own level (Ezek.1), occasionally even to his own people (Isa. 66:21; Mal. 1:11; Zeph. 2:11). Inherited ideas can be universalized; thus the reign of God extends beyond every area and every time (Ps. 103:19; 145:13). To put it another way, the Old Testament expresses with increasing strength the transcendence of God.

The people of Isreal believed Heaven, the abode of God. Heaven becomes God's realm from which the set out, speaks and intervenes in human affairs (Gen. 11:5; 21 : 17; Exo 20 : 22)

Man understood God as a personal God and understands the attributes of God with human behaviours, emotions etc.

God is Eternal-Can not Die

(i) "Are you not from of old, O Lord my God, my Holy one? You shall not die".

Habb. 1:12

(ii) "Before the mountains were brought forth, or ever you had formed the earth and the world, from everlasting to everlasting you are God".

Ps. 90:2

God Who Sees and Hears

"The Israelites groaned under the Egyptian slavery, and cried out. Out of the slavery their cry for help rose up to God. God heard their groaning, and God remembered his covenant with Abraham, Isaac and Jacob. God looked upon the Israelites and God took notice of them" and many other passages like. Neh.9:9,

Gen:21:17, II. Chro. 6:25, I. Sam.9:16, Isa.53:10.

Compassionate God

God is a God of compassion. He not only loves his people but also pity them in their weakness. Bible pictures God as a compassionate God in various places. For e.g.

> "Do not let anything devoted to destruction stick to your hand, so that the Lord may turn from his fierce anger and show you compassion".
>
> *Deut. 13:17*

> "The Lord, the God of their ancestors, sent persistently to them by his messengers, because he has compassion on his people and on his dwelling place".
>
> *II. Chro. 36:15*

> "As the father has compassion for his children so the Lord has compassion for those who fear him".
>
> *Ps. 135:13*

God Felt Sorry

Just like the human beings God felt sorry for some of the happenings in the world. The Bible records some incidents, for example

> "The Lord saw that the wickedness of humankind was great in the earth, and that every inclination of the thoughts of their hearts was only evil continually. And the Lord

was sorry that he had made human kind on earth, and it grieved him to his heart".

—*Gen. 6:5,6.*

Good of Wars

The God of Israel is 'the God of the armies of Israel' (I. Sam. 17:45) and "for more involved in the struggles of his people than Marduk and Asshur were ever thought to be (2. Chro. 20:22)"[23]. God himself is described as a 'man of war' (Exo. 15:3; Isa. 42:13) and one of his titles is 'Lord of hosts'. This title may refer to heavenly hosts (I. Kings. 22:19) or to Israelite armies (I. Sam. 17:45). It was God who led the armies of Israel into battle (Judges. 4:14) so that the earliest account of Israelites triumphs of wars was called "the Book of the Wars of the Lord", (Num. 21:14). At every stage in preparations for battle Israel's dependence upon God was acknowledged. "First enquiry was made as to whether this was propitious moment for attack (2. Sam. 5:23,24); then sacrifice had to be offered"[24].

The battle cry had a religious significance (Judges. 7:18,20) and, further, acclaimed the presence of God as symbolized in the ark of covenant (I. Sam. 4:5,6). Because of the divine presence the Israelites could join battle in confidence of victory (Judges. 3:28; I. Chro. 5:22) even if forces of nature had to be invoked to secure the victory (Josh. 10:11-14).

Alexander Moore has said:

> "Moses made a pact with a fierce god of war, Yahweh, who was to give them the Promised lard, Canaan in Palestine, and smite their enemies in return for obedience to his commandment and adherence to his cult"[25].

Because of the personal relationship and experience enjoyed by the Israelites, they believed that their God is one who fights for his people [26].

God Who Laughs At Man

The knowledge and strength of men is very limited and when he thinks himself as great, God laughs at him.

> "He who sits in the heavens laughs; the Lord has them in derision".
>
> *Ps.2:4*

> "The Lord laughs at the wicked, for he sees that their day is coming".
>
> *Ps.37:13*

God Who Takes Reverenge

To take revenge is a common nature of man and god wants man not to do it but to leave it to him. The belief of the people of Israel is that their God is a God who takes revenge on their behalf.

For example

> "Why should the nations say, "Where is their God?" Let the avenging of the out poured blood of your servants be known among the nations before your eyes".
>
> *Ps. 79:10.*

> "A jealous and avenging God is the Lord, the Lord is avenging and wrathful; the Lord takes vengeance on his adversaries and rages against his enemies".
>
> *Nahum. 1:2*

God-a-judge

The Israelites believed that God is a God of justice and he will. come back one day—the day of Judgement, and on that day as a judge he will judge the whole world both the living and the dead.

"The Lord will judge the ends of the earth".

I. Sam.2:10

"... he comes to judge the earth".

I. Chro. 16:33.

"He judges the world with righteousness; he judges the peoples with equity".

Ps. 9:8

"And the dead were judged according to their works, as recorded in the books".

Rev. 20:12

God as a Friend

God treats his people as friends. Only thing he demands is loyalty.

"Thus the Lord used to speak to Moses face to face, as one speaks to a friend".

Exo. 33:11.

Beliefs Regarding Man

'Man is heaven's master piece' says Francis Quarks. The blind poet John Milton says:

"All those his wondrous works, but chiefly man". The Bible does not provide us with a classified anthropology, but consistently teaches the paradoxical character of human nature. On the one hand, man is `but a little lower than God'; he is crowned with glory and honour and (under God) holds the dominion over the beasts and the whole world of nature"[27]:

On the other hand, man is 'like unto the beasts that perish'.
"Mortals cannot abide in their pomp; they are like the animals that perish".

Ps. 49:12.

His mortality is the outward and visible sign of the inner corruption of his nature.

The Israelites believed all the things and the life in the world are created by God as it is recorded in the Bible. The first man created was given the name Adam and women Eve. Genesis 1st and the 2nd chapters portray the creations of the first man and first woman. God shaped the dust of the Earth in to human form and breathed into the form his own 'breath of life'. The living being God created, shares characteristics with the animals. Actually the first man Adam identified all the animals by names [28].

But man is lifted above all of them by the unique gift of God's image.

"Then God said, "Let us make human-kind in our image, according to our likeness".

Gen. 1:26

The image and likeness of God are expressed in man by:

(i) His personality compared with the animals, he is self-conscious, possesses the power of abstract thought, and has a spiritual nature.
(ii) He normally has a moral resemblance of God. This may be seen in the laws which govern human relationships and human government at their best.
(iii) He possesses dominion, of a limited type, over creation.
(iv) He has characteristics which argue in favour of his hope of immortality[29].

Gen. 1:26 says, "God created man in his own image", after (his own) likeness. It is a much discussed question whether this statement refers to man's bodily form or to his spiritual nature. The Old Testament writers in general seem to have thought of God not as formless spirit as having a form which could be seen (e.g. Num. 12:8).

Therefore, there is no objection to taking the statement to refer primarily to man's bodily form[30].

Another possible belief is there.

Gen. 1:26 says:

> "Then God said, 'Let us make human kind in our image, according to our likeness, and let them have dominion over the fish of the sea, and over the birds of the air, and over the cattle, and over all the wild animals of the earth, and over every creeping things that creeps upon the earth".

The Israelites also believed that man was created by God in his own image means, that man is God's representative on earth to rule over the earth as the image of the kings are placed is the conquered country's court and venerated by the people.

The Israelites also believed that man was created first and the women was created from his rib and thus she is inferior to him. Even Paul says:

> "Wives, be subject to your husbands, as is fitting in the Lord".
>
> *Colo. 1:18.*

And also the Bible tells that Eve, the women and the wife of Adam was deceived by the serpent and so she is called a "weakling". This belief made the Israelites to look down upon the women. Paul says:

> "Indeed man was not made from woman, but woman from man. Neither was man created for the sake of woman, but woman for the sake of man".
>
> *I.Cor. 11:8-9*

So the women are forbidden to take part in the church work. Paul says to Timothy:

> "Besides that, they learn to be idle, gadding about from house to house, and they are not merely idle, but also gossips and busy bodies, saying what they should not say".
>
> *I. Tim. 5:13.*

But it is true that women are also created in the image of God. The Jerome Bible commentary explains the word "IMAGE" like this ...

> ".... the whole man, as a complete personality, had God's image, manifested especially in the resulting ability to rule over other creatures. Man as God's image his representative an earth (status represented the ancient kings in those regions of the empire where they could not be present personally)"[31].

So,

> "From creations follows an unconditional obligations imposed by the divine will. Man is clay which lives by the breath of God (Gen. 2:7). His life is not his own and be must yield it when God recalls the breath of life. Under God, however, man is supreme in the universe and many employ it to his purpose (Gen. 1:26)"[32].

Birth and Death

> "Sons are a heritage from the Lord, children a reward from him".
>
> *Ps. 127:3.*

The Israelites believed that the children are the gifts from God— that too boys. The first born is very special. In Israel's polygamic society, distinctions should be made between the first born of the father and the first born of the mother. The father's first born was considered 'the beginning of his strength' [33].

In the absence of the father, the first born son had authority over his brothers and sisters. e.g. Reuban among the sons of Jacob. (Gen. 24: 55-60). He was ranked highest after the father. The right of the first born was greatly appreciated (Gen. 25: 29-34).In cases of misconduct, it could be shifted to another son [34].

The first born inherited twice as much as every other son and the law forbids the arbitrary removal of this right from the actual first born son to the son of the most highly favoured wife [35].

But, this law does not apply to sons of concubines or handmaids[36].

Among the Kings, the right of the first born implied the succession to his father's rule [37].

But favouritism often played a dangerous role, both among kings and commoners (I. Kings. 1,2; 2. Chro. 11:22, 23; I.Chro. 26:10). In Harran, the first born daughters were given in marriage before their younger sisters.,

Ugaritic literature mentions the shifting of the birth right of the eldest daughter to the youngest one [38].

On account of the sparing of Israel's first born in the night of pass over, the male first born of the mother was considered holy to the Lord [39].

The first born of the generation of the Exodus were redeemed by the consecrations of the Levites [40].

Afterwards every first born son, when a month old, was redeemed by paying five shekels to the priests [41].

Israel is called the first born of the Lord, having a privileged position among the nations.

So the first born had lot of privileges. These privileges could normally be forfeited only by committing a serious offence. (Gen. 35:22; 49:4) or by sale. (Gen. 25:29-34). The incident here is—Jacob the younger son of Isaac is cooking a stew, and Esau the first born of Isaac comes there very tired. When he saw his brother has some food-stuff he requests for some then Jacob says:

> "Jacob said, `First sell me your birth right', Esau said, `I am about to die; of what use is a birth right to me?"
>
> *Gen. 25: 29-34.*

Death and Resurrection

Death is a biological necessity, and it is the most natural of things. The writer of the book of Hebrews says:

"It is appointed for men to die once".

Heb. 9:27

Death seems to be necessary for bodies constituted as ours are. Physical decay and ultimate dissolution are uses capable. Yet the Bible speaks of death as the result of sin. God said to Adam:

"In the day that you eat of it you will die".

Gen. 2:17

Paul tells us that.

"Sin came into the world through one man and death through sin".

Rom. 5:12

"The Hebrew term (Maweth) and the Greek term (ṭhanatos) commonly denote physical death in the sense of the observable dissolution of all living things[42].

and again that,

"the wages of sin is death".

Rom. 6:23

The Old Testament exhibits a certain development in the Israelite ideas of death. The prevailing view in the Old Testament is that death is terminal.

"Every man experiences death. Far from having the effect of turning men aside to take refuge in illusory dreams, Biblical revelation, at whatever level it is examined, beings by clearly facing the fact of death"[43].

The Meaning of Death

In ancient Israel, death, like life, was more a matter of the family than it is now, it was not so much an occasion when an external professional element, represented by priests, lawyers, doctors, nurses and hospitals, broke in upon or set aside the family.

The impression made by death depends partly on belief as to its cause and as to the future of the individual after death. The Israelite and the Jew thought of death as an act of God; more especially a death in early years, or in the prime of life, or under exceptionally distressing circumstances, was often regarded as a judgement upon sin. "Death was not the annihilation of the individual"[44].

The Experience of Death

Every man experiences death. Far from having the effect of turning men aside to take refuge an illusionary dreams, Biblical belief, at whatever level it is examined begins by clearly facing the fact of death:

Death is some thing which each man must envisage for himself since he also "will see death".

Ps. 39&49

Lk.2:26; Jn.8:51

The Influence of Death

A living man senses in death an inimical force. Spontaneously be gives it a countenance and personifies it. "Death is the melancholy shepherd who in hell pens men up".

"Like sheep they are appointed for Sheol; death shall be their shepherd; straight to the grave they descend"[45].

Ps. 49:14

After Death

The dead "are no more"

"You sweep them away; they are like a dream, like grays that is renewed in the morning; in the morning it flourishes and is renewed; in the evening it fades and withers".

Ps. 90:5,6

The first impression is one of non-existence, for what happens after death excapes the grasp of living. According to the belief of primitive peoples, long conserved in the Old Testament, death is nevertheless, not total annihilation. While the body is placed in an earthern grave, something of the dead person, a shadow, perishes in Sheol. These Hells are conceived in a very rudimentary manner: a gaping hold, a deep pit, a place of silence (Ps. 115:17), of prediction, darkness and oblivion (Ps.18:126; Job.17:13). There all the dead share the same miserable lot (Job. 3:13-19) even though there are degrees of ignoring (Eze. 32:17-32); they are given over to dust (Jot. 17:16) and vermin (Isa. 14:11). Their existence is but a sleep (Ps. 13:4, Dan. 12:2), gone is hope, knowledge of God, experience of his miracles, and praise offered to him (Ps. 6:6; Isa. 38:18). God himself forgets the dead (Ps. 88:6). And once the gates of Sheol are entered (Job. 38:17), there is no return what so ever (Job. 10:21b)[46].

The New Testament believes that there is a life after death. They called it as the "eternal life". An Easter Hymn goes on like this:

> "Death and life confronted are another in an awesome struggle, The Lord of Life died : and living, the regions"[47].

Through the resurrection of Christ he emerged victorious.

Hence forth we are dead and our life is hidden with Christ in God (Col. 3:3). This is a mysterious death which is the negative aspect of the grace of salvation. For what we there by dying to is that entire order of things by which the rule of death manifests itself on this earth.

The hope of immortality and resurrection which come to light in the Old Testament has now found a solid foundation in the mystery of Christ. The normal Christian believes that dying for Christ, is in the last analysis, a gain, since Christ is his life (Phi 1:21). His present conditions which binds him to his mortal body is oppressive to him. He would prefer to quit this life in order to go and be with the Lord (2. Cor. 5:8): he is anxious to put on the clothing of glory of the risen, in order that whatever in him is mortal might be absorbed by life (2. Cor. 5:1-4; I. Cor. 15:51-53). He desires to leave in order to be with Christ. (Phil. 1:23).

Death—an Enemy

St. Paul calls death as the last enemy to be destroyed. (I.Cor. 15:26). When God created man be created him to live not to die- and to rule the whole creation as his representative. Because of man's disobedience and sin, death came in to this world. The Biblical belief and teaching is in the Day of Judgement death will be also punished with satan—the great adversary and Hades—

St. John says in the Book of Revelations:

> "Then Death and Hades were thrown into the lake of fire. This is the second death ..."
>
> *Rev. 20:14.*

This second death is the final one. The persons who have accepted Jesus Christ as their personal seriour, will escape this second death. This belief rules even now among the Christians.

Heaven

"Heaven is the future of the earth; salvation is all the more certain because it is already there"[48].

Several words are translated 'heaven' but only important ones are the Hebrew word—Stamazim and the Greek Ouranos. The former is plural, and the later often occurs in the plural. But just as in English, these do not seem to be any great difference between 'heaven' and 'the heavens'[49].

The term is used of the physical heaven, especially in the expression 'heaven and earth'.

> "In the beginning God created the heavens and the earth".
>
> *Gen. 1:1*

The belief of the people of the Bible is expressed by the writers of the Biblical books that heaven as solid, and rather like an invested bowl - the firmament. (Gen 1:8). The sun makes his daily pilgrimage across it [50].

They also believed that there are windows through which rain might descend.

Gen. 7:11,12; Gen.8:2

So the first usage of this word heaven represents the sky - i.e., the firmament.

For the heavens, as far as, the sky is a part of the universe, different form the earth, though in contact with earth. It is for them a global semisphere covering the earth, with the two together making up the universe. For lack of a specific term, this is called "heaven and earth".

Heaven—the Dwelling of God

God is "the God of Heaven" (Jonah. 1: 9) believed the Israelites. Heaven is the dwelling which God first stretched out like a tent, and above the waters he raised the beams of His palace [51].

Then he came forth riding on the clouds. (Ps. 68:5,34; Deut. 33:26), and raising his voice over the great waters in the tumult of the storm (Ps. 29:3). In heaven he has his throne and there the convokes his court, "the army of heaven", that carries out his order even to the ends of the earth. (I.Kings. 22:19; Is. 6:1,8; Job. 1:6-12). They also believed that God is looking down from heaven watches over the world from heaven.

Heaven is the present abode of God and his angels, and the ultimate destination of His saints on earth.

Among many ancient people, there was a belief of a multiplicity of heavens. It has been suggested that the New Testament bears witness to the rabbinic idea of seven heavens, for there are references to paradise.

> "Jesus answered him, I tell you the truth, today you will be with me in paradise".

LK. 23:43.

- and to the third heaven -

St. Paul says:

> "I know a man in Christ, who fourteen years ago was caught up to the third heaven ..."
>
> *2. Cov. 12:2.*

Jesus is also said to have passed through the heavens. (Heb. 4:14). These, however, are slender bases on which to erect such a structure. All the New Testament language is perfectly capable of being understood along the lines of heaven as the place of perfection[52].

The Israelites believed and also desired to go in to heaven. This was expressed in a dream. From the ladder Jacob saw at Bethel, 'setup on the earth with its top reaching to heaven'. (Gen. 28:12)., to the prophetic oracles, like this one of Isaiah, God's distance and proximity are joined:

> "the heavens are my throne ... what kinds of house could you build for me ?...."
>
> *(Isa.66:16, 57:15)*

Heaven—Future House of the Saints

Heaven is also pictured as the future house of the saints. The book of Revelation, the last book of the Bible gives a picture of it. The first heaven and first earth had passed away and a new heaven and new earth are created by God and it is called as New Jerusalem.

"The foundations of the city walls were decorated with every kind of precious stone. The first foundation was jasper, the second sapphire, the third chalcedony, the fourth emerald, the fifth sardony, the sixth cornelian, the seventh chrysolite, the eighth beryl, the nineth top any, the tenth chrysoprase, the eleventh jacinth and the twelth amethyst. The twelve gates were twelve pearls, each gate made of a single pearl. The great street of the city was of pure gold, like transparent glass".

Rev. 21:15-21

This proves the vivid imagery and the belief of the Hebrews. In the new Jerusalem, no temple was there, because the Lord God Almighty and Lamb (Jesus Christ) are its temple. The city needs no sun or moon to shine on it, for the glory of God gives it light, and the lamb is its lamp, (Rev. 21:22,23). It was also believed that a register or a record book is maintained in heaven for the saints called book of life.

Rev. 20:12

"... rejoice that your names are written in heaven" .

Lk. 10:20

In the 4th chapter of the book of Revelation we find a vivid description about the "court of the Lord". God sitting on the throne, angels and some images representing the creatures namely animals, birds, human beings praising God both day and night.

Hell

The Hebrews (like other ancient people) did not think of death as total extinction, a notion which is nowhere found in the Bible. Almost throughout the Old Testament period it was held that the dead continue to exist in the under world, a region of shadows, misery and futility, they lived on as unreal, half—material shades in a land of silence and forgetting[53].

(i) The Hebrew word Sheol - is translated "hell" only in King James version of the Bible; actually means death or the grave. The Greek word is 'Hades'.

(ii) The grave in the Old Testament sense is as in Matt. 11:23. (Jesus tells about the conditions of the town called Capernaum) "Will you be exalted to heaven? No, you will be brought down to Hades". (Matt. 11:23).

(iii) It is the place where the dead await final judgement, as in Luke. 16: 23-28. (Greek word. Gehenna)

(iv) It is also the place of final punishment, as in Matt. 5:22; Mark. 9:43.

The Old Testament talks of a resurrection for the righteous and the wicked (Dan. 12:1-3), but does not deal with the question of what happens to the individual after death. While the New Testament does speak of eternal destiny, only Gehenna shares today's popular meaning of "Hell".

Jesus himself associates 'Gehenna' with fire that burns eternally, and he stated that fiery punishment has been prepared "for the devil and his angels" (Matt. 25:41). Revelation gives us the clearest picture of the eternal destiny of the lost. Describing Satan's doom, Rev.20:10 says:

"The devil who deceived them was thrown in to the lake of burning sulfur, where the beast and the false prophet had been thrown. They will be tormented day and night for ever and ever".

This passage goes on to describe a final judgement. Anyone whose name was not found in Christ's book of life "was thrown in to the lake of fire".

Rev. 20:15

The Hebrews believed that the world is flat and at both corners there are mountains which hold the firmament or the sky like pillors. Above the firmament is the Heaven, the abode of God. The firmament has some windows which will he opened during the rainy seasons. Under the earth there is a place called Sheol, where in all the dead will be accommodated. Another name was "the pit" (Heb. bor) a natural synonym:

> "But you are brought down to the grave, to the depths of the pit".

Isa. 14:15.

The Hebrews believed all the dead are gathered in Sheol—the dead may not return to earth, but the living must eventually go to them.

King David talks about his dead son:

> "... while the child was still alive, I fasted and wept. I thought, `who knows'? `the Lord may be gracious to me

and let the child live'. But now that he is dead, why should I fast? can I bring him back again? I will go to him, but he will not return to me".

II. Sam. 12:22,23

In ancient Israel, the neither world, Sheol is 'the meeting place of all the living' (Job. 30:23). Like many other peoples Israel imagins the after life of the dead as a shadow of existence, without value and with out joy. 'Sheol' is the frame which assembles these shadows 54. It is pictured as a tomb, 'a hole', 'a pit', 'a ditch', (Ps. 30:10; Eze. 28:8), in the deepest regions of the earth (Deut. 32:22), beyond the sub terranean abyss (Job. 26:5; 38: 16b), where a deep obscurity regions (Ps. 88:7,13). It is there that all the living 'descend' (Isa. 38:18; Eze. 31:14). From there, they shall never rise (Ps. 88:10; Job. 7:9). It is total destitution (Ps. 88:6)[55].

The Hell—Place for Sinners

This scandal is one of the provinces of revelation. The tragic aspect of death shows the disorder of the world, and one of the axes of the Israelite religious thought is the discovery that this disorder is the fruit of sin. As this consciousness is affirmed, the features of hell take on a more and more sinister aspect. It opens its jaws to swallow up Korah, Dathan and Abiram (Num. 16:32f); it puts in motion all its power to devour the glory of Zion and its noisy crowd, its cries, its joy (Isa. 5:14); it makes godless men disappear in terror (Ps. 79:19).

Of this terrifying end, Israel knew two esp, expressive images; the burning of Sodom and Gomorrah (Gen. 19:23, Amos. 4:11; Ps. 11:6), and the devastation of the site of Topheth, in the valley of Gehenna, the place of pleasure which is destined to become a place of terror where

"They will see the corpses of those who rebelled against me, where the worms will not die nor the fire be quenched".

Isa. 66:24

This hell promised to sinners could not be the lot of the just, especially when these latter, for remaining faithful of God, had to suffer persecution from sinners and at times death. It is logical that the godless awake to 'the eternal horror' of the 'country of dust', the traditional Sheol, where the intermingled gathering of the body and the godless sleep, while their victims awake' to eternal life' (Dan. 2:12). And while the Lord gives to the just their reward. "He arms creation for punishing his enemies".

The gospels take up this images; "In the abode of the dead", where he is "tortured with flames", the rich man perceives Lazarus in Abraham's bosom: but between them is dug a great abyss "that is unbridgeable". (Lk. 16:23-26). The common belief of the Israelites was fire and abyss, the wrath of heaven and the opening of the earth, the curse of God and the hostility of creation: this is HELL.

Angels and Demons

Every religion believes in some kind of spirit. Judaism also believed in the power of spirits. We can divide them into two categories.

(a) Angels—alias good spirits
(b) Demons—alias evil spirits

Throughout the history of religions, both ancient and modern, primitive and sophisticated, varying kinds and degrees of beliefs have existed in various spiritual beings, powers and principles that mediate between the realm of the sacred or holy. Such spiritual beings, when regarded as benevelant are usually called angels in western religions; those viewed as malevolent are termed demons[56].

> "Both angels and demons are called spirits. The spirit of man is a principle of animal and psychic functions, and its use becomes nearly synonymous with soul"[57].

We may sũm up by saying that the spirit is the divine power immanent in human history, but chiefly in Israel's. It is immanent only because it is essentially transcendent, coming forth out of the supernatural life of a God who dwells directly with men.

The work of the spirit was understood and believed under the following five different aspects in the Old Testament:

(a) The work of the spirit in crations. (Gen. 2:7, Job. 26:13).
(b) The work of the spirit in equiping for service (Exo. 31:3; Jud. 3:10, 14:6).
(c) The work of the spirit in inspiring the prophets. (Amos. 7:14; Hosea. 9:7).
(d) The work of the Holy spirit in producing moral living.
(e) The work of the spirit in fore telling the Messiah. (Isa. 11:2-9).

The New Testament is full of references to the spirit. He is mentioned in every book except 2nd and 3rd John. The Holy spirit's active part is listed with the life of Jesus even from his birth. The Holy spirit is called counsellor and comforter. (Jn. 14:26). The Christians of the early church believed that by the inspiration of the Holy spirit, they can even do miracles. They also believed that the Holy spirit gives them life. (John. 6:63; Rom. 8:11; 2. Cor. 3:6). Even today, the present christian community believes the act of the Holy spirit.

Spirits Good and Evil

Belief in supernatural beings, alive in the woods, in numerous stones and so on is a legacy from primitive religion. The early Hebrew view gives its God control over these spirits. (Jud. 9:23; I.Sam. 16:14; I.Kings. 22:21)[58]

Angels—Good Spirits

The good spirits are normally called angels. This word Angel is used in the Bible to translate Hebrew and Greek words meaning "Messenger", but usually in English it denotes a super human being. In popular Hebrew thought there was a belief that there existed a rich background of supernatural beings attendent on God; they ascend and descend the heavenly ladder (Gen. 28:2) and are distinct from God (Gen. 32:1). These supernatural beings are called sons of God (Job. 1:6; Ps. 89:6; Dan. 3:25), Gods (Ps.8:5) Hosts of Heaven (I. Kings. 22:19), God's Ministers (Ps. 103:21). Later Jewish thought regarded angels as intermediaries between god and man. (Eze. 40:3; Zech.2); they bring God's help (Dan. 3:28; Ps. 91:11; Acts. 8:26; Heb. 1:14); and God's revelation (Mt. 1:20; Acts. 10:3).

Names are also given to individual angels and are arranged in an hierarchy:

(a) Gabriel (Dan.8:16)—a messenger of God.

> "... and I heard a human voice by the Ulai, calling. 'Gabriel, help this man understand the vision'.
>
> *Dan. 8:16*

(b) Michael (Rev. 12:7) - the leader of the army of God.

> "And a war broke out in heaven; Michael and his angels fought against the dragon".
>
> *Rev. 12:7*

It was also believed that God takes the side of the Israelites and often his angels fight the battle on behalf of the people of God. e.g. In Egypt during the deliverance of the Israelites, out of bondage, etc. and at the end the host of heaven under the leadership of Michael fight with the evil forces of Satan and defeat him completely.

"The functions of angels were various. They acted as Jehova's court (Job. 1:2) and as his council (Ps. 89:7); they might be intercessors for men (Job. 5:1), or guardians of the righteous (Ps. 34:7), whom they bear up in their hands (Ps. 91:11f, Num. 20:16); they are the guides and channels of Divine revelation to prophets (Zech. 1:9, 11-14, 19 etc., Dan. 8:16 ff); they inflict punishment on the wicked (Ps. 78:49); some of them guard the nations (Dan. 10:20, 21); and in general they do whatever Yahweh wishes to have done"[59].

An intimate bond links the earthly world with the celestial world, above the angels celebrate a perpetual liturgy, to which is united here below the liturgy of the church. Supernatural presences surround us; the seer of the Apocalypse concretizes these presences in the conventional language sanctified by usage. This demands on our part a reverance, (James. 5:13ff; Dan . 10:9) which is not to be confused with adoration.

Evil Spirits

Every religion in the world believe the existence of the evil powers and demons, and Israelite religion is no exemption. Here the evil power is personified as a single person called Satan and his associates. The Hebrew belief in demons belongs especially to the time after the Exile. There were several causes which led to this belief. James Hastings says:

> "In pre-exilic times, it had been thought that Jahweh did everything, both good and bad. Amos says: 'shall evil befall a city and Jahweh hath not done it ?' (Amos. 3:6). This evil might be accomplished through the agency of non-ethical spirits as in I. Kings. 22:19-23, but Jahweh was in reality responsible for it"[60].

George Arthur Battrick defines Demons like this:

> "A demon may be defined broadly as an anonymous god— i.e., as a personification of one or another of those vaguer, less identifiable powers and influences that were believed to operate alongside the major deities and to condition particular circumstances and experiences"[61].

We find Satan as the chief of the demons in the Bible. Where is he coming from? What is his origin? The Satan is not an animal or monster but one of God's angels, a being of superior intelligence and status; apparently the Israelites saw their intimate enemies not as beasts and monsters but as super human beings whose superior qualities and insider status could make them more dangerous than the alien enemy.

In Biblical sources the Hebrew term Satan describes an adversarial role. It is not the name of the particular character. Although Hebrew story tellers as early as the 6th century B.C, occasionally introduced a supernatural character whom they called the Satan what they meant was any one of the angels sent by God for the specific purpose of blocking or obstructing human activity. The root satan means "One who opposes, obstructs, or acts as adversary". The Greek term Diabolos, latter translated 'devil' literally means one who throws something across one's path.[62]

The Hebrew people believed that the angels were created by God for the purpose of serving and there by glorifying god. In. Rev. 4. we find them praising God, and in Hebrews 1:14; they are called 'ministering spirits' for the purpose of carrying out his bidding. Something happened in the middle and there was a rebellion in heaven and the leader of the angelic rebellion is Satan, also known as Lucifer (Isa. 14:12)[63].

The Israelites were called the people of the book i.e. The Torah, believed the existence of Satan and the evil spirits. The following Bible verses establish this:

> "Give no regard to mediums and familiar spirits; do not seek after them, to be defiled by them".
>
> *Lev. 19:31*

> "and the person who turns after mediums and familiar spirits, to prostitute himself with them, I (God) will set my face against that person and cut him off from his people".
>
> *Lev. 20:6*

Satan—His Origin and Activities

Satan is a fallen angel, a creation of God. He was of the highest order anointed to cover God's throne. He was full of wisdom until iniquity revealed itself in him. (Eze. 28:15).

God did not create Satan as an evil being; he became one when by his own free will be forfeited his position and state. He tried to make himself equal with God, even to usurp God's position (Isa. 14:12-14). Pride and selfish ambition were the reasons he was put out of heaven. In his rebellion he was accompanied by millions of lesser angels who serve as his messengers. He is known by the following names in the Bible:

(a) The adversary *(I. Pet. 5:8,9).*
(b) The god of this world *(2. Cor.4:4)*
(c) The prince of the power of the air *(Eph. 2:1-3).*
(d) Accuser of the brethren. *(Rev. 12:10, Job. 1:6-12)*
(e) The enemy *(Matt. 13:39)*
(f) The tempter *(Matt. 4:3)*
(g) A roaring Lion *(I.Pet. 5:8-10)*
(h) The father of lies *(John. 8:44)*
(i) A deceiver *(Rev. 12:9)*
(j) A Murderer *(John. 8:44)*
(k) Lucifer *(Isa. 14:12)*
(l) Ruler of demons *(Matt. 12:24)*
(m) Destroyer *(I. Cor. 10:10)*
(n) Angel of light *(2. Cor. 11:14)*
(o) Serpent of the old *(Rev. 20:2)*
(p) Great Dragon *(Rev. 12:9)*
(q) Devil *(Rev. 12:9)*
(r) Wicked one *(Matt. 13:19)*

The above names in the Bible reveal something of his nature and his mission[64].

Evil Spirits Mentioned in the Bible

The following evil spirits demons or devils are mentioned in the Bible. Each one is a personality, and the expression or the words used reveals their nature:

(1) Spirit of infirmity *(Lk. 13:11)*
(2) Mute spirit *(Mk. 9:25)*
(3) Dumb spirit *(Mk. 9:25)*
(4) Distrussing spirit *(I. Sam. 16:14)*
(5) Foul spirit *(Rev. 18:2)*
(6) Unclean spirit *(Matt. 10:1)*
(7) Spirit of divination *(Acts. 16:16)*
(8) Spirit of bondage *(Rom. 8:15)*
(9) Spirit of error *(I. Jn. 4:6)*
(10) Spirit of the world *(I. Cor. 2:12)*
(11) Deceiving spirits *(I. Tim. 4:1)*
(12) Jealous spirit *(Num. 5:14)*
(13) Lying spirit *(2. Chro. 18:21)*
(14) Familiar spirit *(Deut. 18:11)*
(15) Spirit of the Antichrist *(I.Jn. 4:3)*
(16) Spirit of Fear *(2. Tim. 1:7)*
(17) Perverse spirit *(Isa. 19:14)*
(18) Sorrowful spirit *(I. Sam. 1:15)*
(19) Spirit of deep sleep *(Isa. 29:10)*
(20) Spirit of harlotry *(Hosea. 4:12)*
(21) Different spirit *(2. Cor. 11:4)*[65].

The non-Israelite deities were called demons, passages like Acts. 17:18; I. Cor. 10:20; Rev. 9:20 prove this. Generally, the practices like magic and sorcery were considered demoniac and forbidden by the spiritual leaders of Israel.

Beliefs Regarding Defilement

Unclean (defiled) is a conspicuous word in the Bible. It occurs more than 100 times in the book of Leviticus 11th to 15th chapters. Almost equally noteworthy is the rare occurrence of the word "sin" (evil, wickedness). This indicates that here the emphasis is on the ceremonial rather than ethical. Yet it does not follow that uncleanness is a matter of minor importance.

Failure to do what God has commanded is considered sin, whether the act be ceremonial or moral. Unclean is the antithesis of holy. Everything which is inconsistent with God's holiness may be described as uncleanness.

The following are unclean in themselves, and association with them conveys uncleanness.

— Sexual intercourse (Gen. 34:5) especially adultery or with in the prohibited degrees. *(Lev. 18);*
— Child birth (Lev. 12; the period is twice as long for a girl as for a boy);
— Sexual or other issues from the body *(Lev. 15);*
— Certain animals. *(Lev. 11; Deut. 14);*
— Leprosy *(Lev. 13f);*
— Dead bodies *(Num. 19).*

Causes of the Belief of Uncleanness

Following reasons are given by some scholars regarding the belief of uncleanness.

Raymond Brown says:

> "The physical health of the Israelites may have been specially in mind. The explanation that the clean animal is that which chews the cud (Deut. 14:6) certainly suggests the possibility of hygenic reasons for the various prohibitions"[66].

Roland J. Faley says:

> "Basically, the distinction between the clean and unclean was related to cult, for it was in terms of service to Yahweh, either in active worship or simply in being his covenated people; that integrity was demanded"[67].

Peakes commentary of the Bible says:

> "The Hebrews acted on the theory that God is concerned with every aspect of life and with the whole of it and this led them to bring all these primitive laws, based on early natural religion, with in their religious systems..."[68].

Lev. 11th chapter and Deut. 14th chapter give a long list of unclean animals and birds. They are considered to be defiled or unclean and forbidden to be eaten.

The Defiled Animals

"Whatever parts the hoof and is cloven footed and chews the cud, among the animals, you may eat. Nevertheless among those that chew the cud or part the hoof, you shall not eat these:

— The Camal, because it chews the cud but does not part of hoof is unclean.
— And the rock budger because it chews the cud but does not part of hoof is unclean.
— And the hare, because it chews the cud, but does not part the hoof is unclean.
— And the swine, because it parts the hoof and is cloven footed but does not chew the cud is unclean.
— Of their flesh shall not be eaten, and their carcasses you shall not touch, there are unclean"

Lev. 11:3-8

"Of all the animals that walk on all fours, those that walk on their paws are unclean..."

Lev. 11:27

"Of the animals that move about on the ground, these are unclean for you: the weasel, the rat, any kind of great lizard the gecko, the monitor lizard, the wall lizard, the skink and chameleon. Of all these that move along the ground, these are unclean for you".

Lev. 11: 29-30

Eating the feresh of a dead animal is also considered to be unclean. The cleaning process is,

> "when one of them dies and falls on something, that article, whatever it's use, will be unclean whether it is made of wood, cloth, hide or sackcloth. Put it in to water; it will be unclean till evening, and then it will be clean. If one of them falls in to a clay pot, everything in it will be unclean, and you must break the pot".
>
> *Lev. 11:32,33.*

The Defiled Birds

Out of the birds of the sky, the Israelites were forbidden to eat the following birds. They are recorded in Lev.14:11-20.

They are:

> The eagle; the vulture; Osprey; the buzzard, the kite and their kinds; every raven after its kind; the Ostrich, the night-hawk the sea-gull; the hawk, after their kinds; the little owl and the great-owl the water hen and the pelican, the carrion vulture and the cormorant, the stork the heron, after their kinds, the hoopoe and the bat and all the winged insects.

The Unclean Beings of the Water

There are some creatures in the water were also considered unclean.

> "Of all that are in the waters you may eat these: whatever has fins and scales you may eat. And whatever does not have fins and scales you shall not eat, it is unclean for you"
>
> *Lev. 11:9-10*

The Dead—Unclelan and Forbidden to Eat

The dead ones were believed to be unclean and the command that the Israelites were not allowed to eat anything may formed already dead (Deut. 14:21) was probably determined by the earlier regulation about not eating blood (Deut. 12:23). For that reason such food might be passed on to those who were not bound by the rules of the covenant:

"You may give it to an alien living in any of you known:

The prohibition about eating unslaughtered animals may also lead further support to the idea that God was specially concerned here for his people's health"[69].

Uncleanness Due to Child Birth

The Israelites believed that a women becomes defiled due to her child birth and for purification, certain ritual requirements are given in the Bible. Leviticus 12th chapter gives the laws regarding it.

If a woman conceives, and bears a male child, then she shall be unclean for seven days; as at the time of her menstruations; she shall be unclean. And on the eighth day, the flesh of his fore skin shall be circumcised. Then she shall continue for thirty-three days in the blood of her purifying; she shall not touch any hallowed thing, nor come into the sanctuary, until the days of her purifying, she shall not touch any hallowed thing, nor come into the sanctuary, until the days of her purifying are completed. But if she bears a female child, then she shall be unclean for two weeks, as in her menstruation; and she shall continue in the blood of her purifying for sixty six days.

Cleaning Rituals

And when the days of her purifying are completed, whether for a son or for a daughter, she shall bring to the Priest at the door of the tent of meeting a lamb, an year old for a burnt offering, and a young pigeon or a turtle dove for a sin offering, and he shall offer it before the Lord, and make atonement for her; then she shall be clean from the flow of her blood. This is the law for her who bears a child either male or female[70].

Cleanness is indispensable for being sanctified: no one may enter the sactuary or touch sacred objects when they are unclean (So in Deut. 12:15 clean/ unclean mean ready/unready for religions duties; Lev.22). This is especially true of the priest (Exo. 30:19), who may also be disqualified if he is branded as abnormal by a physical defect (Lev. 21:17ff; so also the sacrificial animal. Lev. 22:20ff)[71].

Many forms of uncleanness may be removed by WASHING. (e.g. Lev. 22:6f), but an offering is necessary:

(a) for a woman after child birth. (Lev. 12:7f).
(b) after contact with the dead (Num. 19)[72].
(c) and for a cleanned leper (Lev. 14).

Uncleanness Due to Leprosy

In the Old Testament, leprosy is dealt with solely from the stand point of the uncleanness which it contains. It is most frequently called "the plague" or "the plague of leprosy"[73]. The man who has it or is suspected of having it, is unclean, so unclean that he must be shut up (mentioned 8 times), apparently outside the camp[74] while his case is being decided. They if the verdict is unfavourable, he must be removed from the camp until he is healed[75].

According to the Jewish Law, The Torah, leprosy is contageous impurity whose victim is excluded from the community until he has been healed and ritually purified, for which a sin offering is required (Lev. 13-14). Leprosy is "the plague" par excellence with which God strikes sinners.

"Israel is threatened with it. (Deut. 28: 27,35); the Egyptians are afflicted with it (Exo. 9:9ff); as are Miriam (Num. 12:10-15) and Uzziah (2. Chro. 26:19-23). In principle, therefore, it is a sign of sin"[76].

The possibility of recovery is thus plainly included in the decree of banishment. But it is to be noted that while elaborate rules are laid down for the recognition of leprosy and for distinquishing true leprosy from other diseases with which it might easily be confused, nothing is said about the treatment of the disease. This has led some to the conclusion that it was incurable, and even that it was not an ordinary disease, but a visitation of God. The case of Miriam (Num. 12:10-15), Gehazi (2Kin. 5:27) and Uzziah (2. Chro. 26:19-23) are appealed to as proof of this:

"Medically considered, the symptoms described in Lev. 13, 14th chapters are not those of the disease known today as leprosy, more accurately called 'Hansen's disease', a malody now amenable to treatment. Leprosy in the Bible, as in Num. 12:10-15; 2. Kings. 5; Luke. 5:12-14; and imparts of Lev. 13,14 was some thing much worse"[77].

Leprosy in the Bible speaks of sin as:

— becoming overt in loath some ways; and
— as incurable by human means.

The antitype as applied to the people of God is 'sin', demanding self-judgement (I. Cor. 11:31); and 'sins', demanding confession and cleansing (I.Jn. 1:9).

Beliefs Regarding Magic and Sorcery

Magic is born of the emotional tension of specific situation. The primitive man experienced and witnessed countless events and made his own opinion about them. This opinion or belief was responsible for the growth of primitive human beliefs about spirits, that they were capable of doing harm or good to human beings[78].

Magic and sorcery attempt to influence people and events by supernatural or occult means. The magician tries to compel a god, demon or spirit to work for him; or he follows a pattern of occult practices to bend psychic forces to his will.

John L. McKenzie says:

> "Magic is the art which claims or is believed to produce effects by the assistance of supernatural beings or by a

> mastery of secret forces in nature. It is characteristic of magic that it is occult; its powers are concealed from all but the few who are enabled to employ them. It is infallible, recognizing no higher power. It is disproportionate; the means which it employs are not adapted to the end which is desired and there can be no question of the natural operation of there means"[79].

Magic is as old as mankind Paul Radin says:

> "In the beginning, there was magic and magic was with God and God was magic"[80].

Emile Durkheim says:

> Magic, too is made up of beliefs and rites like religion, it has its myths and its dogmas; only they are more elementary, undoubtedly because, seeking technical and utilitarian ends, it does not waste its time in pure speculation. It has its ceremonies, sacrifices, prayers, chants and dances as well. The beings which the magician invokes and the forces which he throws in play are not merely of the same nature as the forces and beings to which religion addresses itself; very frequently, they are identically the same"[81].

The Bible always condemned magic and sorcery. The three great Mosaic codes of law forbid magic under pain of death (Lev. 19; Deut 18; Exo. 23). Similarly, practices connected with magic are also forbidden (Deut. 22:5,11; Lev. 19:19), the death penalty for witchcraft is explicit in Exo. 22:17. That these prohibitions were not idle is evident not only from the background sketched above, but also from numerous allusions to the practice of magic in Israel (2. Kings. 21:6; 23,24, abolitions of magic by Josiah; 2. Kings. 9:22, sorceries of Jezebel; 2. Kings. 17:17; 2. Chro. 33:6; Isa 3:3; 57:3; Jere. 27:9; Eze. 13:8f; Mich. 5:11; Mal. 3:5). The nature of these practices is not indicated except in Eze. 13:8f, and the allusion here is obscure; it seems to refer to the use of bands and knots, which are extremely common in magical rites.

Moses and Aaron surpassed the feats of the magicians of Egypt (Exo. 7:10-13; 19-23; 8:1-7; 17f; 9:8-12). Nahum. 3;4 calls Assyria a witch. The magic of Babylon is alluded to in Isa. 47:12. there allusions to foreign magic are always contemptuous; magic is in effectual.

Conclusion

There cannot be any religion without beliefs sometimes seem to be silly. But, since we respect the person who believes some thing as sacred or related to God—we also respect the beliefs. So the beliefs of the Israelites are folk in character since the Israelite community is a tribal folk community.

NOTES

1. Tristram, Coffin (Ed), *American Folk Lore* (Washington voice of America Forum Lectures. 1974). p. 243.
2. Lucy, Mair, *An Introduction to Social Arthopology* (New Delhi, Oxford University Press. 1987.) p. 211.
3. Thomas, F. O'Dea, *The Sociology of Religion* (Englewood Cliffs, N.J. Prentice Hall. 1966) p. 2
4. Mircea, Eliade, '*A History of Religious Ideas*' (London, Collins, St. James's place. 1979) p. 13.
5. Emcile, Durkheim, '*The Elementary Forms of the Religious Life*' (London George Allen & Unwin Ltd., 1976) p. 101.
6. Herbert, Lockyer, '*All the Doctrines of the Bible*' (Midnigan: Zondervan Publishing House, Grand Rapids, 1992) p. 13.
7. Ibid. p. 25.
8. Lev. 19:2.
9. James 1:17
10. Deut 32:4
11. Rom. 3:24
12. Ps. 86:5; Ps. 100:5
13. Deut. 32:4; Heb.10:23
14. W.J.Toconsend, *A Handbook of Christian Doctrine* (London Burroughs, 1986). p.87.
15. Rom. 1:18-20

16. Deut. 29:23; Nahum. 1:2-8
17. J.D.Douglas (Ed), '*The New Bible Dictionary*' (Norwich, Interversity Press. Fletcher & Son Ltd. 1976) p.1341.
18. Isa 30:27-33.
19. Num.12:1-10.
20. Jer 6:11: Jer.15:17
21. J.D. Douglas (Gen.Ed), *New Bible Dictionary. II Edition* (England IV Press, Leicester. 1986) p.427.
22. Werner H. Schmidt, *The Faith of the Old Testament*. (Oxford Basil Blackwell. 1986) p.282.
23. Op cit. p. 1241.
24. Ibid p. 1241
25. Alexander Moore, *Cultural Anthropology*. (NewYork Harper & Row Publishers 1978) p.279.
26. Exo. 14:14; Deut. 1:30, Deut. 20:4, Isa. 31:4, Jer.21:5
27. Psalms. 8: 4-8.
28. Gen. 2:19
29. T.C. Hammond, "*In understanding be men*", (London Inter-versity Fellowship- 1965) p. 74.
30. Alan, Richardson (Ed.), *A Theological Word Book of the Bible* (London: Scm Press Ltd. 1988) p. 110.
31. Ragarone, E. Brown (Ed), *The Jerome Biblical Commentary* (Bangalore; Theological Publications in India. 1972) p. 11
32. John. L. Mc Kenzie S.J, *Dictionary of the Bible* (Bangalore: Asian Trading Corporation 1984) p. 538.
33. Deut. 21:17
34. I.Chro. 5:1
35. Dent. 21:15-17
36. Gen. 21: 9,10
37. 2. Chro. 21:1-3
38. J.D.Douglas, *The New Bible Dictionary* (Norwich Inter-versity Press,1976) p. 423.
39. Exo. 13:1,2
40. Num 3:40, 41
41. Num. 18:16
42. Alan, Richardson (Ed), *A Theological word Book of the Bible*. (London SCM Press Ltd. 1988) p. 60.
43. Xavier Leon-Dufour, *Dictionary of Biblical Theology*. (Bangalore Theological Publications in India. 1973) p. 114.
44. James, Hastings, *Encyclopaedia of Religion and Ethics*. Vol. IV" (Edinburgh. T&T. Clark., 1967) p. 497.
45. Ibid. p. 115
46. Ibid. p. 114
47. 2. Cor. 5:14, 15

48. Werner H. Schmidt, *the Faith of the Old Testament*. (Oxford Basil Blackwell Ltd., 1983) p. 266.
49. J.D. Douglus, *The New Bible Dictionary* (Norwich Interversity Press. 1976) p. 510.
50. Ps. 19:4-6
51. Ps. 104: 2,3
52. J.D. Douglas, *The New Bible Dictionary* (Norwich. Inter versity Press. 1976) p. 510.
53. Alan, Richardson, *A Theological Word Book of the Bible*. (London: SCM Press Ltd. 1982) p. 106.
54. Xavier L'eon Dufoue, *Dictionary of Biblical Thought*. (Bangalore Theological Publications of India. 1973) p. 233.
55. Ibid. p. 233.
56. *Encyclopaetia Britanica* - Vol.I. p. 871.
57. John L. McKenzie S.J. *Dictionary of the Bible* (Bangalore: Asian Trading Corpoation 1984) p. 842.
58. Alan, Richardson, *A Theological Word Book of the Bible*. (London SCM Press Ltd. 1982) p. 234
59. James Hastings: *Encyclopedia of Religion and Ethics*. Vol IV. (Edinburgh. T & T. Clark - 1967) p. 597.
60. Ibid. p. 597.
61. George, Arthur Buttrick (Ed), *The Interpreter's Dictionary of the Bible—Vol.II*. (New York Abington Press. 1976) p. 817.
62. Eliaine Pagels, *The Origin of Satan*. (New York. Vintage Books, Random House Publications. 1996) p. 39
63. John, Mac Arthur (Jr), *God, Satan and Angels* (Bombay Gls Press. 1983) p. 70
64. Billy, Graham, *The Christian Worker's Hand Book*. (Minneapolis. USA. World wide Publications. 1965) p. 210.
65. H.A. Maxwell Whyte, *Demons deliverance* [Springdale (USA) Whitakan House. 1989] p. 55.
66. Raymond, Brown, *The Message of Deuteronomy* (London. Inter versity Press. 1993) p. 160
67. *The Jerome Biblical Commentary* (Bangalore Tehnological Publications in India. 1972) p. 74
68. *Peake's Commentary on the Bible* (London Nelson. 1967) p. 246.
69. Raymond Brown, *The message of Denteronomey* (London. Interversity Press. 1993) p. 161
70. Levities. 12th Chapter. Alan Richardson. *A Theological word Book of the Bible* (London. SCM. Press Ltd. 1988) p. 272
71. Levities. 12th Chapter. Alan Richardson, *A Theological word Book of the Bible* (London. SCM. Press Ltd. 1988) p. 272
72. (It is noted to be that kind David's conduct over his son, II. Sam. 12:15ff, strikes at the root of the old idea of the unclearness of death).
73. Lev. 13:2.

74. Deut. 14:3
75. Deut. 13:45f.
76. Xavier L'eon-Dufour, *Dictionary of Biblical Theology.* (Bangalore Theological Publications in India. 1973) p. 308.
77. C.I. Scofield (Ed), *The New Scfield Reference Bible* (London Oxford University Press. 1967) p. 141
78. Frazer, J.G., *Golden Bough* (London-Macmillan & Co. 1911) p. 146.
79. John, L. Mckenzie S.J., *Dictionary of the Bible* (Bangalore Asian Trading Corporation. 1984) p. 534.
80. Paul Radin, *Primitive Religion.* (New York Dover Publications. Inc. 1957) p. 60
81. Emile, Durkheim, *The Elementary forms of the Religions Life* (London George Allen & Unwin Ltd. 1976) p. 42.

7

FOLK GODS IN THE BIBLE

Introduction

Religion is inherent in man. It is one of the forms of social consciousness, a reflection of reality in illusionary, fantastic images conceptions and concepts. Engels was to write that essentially,

> "...all religion ... is nothing but the fantastic reflection in men's minds of those external forces which control their daily life, a reflection in which the terrestrial forces assume the form of supernatural forces"[1].

Karl Marx has said, "Religion is the sign of the oppressed creative, the sentiment of a heartless world and the soul of soulless conditions. It is the opium of the people".[2]

For our study, it is important to know the meaning of Religion and God. The Pedagogy of religion needs a detailed study. Religion cannot be defined except by the characteristics which are found wherever religion itself is found.

One idea which generally passes as characteristic of all that is religious are that of the supernatural. By this, it is understood all sorts of things which surpass the limits of our knowledge; the supernatural in the world of the mysterious of the unknowable of the ununderstandable. Thus religion would be a sort of speculation upon all that which evades science or distinct thought in general.

"Religions diametrically opposed in their overt dogmas", said Spencer, "are perfectly at one in the tacit conviction that the existence of the world, with all it contains and all which surrounds it, is a mystery calling for an explanation," he thus makes them consist essentially is "the belief in the omnipresence of something which is inscrutable". In the same manner, Max Muller sees in religion a struggle to conceive in conceivable, to utter in unutterable, a longing after the infinite.[3]

So religion is the determination of human life, by the sentiment of a bond uniting the human mind to the mysterious mind, whose domination of the world and itself it recognizes and to whom it delights in feeling itself united.

Meaning of God

"Is there a God?" is the question, that lot of scientists and philosophers raise. How can this be proved? What is the origin of this concept of God? The Dictionary for Believers and Non-believers defines God as follows :

> "God an illusory being endowed with supernatural qualities, who is the main object of worship in almost all religions. All advanced religions attribute to God the qualities of a perfect person who created the world and rules it in accordance with his own wishes"[4].

Man was born with fear. The early man started to worship all objects, natural forces, animals, reptiles etc. which were stronger than him. This thing started with nature worship, later became worshipping human beings—slowly changed into formulating God. But none has said that this is how God came. The customs and beliefs play an important role among all individuals. It is the belief, invariably found associated with the specific feeling, in spirits outside of man, to whom are ascribed powers greater than his and who are depicted as in control of everything on which man lays most stress. This, we call as the religious feeling. The specific quality of the religious feeling is thus conditioned by that background. It is the emotional correlate of the struggle for existence in an insecure physical and social environment.

"This struggle for existence must not be interpreted too narrowly. It had, particularly in the early phases of man's history, a spiritual side was concerned with the battle of that reflective consciousness which is the especial earmark of the human as opposed to the animal mind, with the physical make up he has in common with his animal ancestors. This mentality has expressed itself most clearly in what might be called the social precipitates of fear"[5].

Another idea by which the attempt to define religion is often made, is that of divinity.

> "Religion", says M. Reville, "is the determination of human life by the sentiment of a bond writing the human mind to that mysterious mind whose dominations of the world and itself it recognizes, and to whom it delights in feeling itself united"[6].

Thus we arrive at the following definition. A religion is a unified system of beliefs and practices relative to sacred things, that is to say, things set apart and forbidden-beliefs and practices which unite into one single moral community called a church / temple / mosque, all those who adhere to them.

The Understanding of God in the Ancient Neighbouring Countries of the Jews

The neighbours had a great influence on the Hebrews in socio-politico and religious fields. Without a basic knowledge of the neighbours of Israel, it is quite impossible to understand the Hebrews.

Polytheistic Religion of Ancient Egypt

Many Gods and Goddesses were worshipped in ancient Egypt. Most of their deities were cosmic deities. Thus not only did they worship sky, sun, moon and the river. Nile but also considered mountains, trees, arians and creatures to be the abodes of Gods. Egyptian religion was never a unitary whole. "There were always local gods up and down the land, among whom were Ptah, artifier—god of Memphis; Thoth god of learning and the moon at Hermopolis;

Amin 'the hidden', god of Thebes, who over shadowed the war god Mentu there and became state god of 2nd millennium Egypt; Hathor, goddess of joy at Dendera; and many more. Then there were the cosmic gods; first and foremost Re or Atum the sun-god, whose daughter Ma et personified Truth, Justice, Right and the cosmic order; then Nut the sky goddess and Shu, Geb and Nu, the gods of air earth and primordial waters respectively"[7].

Egyptian Worship

Egyptian worship was a complete contrast to Hebrew worship in particular, and to semitic in general. The temple was isolated with in its own high walled estate. Only the officiating priesthood worshipped in such temples; and it was only when the god went forth in glittering procession on great festivals that the populace actively shared in honouring the great gods. Apart from this, they sought their solace in house hold and lesser gods. The cult of the great gods followed one general pattern, the god being treated just like an earthly king. He was awakened from sleep each morning with a hymn, was washed and dressed (i.e. his image), and break fasted (morning offering), did a morning's business, and had midday and evening meals (corresponding offerings) before retiring for the night.

Funerary Beliefs of the Egyptians

The Egyptians elaborate beliefs about the after life found expression in the concerete, material terms of a more glorious, other worldly Egypt ruled by the deity Osiris. "The body was a material attachment for the soul; mummification was simply an artificial means of preserving the body to this end, when towards early became to elaborate for the sun's rays to desicate the body naturally, as it did in prehistory's shallow graves. Objects in tombs left for the use of the dead usually attracted robbers. Egyptian concern over death was murbid; this cheerful, pragmatic, materialistic people simply sought to take the good things of this world with them, using magical means so to do. The tomb was the desecrated eternal physical dwelling[8].

The Idol Worshippers of Babylonia

From the 3rd millennium BC onwards lists of the names of deities with their titles, epithets and temples were compiled. Although in the final library version at Nineveh in the 7th century B.C. these numbered more than 2500, many can be identified as earlier Sumerian deities assimilated by the semites after the time of the 1st Dynasty of Babylon (c.1800. B.C.), so that the actual number of deities worshipped in anyone period was considerably less.

The Gods of Babylonia

The chief gods were Anu, the heaven god, with his principal temple E, anna at Uruk. He was the Semiti 'El, and his wife Innana, or Inani, was Caltu confused with Ishtar.

Many gods and goddesses were worshipped in the Babylonian religion. In the 9th century B.C., the number of gods had increased to 65,000. The inhabitants of Babylonia borrowed their gods from Sumeria and gave them Semitic names. Babbar, Nannar, Inani and Enlil of Sumeria became 'Shams, sin, Ishtar and Bal' respectively in Babylonia[9].

Goddess Ishtar was the carnation of Beauty and Love and was attributed the noble sentiments of motherhood. She was the goddess of both love and war. When Babylonian Empire was founded, its chief deity "Marduk" gained tremendous importance. He was considered to be the God of Empire. Other gods continued to be worshipped.

Worship and Festivals

There were many classes to temple servants, with the king or ruler as the supreme pontiff at certain solemn festivals. In early sumerian times the whole economy was centred on the temple, (just like the Hebrews had around the temple during the time of Jesus[10]), where the chief official was 'the Lord of the manor'. In the worship of sin, the high-priestess was usually a royal princess.

In man's approach to the god many specialists might play a role. The exorcist could remove the evil spirit or spell with the incantations or ritual prescribed in the texts, involving symbolic substitutions, purification by priests or by those who cleansed by water. There are many documents describing the action to be taken against evil spirits, demons of fate, demons plaguing women or taboos. The regular service included giving the gods something to eat and drink. Statues were dressed and ornamented and votive figures of worshippers set near by. Sacrifices played on altars were subsequently allocated, wholly or in part, to the priests. The gods had their own chairs chariots and boats for use in processions[11].

Most cities and temples had their own distinctive festivals and sacred days. At Babylon, Erech and Ur, as at Assur, Ninoveh and Calah, the New Year festical was the most outstanding, held in the spring, but not exclusively, and with varying practices at different centres and periods. Royal festivals included the coronation of the king, celebration of victories and the inaugurations of a city or temple. Personal festivals include celebration of birth, marriage and the installations of girls as priestesses.

Polytheistic Religion of Ancient Greece

Many gods and goddesses were worshipped by the ancient Greeks. Cosmic powers were worshipped. Zeus was the god of sky. He was the chief deity of Greeks. Zeus' son Ares was the God of war. Apollo was the god of light and Posedien of the sea. Hephaestus was the god of fire and Hades of the underworld. Greeks viewed life after death with great pessimism. They believed that dead souls were sent to live in Hades or the underworld in complete darkness.

Greek was never a political entity. But the supremacy of the Greek Philosophy had a strong impact on the Jews-especially of the New Testament Jews. The Greeks provided not only education but brilliant entertainment and a wider range of health and welfare services than most modern communities. It was membership in such a Republic and use of the Greek language that marked a man as civilized (Acts. 21:37-39). Such a person might be called a Greek, whatever his race (Mk.7:26); all others were 'barbarians' (Rom. 1:14).

The term 'Hellenists" in Acts. 6:1; 9:29 presumably shows that this distinction applied even with in the Jewish enthnic community.

The Assyrian Religion

Assyria was one of the great empires in the past. It was situated in the upper Mesopotomian plain, bounded on the west by the Syrian desert, on the South by the Jebel Hamrin and Babylonia, and as the North and East by the Urartian (Armenian) and persian hills.

> "Assyrian religion was that of Babylonia, with the exception of its national god Assur, who gave his name to the city and the people, Assur was primarily a warrior and a conqueror, whose symbol was an archer with in a winged desk"[12].

All the victories of wars were ascribed to Ashur, and some scholars have explained Assyrian militarism as religiously motivated. The Assyrian King acted as regent on earth for the national god Ashur, to whom he reported his activities regularly.

Legends say in 3500 B.C. some Sumerians migrated to Assyria and the name of their god was "Ashr" or "Assur", which is the sun god. "Assur was considered to be martial and fierce when Assyrians were victorious in any war, they offered sacrifice of the war—captives to Assur"[13].

Assyrians believed in ghosts and spirits. Their view was that all physical and mental ills were caused by ghosts and evil spirits. Magical chants; magical rites and to terms prevailed toward off the evil efforts. Several prayers, rites and rituals were observed by the Assyrians to propitiate their gods. The gods were harsh but could forgive if an individual accepted his faults and did penance. Great importance was accorded to good and bad omens.

Religion of the Canaanites

Canaan is the important country which influenced the Israelites both religiously and culturally the most. The Israelites believed that Canaan was the country promised by God to them.

Only on this promise the people who were in bondage in Egypt left out on exodus under the leadership of Moses, later conquered the land of Canaan under the leadership of Joshua.

The Canaanites had an extensive pantheon, headed by E1, More prominent in practice were Baal ('Lord'), i.e. Hadad the storm god, and Dagon, with temples in Ugarit and elsewhere. The goddesses Asherah, Astarte (Ashtaroth) and Anath—like Baal - had multi-columned personalities and violent characters; they were goddesses of sex and war, Kothar-and-Hasis was artificer god, and other and lesser deities abounded [14].

The title of the high priest is attested for Canaanite religion at Ugarit - (the inscriptions found by the archaeologists), that the texts of the Ugaritic texts were cult prostitutes is very possible, which was forbidden to Israel[15]. Human sacrifice in 2nd millennium Canaanite religion has not yet been isolated archaeologically with any certainity, but there are indications that it was customary. Canaanite religion appealed to the bestial and material in human nature is clearly evidenced by the Ugaritic texts and in Egyptian texts of semitic origin in inspiration.

With this background of the neighbours we can see about the religion and the concept of God, of the Hebrews.

Folk Gods

In the beginning, man was afraid of nature. By worshipping nature, he thought he can escape the wrath of it. Arnold Toynbee says:

> "If we set out to make a survey of the religious that have been practised at different times and places by the numerous human societies and communities of whom we have some knowledge, our first impression will be one of a bewilderingly infinite variety. Yet, on considerations and analysis, this apparent variety resolves itself into variations on man's worship or quest of no more than three objects or objectives; namely nature: Man himself; and an absolute

reality that it is not either nature or man but is in them and at the same time beyond them"[16].

Basically fear is the root cause of the envergence of religion. This concept is supported by Sigmund Freud[17]. Following this Animism, Totemism, Fetishism, Ancestor worship came into existence.

Characteristics of Folk Gods

(1) Folk gods were formed by human emotions.
(2) There were sacrifices of the living things.
(3) People had no set rules for the festivals and rituals.
(4) Non-Vegetarian food was offered.
(5) They were created and maintained by people.
(6) They had stories and myths of their own.
(7) Belonged to the little traditions.

Sakthivel divides the folk gods into five categories. They are:

(1) Masculine Deities.
(2) Feminine Deities.
(3) Cult Deities.
(4) Caste Deities, and
(5) Village Deities.[18]

People believed that the folk gods are responsible for destruction and creations. They are responsible for all natural things. They guard the rivers and ponds and save people from epidemics and also save the cattle from destructions. A particular god was in charge of each and every aspect of nature.

With this background, we can see how the religion of Israel recorded in the Old Testament show its characteristics of a folk religion and folk gods.

Important Non-Isralite Gods Mentioned in the Bible

Asherah (2. Chro. 24:18)

Asherah is a Canaanite goddess of fertility and originally the consort of El, but in Biblical times of Baal. Known also in the Bible as Ashtoreth and by the plural-form Ashtoroth[19]. Asherah is linked with other fertility goddesses of the ancient near East such as the Sumerian Inanna, the Mesopotamian Ishtar, the Babylonian Ashratum, Phoenician, Ashirat, and the Greek Astarte[20].

The name Asherah is used also of an image made for that goddess (I.Kings. 15:13) which consequently came to represent her. The Isralites were commanded to cut down (Ex. 34:13) or burn (Deut. 12:13) the Asherim of the Canaanites, and like wise forbidden themselves to plan "an Asherah of any kind of tree" beside God's altar (Deut.16:21). From these references it appears that the object was of wood, and was presumably an image of some kind.

Ashtoroth, Ashtoreth : (I. Kings. 11:5)

It is a mother goddess with aspects as goddess of fertility, love and war, known to the Israelites through the canaanites (I.King. 11:5). The name was common in one form or another, among many of the Semitic-speaking peoples of antiquity. The Israelites turned to the worship of Ashtoreth soon after arriving in the land (Jud. 2:13, 10:6); it was rife in the time of Samuel (I.Sam. 7:3-4; 12:10) and was given royal sanction by Solomon (I. King. 11:5; 2 Kings. 23:13). After Saul had been killed by the Philistines, his armour was placed in the temple of Ashtoroth at Beth-shan (I. Sam. 31:10).

Baal : (Jud. 2:13)

The Baal cults affected and challenged the worship of Yahweh through out Israelite history.

Baal in Canaanite Mythology

Literature recovered from Ras Shamra, dating to the 1400s B.C., contains a number of mythical stories about Canaanite gods, known as the Baal cycle. These stories seems to suggest the gradual replacement of El by Baal as chief god of the Canaanites. The myths portray Baal as god of the sky and rain, struggling with Mot, who represents drought, Baal also is in conflict with Yamm, in a struggle between fertility and sterility. The annual pattern of early and later rains in Palestine, alternating with hot, dry summers, was explained in terms of the victories of one god over the other. As god of rain and fertility, Baal was of primary importance in agricultural Palestine.

In the myths Baal is also portrayed as blood thirsty and highly sexed. The erotic element in Baal worship was intended to stimulate the good to mate with his consult (who in biblical times was called Asherah or Astarte), and so bring rain and fertility to the land. The Bible identifies ritual prostitutions as one depraved element in Baal worship (Jud. 2:17; Amos. 2:7,8).

Baal and Israel

The greatest challenge of Baal to the worship of Yahweh came in the Ninth century B.C., when Ahab and Jezebal actively promoted a virulent form of Baal worship imported from Phoenicia (I.Kings. 16-2 Kings. 10). In this period Elijah was God's primary proponent. The struggle culminated in a great contest with 450 prophets of Baal on Mount Carmel. Elijah's resounding victory stimulated a popular uprising against Baalism, caused the death of Baal's prophets, and laid the ground work for Jehu's subsequent extermination of Baal worship in Israel.

Despite the victory over Phoenician Baalism, traditional Canaanite worship of Baal persisted in Israel. Centuries after the Hebrew people had entered Canaan, as the Babylonian armies were advancing on Judah, one could find, on the very streets of Jerusalem and on the roofs of their houses, altars where incense was burned to honour Baal. (Jer. 11:13; 32:29)[21].

Molech, Moloch : (Zeph. 1:5)

The Old Testament often speaks of the fact that Israelites at times of apostasy made their children 'go through the fire to Moloch'. (2 Kings. 23:10; Jer.7:31; 19:5). The deity is associated with Ammon in I. Kings. 11:7, where reference is made to 'the abomination of the Ammonites'. The worship of Molech seems to have been associated with the sacrifice of children in the fire (Lev. 18:21; 20:2-5; 2.Kings. 23:10; Jere. 32:35; 2.Kings. 17:31).

Moloch is known as the national god of Ammon in I. Kings. 11:7. He may be identified with the deity Muluk worshipped at Mari about 1800 B.C., and Malik, known from Akkadian texts, and appearing in the compound forms Adrammelech and Anammelech in 2 Kings. 7:31.

The practice of offering children as human sacrifices was condemned in ancient Israel. The law of Moses demanded the death of anyone who offered his child to Molech or as a sacrifice (Lev. 18:21; 20:2-5). Solomon, however, built a high place for this god in 'the hill that is before Jerusalem., i.e. the Mount of Olives (I. Kings. 11:7). Several references in the Old Testament to child sacrifice, while not referred specially to Molech, may be included here (Ps. 106:38; Jer. 7:31; 19:4-5; Eze. 16:21; 23:37;39). King Ahaz (c.739 BC) burnt his children in the fire (2.Chr. 28:3) and Manasseh did the same (2. Ki. 21:6).

Samaria was judged for this sin (2.Ki. 17:17). Josiah, in Judah, destroyed in high places of Molech (2. Kings. 23:10,13)[22].

Succoth-Benoth : (2.Kings. 17:30)

Succoth-Benoth is the name of an object made by Babylonians exiled in Samaria c.722. B.C. and named among the pagan deities worshipped there (2. Kings. 17:30). 'The both of daughters has been explained either as places of prostitution or as shrines in which were carried images of female deities.

Folk Gods in the Old Testament

A common man needs God as a source of courage and help during his trials and tribulations. The Bible says that God is our refuge and strength, a very present help in trouble[23]. At the outset it is essential to realize that according to the Bible, the knowledge of God is not perceived by abstract speculations as in Greek philosophy, but in the actual everyday business of living of social relationships and of current historical events. Alan Richardson says:

> "God is known not by thinking out ideas about him, but by seeking and doing His will as made known to us by prophetic men and by our own consciousness of right and wrong"[24].

The Bible reveals God as a monotheistic being. The Biblical community in the beginning was a folk community. The Israelite community was made up of twelve tribes. We read different accounts in the Bible. Sometimes it seems to give contradictory statements. The following may be the reason for this.

The Bible was not written in a single sitting and by a single author and in a stipulated time. It covers a period of nearly 3000 years, by various authors. Some of the early writings of the Bible were collected from the Oral tradition.

Animism in the Old Testament

The early anthropologists believed that primitive man thought all things were in some sense alive—this they called animatism.

> "If man eventually came to believe in souls (as they thought he did on the basis of dreams in which some thing in one seems to leave the body), then he believed that the life in a thing is a kind of spirit of that thing"[25].

Seeing the power of nature, man started to have fear over it. The power of fire, thunder, lightening, rain etc., made man to believe that nature has life. So in order to get favour from it, he started worshipping nature. In the Bible we see this kind of worship.

Tree

Gensis 12:6 talks about '*the great tree of Morah*'. The Hebrew word for this it "Elon Morah". Elon means 'terebinth'. Normally this word Elon refer the worshipping places in the Old Testament[26]. People used to gather under these kinds of trees to hear the word of God. We read that God appeared to Abraham under this tree. These trees are called "Great Trees of Mamre", and Abraham built an altar to the Lord under the tree.

Exo. 3:2-5 talks about the burning bush in which God appeared to Moses. It tells two important things to us:

(1) Fire represents the presence of God.
(2) Tree (bush) an abode of God.

Deuteronomy 33:16 says, " ..... and the favour of him (God) who dwelt in the burning bush". But in the later days, the practice of the tree worship was condemned by the prophets of Israel [27].

Rivers, Streams and Brooks

The early Babylonians believed that there was life in water. In the stone engravings of Hammurabi, a god of river is mentioned by the name called NARU[28]. In India too, we have gods related to rivers. e.g. Ganga Devi, Kaviri Amman most of the worshipping places are situated on the banks of rivers. The same kind of setting, we find in the Old Testament.

In Genesis 14:7, a place called Kadesh is called "En Mishpat", which means "a brook of Justice".

Joshua. 15:7 and 18:17 talks about the 'waters of En Shemesh' which means 'the brook of Sun', which shows that this brook had connection with the sun worship. The running rivers are called sacred (Deuteronomy 21:4; Judges. 5:21; I.Kings. 18:40). The tribes of Manasseh, Ruban and Gad built altars on the banks of river

Jordan. (Josh. 22:10). There was a belief that the river Jodan has the power of curing e.g. Naaman's leprosy was cured by taking seven dips in the river Jordan[29]. Man born blind curing by washing in the pool of Siloam[30], and the pool near the Sheep Gate at Jerusalem had the power to cure a person who got in to it when the angel of the Lord disturbed the water[31].

Rocks and Mountains

Normally people believed that the mountains are the abode of gods. In the Indian Myths, we find this idea. Mount Kailash is considered to be the abode of Lord Siva, Palani - Murugan, Tirupathi - Venkatachalapathi etc. The religion of Israel is not exempted from this. Old Testament gives lot of evidences about this:

- — Mount Carmel was considered to be holy and the altars were built on it (I. Kings. 18).
- — Mount Taber was also considered to be holy[32].
- — Mount Gibeah is called Gibeah of the Lord[33].
- — Mount Olives was one of the important worshipping places for the Israelites[34].

Abraham took Isaac to Mount Moriah to be given as a sacrifice to God, and there God spoke to him. (Gen.22:2). Mount Horeb was called as the mountain of the Lord and Mount Sinai and Mount Horeb were considered to be the place where God revealed himself (Exo. 3:2).

Like the mountains, even stones had their importance in the worship. Jacob, one among the three patriarchs of Israel kept a stone under his head and slept over it and a vision of God, and he called that place Bethel, which means "House of God"[35]. He planted that stone, poured oil over it and worshipped the Lord who was present in that stone. Joshua plants a big stone in Shechem as the covenant stone under the Oak tree [36]. When Joshua crossed the river Jordan, he placed twelve stones and they were monuments representing twelve tribes[37]. Stones were given names with some importance and they were also considered to be of Animistic value. e.g. Ebenezer stone of help[38].

Ancestor Worship

Most premitive pagan people believe in the existence of spirits, good and evil, and many consider that among these are the spirits of the dead. The desire to provide for the comfort of the benevolent and placate the ill-will of the malevolent, among these, often leads to a 'cult of the dead', where such services as fitting burial and provision of food and drink are performed to achieve these ends.

> "The overt worship of the dead in the sense of adoration or even deification is, however, comparitively rare; the best known example is that of Confucian China. It is more appropriate therefore to speak of a `cult of the dead' than of `ancestor worship', since there is no question of the latter's being found in the Bible"[39].

The name of the father of the tribe came as the name of a god and it can be an example of the ancestor worship.

In the ancient near East belief in the after life led to wide spread cult practices connected with the dead. The provision by the Egyptians for the comfort of the deceased, in what was believed to basically enjoyable future existence, were eleborate. In Mesopotomia less is known of the funeral rites of individuals, but a gloomy view was taken of the life to come, and it was in consequence important to ensure, by the provision of necessities as well as by ritual and liturgy, that the dead did not return as dissatisfied spirits to molest the living[40].

Few cemeteries or tombs of the Israelite period have been excavated in Palestine, but those which have show, perhaps, a decline in furniture from the Canaanite Bronze Age, or, in other words, a decline in the cult of the dead. That the Israelites, however, were continually falling away from the right path and adopting the religious practices of their neighbours is clearly stated in the Bible.

It is to be expected that among these practices should have been some associated with the cult of the dead. Thus the declarations in Deut. 26:14:

("I have not eaten there of in my mourning neither have I taken away ought thereof for the dead: but I have hearkened to the voice of the Lord my God, and have done according to all that thou hast commanded me....") suggest that it was necessary to prohibit offerings to the dead; it appears that it was expected that incense would be burned for, Asa at his burial (2. Chro. 16:14), and at Zadekiah's funeral (Jer. 34:5); and Ezk. 43:7-9 implies that there was worship of the dead bodies of kings. The practice of Necromancy (Divination) is also attested (I. Sam. 2:7), though clearly condemned. (Isa. 8:19; 65:4).

Other Biblical passages are sometimes cited as evidence that such practices were acquieseed in or accepted as legitimate. Thus in Gen.35:8 it is described how the Oak under which Rabekah's nurse was buried was called Allon-bacuth. 'Oak of weeping', and again in Gen. 35:20 Jacob setup a 'pillar' over Rachel's grave. These actions have been taken to indicate a belief in the sanctity of graves, and as a consequence, cult practices associated with the dead. But weeping over the dead may just as well be genuine as ritual, and there is no evidence to suggest that the raising of a memorial pillar necessarily implies a cult practice. The custom of levirate marriage (Deut. 25:5-10) has been interpreted as partly aimed at providing some one to carry out the cult of the dead for the deceased. This interpretation, however, is again one which exceeds the simple testimony of the text. Despite various theories, the participations in family sacrifices (I. Sam.20:29) provides no evidence of a cult of the dead. It has been further suggested that some of the mourning customs show signs of a cult of, or even worship of, the dead. But such of these practices as were legitimate (Lev. 19:27-28; Deut. 14:1) may just as well be explained as manifestations of sorrow over the loss of a dear one.

It is thus clear that neither ancestor worship nor a cult of the dead played any part in the true religion of Israel.

Polytheism

Hebrew religion is strictly monotheistic. But in the early period, this monotheism was not in practice fully. The patriarchs, namely Abraham, Isaac and Jacob worshipped God. But no single name was given for God at that time. He was known and worshipped in different names. The name of God is given in the book of Exodus 3:14; for the first time in the Bible. Here too, it is not given in direct form. It is said "I AM WHO I AM". This has its origin from the Hebrew "YHWH". But through out the Old Testament we find different names for this God, based on His power, attitude and functions.

The names are given below with the Biblical references and the meaning:

Hebrew	*Meaning*
(1) El Elyon (Gen. 14:18-20)	God most high.
(2) Shapat (Gen. 18:25)	God the Judge.
(3) El Olam (Gen. 21:33)	The Eternal God.
(4) Yahweh Jireh (Gen. 22:14)	The Lord provides
(5) El Elohe- Yisra'el (Gen. 33:20)	God, the God of Israel
(6) El Shaddai (Gen. 49:25)	God of Mountains
(7) Yahweh-Nissi (Exo. 17:25)	The Lord my Banner
(8) Yahweh - Shalom (Jud. 6:24)	The Lord is Peace
(9) El Berit (Jud. 9:46)	God of the covenant
(10) Yahweh-Seba'ot (I.Sam. 17:45)	God of armies
(11) Adonai (Ps. 2:4)	Lord, Master
(12) Qedesh Yisrae'l (Isa. 1:4)	The Holy One of Israel
(13) Yahweh-tsidkenn(Jer.23:6)	The Lord our righteousness
(14) Yahweh Shammah (Eze. 48:35)	The Lord is there.

Aramaic

Attiq Yomin (Dan. 7:9) (Dan. 7:18)	Ancient of DaysIllya Most High [41]

The primary meaning of the name "LORD". (Perhaps Pronounced Yahweh, in English Jehovah) is the self existent one; literally (as in Exo. 3:4), "He that is who He is", therefore the eternal I am.

It is significant that the first appearance of the name Jehovah in scripture follows the creation of man. It was God (Elohim) who said, "Let us make man in our image"[42]; but when man, as in Gen. 2, is to fill the scene and become dominant over creations, it is the LORD GOD (Jehovah Elohim) who acts (Gen. 2:4ff). This clearly indicates a special relation of deity in His Jehovah character, to man, and all scripture emphasizes this.

Jehovah is distinctively the redemptive name of Deity. When sin entered the world and man's redemption became necessary, it was Jehovah Elohim who sought the sinning ones[43], and clothed them with coats of skins (Gen. 3:21), a beautiful type of the righteousness provided by the Lord God through sacrifice (Rom. 3:21-25). The first distinctive revelation of Himself by his name Jehovah was in connection with the redemption of the covenant people out of Egypt[44].

As redeemer, emphasis is laid upon those attributes of Jehovah which the sin and salvation of man bring into exercise. These are:

(a) His holiness[45].
(b) His hatred and judgement of sin [46].
(c) His love for and redemption of sinners but always righteously[47].

Salvation by Jehovah apart from sacrifice is unknown in scripture.

Lord is also the distinctive name of Deity as in covenant with Israel[48].

Lord God is the first of the compound names of God. Lord God is used distinctively:

(1) Of the relation of Deity to man.
    (a) as creator (Gen. 2:7-15)
    (b) as morally in authority over man (Gen. 2:16-17)
    (c) as creating and governing the earthly relationships of man (Gen. 2:18-24; 3:16-19, 22-24); and
    (d) as redeeming man (Gen. 3:8-15, 21).
(2) Of the relation of Deity to Israel (Gen. 24:7; Dent. 1:11,21; Josh.7:13,19-20; Jnd. 2:12; I. Sam.2:30; I.Kings.1:48; II Kings. 9:6; I Chro. 22:19; II. Chro. 1:9; Ezra. 1:3; Isa.21:17).

In God's redemptive relation to man, various compound names of Jehovah are found which reveal him as meeting every need of man from his lost state to the end. These compound names are:

(a) Jehovah-Jirreh, "the lord will provide" (Gen. 22:13-14) i.e., will provide a sacrifice.
(b) Jehovah-Rapha, " the Lord who healeth" (Ex. 15:26). That this refers to physical healing, the context shows, but the deeper healing of soul malady is implied.
(c) Jehovah-Nissi, "the Lord my banner". (Exo. 17:8-15). The name is interpreted by the context. The enemy was Amalek, a figure for the flesh, and the conflict that day illustrates the conflict of Gal.5:17-the war of the spirit against the flesh. Victory was wholly due to divine help.
(d) Jehovah-Shalom, "the Lord our peace", or "the Lord send peace" (Jud. 6:24). Almost the whole ministry of Jehovah finds expression and illustration in that chapter. Jehovah hates and judges sin (vv.1-5); Jehovah loves and saves sinners (vv.7-18), but only through sacrifice (vv 19-21).
(e) Jehovah-Tsidkenu, "the Lord our righteousness" *(Jer. 23:6).*

This name of Jehovah occurs in a prophecy concerning the future restoration and conservation of Israel. Then Israel will hail him as Jehovah - Tsidkenu - "the Lord our righteousness".

(f) Jehovah - Shammah, " the Lord is Present" (Eze. 48:35). This name signifies Jehovah's abiding presence with this people.

There are also descriptions in the Old Testament of the activities of the Lord which are in some cases similar to compound names of Jehovah, but are not properly so. (eg. Ps.32:1; 27:1; 28:1; 61:3-4; 62:6-7)[49].

El, is the name of the supreme god in the Uganistic traditions and myths. And there is also a view that "El and Elohim" are from the earliest times, the general names applied to the spirits or demons associated with the popular belief in certain localities or natural objects such as trees, wells, rocks, stones .... etc. Some of these numerous vague spirits attained in the course of time to a more definitely presonal quality advancing as the protective spirits of places and tribes to the stage of deity[50].

In the Old Testament, non-Israelite gods were called as Pagan gods. They are:

	Name	*Worshippers*	*Reference*
(1)	Adrammelech	Sephravaim	2.Kings. 17:31
(2)	Anammelech	- do -	- do -
(3)	Asherah	Canaanites	2. Chro. 24:18
(4)	Ashima	Hamathites	2 Kings. 17:30
(5)	Ashtoreth	Sidonians	I.Kings. 11:5
(6)	Baal	Canaanites	Judges. 2:13
(7)	Baal - Zebul	Philistines	2 Kings. 1:2
(8)	Bel	Babylonians	Jer. 51:44
(9)	Chemosh	Moabites	I. Kings. 11:7
(10)	Dagon	Philistines	I. Sam. 5:27
(11)	Destiny	Canaanites	Isa. 65:11
(12)	Fortune	- do -	- do -
(13)	Marduk	Babylonians	Jer. 50:2
(14)	Molech	Ammonites	Zeph. 1:5
(15)	Nebo	Babylonians	I sa. 46:1
(16)	Nergel	Cuthites	2. Kings. 17:30
(17)	Nibhay	Avvites	2. Kings. 17:31
(18)	Nisroch	Assyrians	Isa. 37:38
(19)	Succoth Benoth	Babylonians	2. Kings. 17:30
(20)	Tammuz	- do -	Eze. 8:14
(21)	Tartak	Avvites	2. Kings. 17:31 51.

Worshipping Systems in Israel

The 'worship of God' and the 'service of God' are practically synonymous terms in the Old Testament. The connection between these ideas goes back to primitive times when the deity was conceived anthropomorphically as a being with human wants and appetites (Gen. 8:21). The true worship of God was therefore regarded as dutiful ministration to these wants by sacrifice and obedience to his behests. In the Old Testament there are instances of individual worship (Gen. 24:26f; Ex.33:0-34:8). But the emphasis is upon worship in the congregation (Ps.42:4; I chro.29:20).

The Old Testament shows people responding to God in many ways. The ancient Israelite showed his reverence for God by giving thanks, by praising, by making required and voluntary donation, by maintaining ritual purity, and by obeying the Law's moral precepts, as well as by taking part in the worship rituals established in the law. Specific acts of worship in Old Testament times can be categorized as corporate ritual, corporate non-ritual, individual ritual and individual non-ritual.

Corporate Ritual Worship

While God ordained the ritual by which he was to be worshipped— and that ritual was to be performed exactly as he ordained— corporate ritual worship was unacceptable unless it was a true expression of the community's heart for God. This was expressed not through the ritual, but by committing oneself to the moral and ethical precepts in Israel's law[52]. A true heart for God was also expressed in the worship joy. Many of the Psalms chanted or sung in public worship capture the sense of joy the true believer found in his or her relationship with the Lord. This is perhaps best exemplified by David, who leaped and danced before the Lord "with all his might" as he led the procession bringing the ark of God to Jerusalem (2.Sam.6:14-16).

Corporate Non-Ritual Worship

During the Babylonian captivity, the synagogue gathering was introduced. The practice of assembling on the Sabbath for study of the law, praise and prayers were maintained by the Jews scattered through out the ancient world and by the relative few who returned to Israel. As long as the restored Jerusalem Temple stood, the synagogue's corporate non-ritual worship existed along side the ritual worship conducted at the Temple. Since the Temple's destruction in A.D.70, the synagogue has been the main centre of Jewish worship.

Individual Ritual Worship

Old Testament law calls for individual acts of ritual worship. Those who sinned unintentionally were to offer specified sacrifices. Observing rules of uncleanness and cleansing was part of the individuals were also able to express their appreciation to the Lord in personal vows and voluntary offerings.

Individual Non-Ritual Worship

The Old Testament contains many examples of personal worship apart from sacrifices and vows. Abraham's servant praised God for answering his prayer (Gen. 24:26,27). Jacob erected a pillar to commemorate his vision of God (Gen: 28:10-22). Hannah's Psalm of praise is among the most beautiful expressions of personal non-ritual worship (I. Sam. 2:1-10). The primary models for personal worship are the Paslms, in which the most intimate of human emotions are freely expressed to God and in which the most exalted expressions of praise to God can be found. The worship of the Hebrew religion will be incomplete without the sacrifice.

Sacrifices and Offerings

We can trace the biblical practice of making sacrifices back to God's killing of an animal to provide coverings for Adam and Eve after their sin (Gen. 3:21). Later, cain is rebuked because in beginning fruits of the soil to offer God rather than an animal of the flock, as his brother Abel did, Cain failed to "do what is right" (Gen. 4:3-7). Thus the Bible suggests that early man's practice of bringing animal sacrifices war rotted in a tradition established immediately after man's fall. Animal sacrifices continued to be the norm as illustrated by the offerings of Noah (Gen. 8:20,21), and Abraham and the other Patriarchs (Gen. 12:8; 13:4; 26:25), long before Moses' law was established.

Motives underlying Sacrifice

The motives which prompted early man to offer sacrifices were complex. There are fairly easily discernible, though it is by no means easy to decide, in a particular class of sacrifice, which of them was uppermost in the intention of the offered. Sacrifices might be either public - offered on behalf of the community, or private. They are, sacrifices as:

(1) gifts of God
(2) means of entering into communion with God
(3) means of releasing life, whether for the benefit of God himself, or of the worshipper[53].

In regard to this third motive, it should be clearly understood that the object in offering a sacrifice was never to present the dead carcass of an animal, but to release its potent life. This 'life' was conceived to be resident in the blood, which was dashed against the altar.

In the Old Testament, sacrifices of animals, birds, food grains and human beings are recorded.

Burnt offering : (Lev.1; 6:8-13)

In which bull, ram, he-goat or male dove or young pigeon (for poor) without defect was given. It signified the complete surrender to God and also devotion and commitment.

Grain offering : (Lev. 2; 6:14-23)

In which flour, baked bread or crushed grain made with olive oil and salt; were given. The procedure for this sacrifice is, the food was prepared by the offerer and brought to the altar. Priest used to burn a "memorial portion" (handful) of the offering and keep the rest as his food. This voluntary offering accompanied fellowship offering.

Fellowship offering : (Lev. 3; 7:11-36)

In which any animal without defect from herd or flock and variety of breads were given. The procedure for this is the offerer laid hands on the head of the sacrifice and killed it at the door of the outer tabernacle or Temple court. Priest collected the blood, threw it against the altar. Selective parts of the animal were burnt. Part of the animal was given to the priest. The offerer and his family ate the rest as a communal meal. The significance is the communal meal symbolized fellowship with God. This voluntary offering could be a thank offering for a blessing bestowed, a ritual expression of a vow or a freewill offering to be brought to are of the three required religions convocations.

Sin offering : (Lev.4:1-5,13; 6:24-30; 12:6-8;14:12-14)

In which suitable animal was sacrificed without defect such as:

— a young bull for high priest and congregation
— a male goat for leader
— female goat or lamb for a common person
— dove or pigeon for the poor
— Tenth.of an ephah of five flour for the very poor will be given.

The procedure for this sacrifice is that the offerer laid hands on animals head, then killed it at the North side of the altar. The priest poured blood on the horns of the altar and at its base. The choice parts were burnt. The priest received what was edible, except in the case of a bull. It signified that this mantatory offering was made, by a person who sinned unintentionally or was ritually unclean. The worshipper identified himself with the sacrifice before it was killed for his atonement.

Guilt offering : (Lev.5: 14-6:7; 7:1-6; 14:12-18)

In which ram or lamb without defect and of proper value was offered. The offerer first made full restorations plus one fifth, then lay hand (s) on the animal's head and kill it on Northern side of the altar, choice parts were burnt. The priest received what was edible. It signified that mandatory offering was made when a person deprived another of his rights as by theft or leprosy; in the latter case. God deprived the leper's worship when he or she was un clean.

Human Sacrifice

Was human sacrifice ever part of Israelite religion? Some have answered this question in affirmative and conclude that the animal or later sacrificial custom was considered a victim in substitutions for the donor who should have been the victim. An important preliminary consideration in this discussion is the fact that Israel was a late comer among the nations of the Ancient Middle East. Joseph Fitymyer says:

> "If the Israelites did practice human sacrifice, they presumably would have borrowed it from some already existing ritual system"[54].

The only clear information on the subject comes from Phoenician sources and it is important to note that Israel was in close contact with Phoenicia. Joseph. A. Fitymyer again says:

> "The Canaanites evidently had a custom of slaying infants and burying them as foundation sacrifices when they were about to put up a new building"[55].

The Bible has references in so many places regarding the human sacrifices[56].

According to I.Kings 16:34, when Hiel rebuilt Jericho, "at the price of his first born he set up his gates". The story of Jephthah's sacrifice of his daughter (Jud. 11:30-40) is narrated as something extraordinary and horrifying, as is the story of the king of Moab's sacrifice of his only son to avert defeat at the hands of the Israelites. (2 Kings. 3:27).

Arnold Toynbee says:

> "The rite of sacrifice one's first born son by burning his alive was, in truth, practised both in Canaan and in the Canaanite Colonies overseas in North-West Africa. There is like wise evidence of the practice for Israel, Moab, Judah and Carthage; and for Carthage there is archaeological evidence as well"[57].

In Jadah, King Ahaz (741-725 BC) and king Manasseh (696-641 BC) are recorded each to have "made his son pass through the fire" (2 Kings. 14:3; 21:6). An un answerable verdict as the site is given in a passage appended to the Book of the Prophet Micah: "Shall I give my first born for my transgression"? (Mic. 6:7).

Among the non-Israelite gods referred in the Old Testament, the following gods demanded child sacrifice:

Adrammelech and Anammelech worshiped by Sephraveion (2.Kings. 17:31) and Molech worshiped by Ammonites (Zeph. 1:5). Can there by a folk religion without festivals? As a folk community, the religion of the Hebrews, had lot of feasts and festivals.

Feasts and Festivals

"The Hebrew word for festival is 'hag', generally translated as FEAST. It is cognate with the Arabic "hajji", a title given to anyone who has made the pilgrimage to Mecca, to attend a 'hag' involved the making of a journey. Before the centralization of sacrificial worship at the Jerusalem Temple the journey required would be short, perhaps on farther than to the local sanctuary or "high place"[58].

Feasts, festivals and feasts, religious observances punctuated the Jewish year. The terms 'feast' or 'festival' convey joyful celebration. Specific activities and ritual varied from festival but they all included sacrifices, prayers, special meals, ceremonies and customs.

Unlike other religions of the ancient Near East. However, the origins of seasonal rituals were subserviant to the greater purpose of acknowledging God's forgiveness, favour and provisión. (Exo. 10:2;12:8-14; Lev. 22:31-23:2; Deut.16:1-17). These events drew God's people to gether to worship and to remember their heritage. They also provided a vital means of deepening Israel's faith. God expressed displeasure with the Isralites when, despite their external observance of feasts, they were unjust and disobedient to God's Law. (Isa. 1:10-20).

Fasts, by their nature, were times of mourning or reflection on one's sin. Many fast days were noted on the religious calendar of Israel, but only one fast day was ordained by Mosaic Law - the day of Atonement.

Following are some of the festivals celebrated by the Israelites.

Passover Festival : (Exo.12; Lev. 23:5-14)

The feast of Unleavended Bread (Ex.23:15) or Passover (Lev. 23:5) was established to commemorate the historical deliverance from Egypt. (Exo. 10:2; 12:8,14). It was one of the three annual festivals, and was observed on the fourteenth day of the first month. For seven days unleavended bread was eaten and no servile work done. The first and the last day being 'holy convocations', sacrifices were offered. (Num. 28:16-25; Deut.16: 1-8).

Feast of Weeks : (Exo. 34:22; Lev. 23: 15-21)

It is also called the 'feast of harvest' and 'the day of first fruits' (Exo. 23:16: 34:22; Num. 28:26). Later it was known as Pentecost because it was celebrated on the fiftieth day from the sabbath beginning the passover. It was marked by a holy convocation and the offering of sacrifices.

Feast of Tabernacles

The feast of Tabernacles or 'the feast of booths', is also called the 'feast of ingathering' (Exo. 23:16; 34:22; Lev. 23:34; Deut. 16:13). It lasted seven days the first and last days being holy convocations. Fruit was gathered in and people dwelt in booths made of branches and boughs of trees (Lev 23:39-43; Num 29:12-38).

The Sabbath

This is regarded as a feast in Lev. 23:2-3, and called a 'Sabbath of rest'. It was marked by a solemn assembly (Isa. 1:13), and cessation from all labour. It was also a day of joy (Isa. 58:13).

The Day of Blowing of Trumpets : (Num 29:1)

In Lev. 23:24, it is called a memorial of blowing of trumpets and a sabbath. Sacrifices were offered and hard labour ceased.

The Day of Atonement : (Lev. 23: 26-31)

It was observed on the tenth day of the seventh month, and was a day of 'holy convocation' in which souls were afflicted and an atonement made for sin. It was observed but once in the year (Ex. 30:10).

The Feast of Purim

Described in Esther 9. Established by Mordecai in the time of Ahasuerus to commemorate the remarkable deliverance from the intrigues of Haman, this was a day of feasting and gladness.

Idolatry

Idolatry is one of the main characteristics of folk religion. "The story of the Old Testament religion could be told for the most part in terms of a tension between a spiritual conceptions of God and worship; the hall mark of the genuine faith of Israel and various pressures such as idolatry, which attempted to debase and materialize the national religious consciousness and practice"[59].

In Biblical times, idols were shaped in human and animal forms. A stone or tree trunk might serve as an idol. At times, idols were treated as if they were themselves gods (Isa. 44:17-20). However, most idols probably represented the god or goddess, with the likeness between the image and the deity serving as a link between material and spiritual worlds. As male Canaanite gods are often portrayed riding on a bull, many believe the golden calf of Exo. 32 and the calves or bulls Jeroboam I erected at Bethel and Dan were intended to serve as thrones for an invisible deity (I. Kings. 12:25-33).

Idolatry constantly tempted the people of Israel up to the time of the Exile (Exo. 32; Josh. 24:14; I.Kings. 18; 2.Kings. 21:7). Thus, idolatry was not an evoluationary step towards monotheism but just the opposite a turning away from the worship of the "One true God". The Exile experience, however, purged God's Old Testament people of their yearning for idols.

Nevertheless, idolatry remained dominant in surrounding cultures. It was well entrenched in the first-century world when the Christian church exploded out of tiny Palestine.

The Old Testament takes a strong stand against idolatry. The Ten commandments state. "You shall not make for yourself an idol in the form of anything is heaven above or on the earth beneath or in the waters below. You shall not bow down to them or worship them" (Exo. 20:4,5).

Following are the important reasons, why idolatry was condemned by the Ten commandments and the Law of Israel:

(a) Idolatry distorts the concept of God (Deut. 4:15,16)
(b) Idolatry represents human arrogance. (Isa. 2:8-22)
(c) Idolatry leads to immorality (Hos. 9:10)
(d) Idolatry serves as a point of contact with the demoniac. (Deut. 12: 1-3; 18:9-14)[60].

There are certain events ali associated with a Patriarch Jacob, which might appear to show Patriarchal idolatry. For example, Rachel stole her father's Teraphim (Gen. 31:19). It is urged that Jacob's pillars (Gen. 28:18, 31:13,45; 35:14, 20) are the same as the idolatrous stones with which Canaan was familiar. The pillar at Bethel was associated with Jacobs vow (Gen. 31:13) and could more easily belong to the category of memorial pillars (Gen. 35:20; Josh.24:27; I Sam. 7:12; II. Sam. 18:18).

Teraphim

Which Rachel stole from her father's house (Gen. 31:19) is a figure or image associated with pagan worship and the occult practice of divination. The Hebrew word is typically translated "home hold gods" or "idols". Teraphim are reported in all periods of Old Testament history, showing the persistence of Pagan practices in Israel (Gen. 31:19; Jud. 17:5; I. Sam. 15:23; 2. Kings. 23:24: Eze. 21:21; Zech. 10:2). Teraphim are specifically condemned in most contexts where they are mentioned.

The Bible condemns idolatry because it distorts the truth and leads people away from God. Thus idols need not be only graven images; they may be money (Colo. 3:5), sexual desires (Eph. 5:5), covetousness (Gal. 5:19,20). etc.—whatever serves to turn on attention away from God.

Conclusion

All these rituals, practices and worship patterns are typical which belong to little tradition. But after the period of Jesus Christ, the Little tradition became great tradition, i.e., the christianity has become more sophisticated. But it is a fact that the religion of the Old Testament is a folk religion and the gods mentioned are folk gods.

NOTES

1. *Dictionary of Believers and Non-believers* (Moscow : Progress Publishers, 1989), p.474.
2. Ibid. p.474.
3. Emile Durkhein, *The Elementary Forms of the Religions Life* (London: George Allen and Unwin Ltd., 1976), p.25.
4. Op cit. p.222.
5. Paul, Radin, *Primitive Religion* (New York : Dover Publications, Inc., 1957), p.5.
6. Emile, Durkheim, *The Elementary Forms of the Religions Life.* (London:George Allen and Unwin Ltd., 1976), p. 24.
7. J.D. Douglas, *New Bible Dictionary* (England, Leicester : Inter versity Press, 1986) p. 309.

8. Ibid. 309
9. Rajendra Kumar Rajeev, *World famous Religions—Doctrines and Sects.* (Delhi - Pustak Mahal. 1992) p. 98.
10. Matt. 21:12-17, LK.19:45-48, Jn. 2:12-16.
11. J.D.Douglas, *New English Bible Dictionary* (Leicester. Interversity Press. 1986) p. 118.
12. John L. Mckenzie, *Dictionary of the Bible* (Bangalore Asian Trading Corporation. 1984) p. 66.
13. Rajendra Kumar Rajeev, *World Famous Religions, Doctrines and Seets.* (Delhi. Pustak Mahal 1992) p. 106
14. J.D. Douglus, *New Bible Dictionary* (Lelcester Inter Versity Press. 1986) p. 166
15. Deut. 23:17-18
16 Arnold Toynbee, *An Historian's Approach to Religions* (Oxford: Oxford University Press. 1979) p. 16.
17 S. Sakthivel, *Nattupura Iyal Aayvu* (Madras : Manivasagar Pathippagam. 1992) p. 139
18. Ibid. p. 217
19. Exo. 34:13, 2 Kings. 23:4-15.
20. Opcit. p. 106
21. Ibid. p. 118
22. J.D. Douglas (Ed), '*New Bible Dictionary*' (Leicester, Inter versity Press. 1986) p. 789
23. Ps. 46:1
24. Alan, Richardson, *A Theological word book of the Bible* (London: SCM Press Ltd. 1982) p. 89
25. John, Lewis, 'Anthropology - made simple' (London: William Heini Mann Ltd. 1982) P.176.
26. Gen. 13:18; 14:13; 18:1; Josh. 19:33; Judges.4:11; 9:6,37; I.Sam. 10:3)
27. I. Kings. 14:23; II. Kings.16:4;17:10; Isa.1:29, 57:5; Jer.2:20; 3:6; 17:2; Eze.6:15; 20:28 and Hosea. 4:13,14.
28. Gnana Robinson, *Isravelarin Samayam* (The religion of Israel Madras: TTBC. CLS., 1969) p. 59.
29. 2 Kings 5:14
30. Jn.9:1-12
31. Jn. 5:1-14
32. Deut. 33:19; Josh. 19:22; I.Chro. 6:17; Hos.5:1
33. I. Sam. 10:3; 22:6; 2 Kings. 23:8.
34. I. Kings. II:7
35. Gen. 28:11-22
36. Josh. 24:25-27
37. Josh. 4:3-9
38. I.Sam. 4:1, 5:1
39. J.D. Douglas, *New Bible dictionary* (Leicester: Inter - Versity Press. 1986) p. 35

40. Ibid. p. 36
41. Lawrence O. Richards (Ed.), *The Applied Bible Dictionary*: Sussex (UK): Kingsway Publications 1990) P.440
42. Gen. 1:26
43. Gen. 3:9-13
44. Exo. 3:13-17
45. Lev. 11:44-45; 19:1-2; 20:26; Hab. 1:12-13
46. Deut. 32: 35-42
47. Isa. 53:5-6, 10
48. Exo. 19:3; 20:1-2; Jer. 31:31-34
49. C.I. Scofield, (Ed), *The New Scofield Reference Bible* (London: Oxford University Press. 1967) p. 117.
50. Alan Richardson (Ed), *A Theological word book of the Bible*. (London. SCM Press Ltd. 1982) p. 94.
51. Lawrence, O. Richards (Ed), *The Applied Bible Dictionary* (Sussex. UK: Kings way Publications. 1990) p. 440.
52. Ps. 50:12-15; Isa. 1:11-17; Amos. 5:21-24.
53. Alan Richardson (Ed), *A Theological Word Book of the Bible*. (London. S.C.M. Press Ltd. 1988) p. 206.
54. Joseph A. Fitymyer. S.J. (Ed): The Jerome Biblical commentary "(Bangalore: Theological Publications India. 1968) p. 723
55. Ibid. p. 723
56. Gen. 22:1ff; Jud. 11:31ff; I.Sam.15:3,33; 2.Kings.3:27; 16:3; 21:6; 23:10; Jer.7:31; 32:35; Eze.23:39; Hos.13:3,7.
57. Arnold Toynbee, '*An Historian's Approach to Religion*'. (London. Oxford University Press. 1979) p. 37.
58. Alan Richardson(Ed). *A Theological Word Book of the Bible* (London. S.C.M. Press Ltd. 1988) p. 211
59. J.D. Douglas (Ed), '*The New Bible Dictionary*' (Leicester England. Interversity Press. 1986) p. 551.
60. Lawrence, O. Richards : "*The Applied Bible Dictionary*" (E. Sussex Kingsway Publications. 1990) p. 511.

8

FOLK MUSIC AND SONGS IN THE BIBLE

Introduction

A natural expression of man which probably began with speech - singing and developed into songs, which were then accompanied by instruments. Music as we know it has become quite complex, a luxury and entertainment, music in antiquity, however, was a functional expression of daily life, work and worship.

The folk song is a song, i.e. a lyric poem with melody, which originated anonymously, among unlettered folk in times past and which remained in currency for a considerable time, as a rule for centuries[1].

Classification of Folk Songs

Maria Leach classifies folk songs into five categories:

(1) Emotional Songs
(2) Daily Life Songs
(3) Crucial Moments of Life Songs. Such as:
    (a) Birth
    (b) Marriage
    (c) Death
    (d) Parting
    (e) Nostalgia
    (f) War
(4) Children Songs
(5) Religious Songs

Bowra Classifies them under six headings:

(1) Nature songs
(2) Love songs
(3) Marriage songs
(4) Lullaby songs
(5) Work songs
(6) Festival songs

Kemmeth Peacock divides them into eight categories.

(1) Children songs.
(2) Commic ditties.
(3) Fishermen songs.
(4) Lamentations.
(5) Pirate songs.
(6) Sailors songs.
(7) War songs.
(8) Miscellaneous songs.

Instrumental and vocal sounds having rhythm, melody, or harmony - secular and sacred music played no less role in the lives of the people of Biblical times than it does in our own day. It added to the pomp of national celebrations, bolstered the soldier's courage, enlivened work and play, lent comfort in times of sadness, and provided inspiration in religious expression. "The sound of early Near Eastern music would seem less strange to the modern ear than previously thought. Though we are not informed about ancient rhythms and tempos, we do know that heptatonic, diatonic scales, familiar to us from western music, also existed in antiquity"[2].

A number of stringed instruments would have produced sounds similar to modern small harps, lyres and lutes. Other instruments, notably wood wind, percussion and the simpler stringed instruments, were merely less sophisticated forms of modern orchestral or folk instruments, and some are still in use in the traditional cultures of the contemporary Near East.

Origin of Hebrew Music

Hebrew tradition ascribes the origin of music to Jubal, one of the three sons of Lamech. "He was the father of all such as handle the harp and organ" says Gen.4:21. He has an elder brother Jabal, who is like wise described as 'the father of such as dwell in tents, and of such as have Cattle'. (Gen.4:20). The close relation thus assigned to the fathers of the pastoral and the musical arts—they are represented as being born of the same mother, while Tubelcain, the first smith, was the son of the other wife of Lamech—witnesses to the belief that the origin of music is to be found among a people of pastoral habits. The shepherd playing on his pipe to call the sheep (Jud.5:16), or to beguile the tediousness of his watch, appeared to the Hebrew mind the earliest type of musician. It may be that the inclusion in Cain's family tree of the originator of the art of music indicates a tendency on the part of the compiler to view with disfavour the arts which had banished the severe simplicity of primitive times. But, if so, this is a view, which, so far as music is concerned, finds no further expression in the Bible, where music is consistently regarded with favour as the natural utterance of the joy which fills the heart, and the fitting channel where by the voice of man may convey to God his gratitude and devotion.

References to the popular enjoyment of music are common in early Biblical history. It was always a part of celebrations, whether a farewell party with 'mirth and songs, with tambourine and' Lyre and harp, timbrel and flute and wine" (Isa. 5:12)3. Singing accompanied work as well as play, and many work songs or chants have been recorded, e.g., those of the well diggers (Num. 21:17-18), the watchmen (Isa.21:12), and the pressers of grapes (Jer. 25:30; 48:33).

Warfare gave rise to martial songs. Such heroic ballads were probably set down in the lost "*Book of the Wars of the Lord*" (Num.21:14), and the "*Book of Jasher*" (Josh. 10:13; 2.Sam. 1:18), and were no doubt sung by itinerant minstrels and bards (Num.21:27-30). Miriam sang of Moses' final defeat of Pharaoh (Exo. 15:20-21); and Deborah celebrated Israel's victory over Jabin with a song of triumph (Jud.5). Samson exulted over his victory over his slaying of the Philistines (Jud. 15:16) in a rhythmic victory chant like the one the women sang back and forth at Saul's home coming (Isam.18:6-7). But Israel was not always victorious, and songs were also composed for fallen heroes, such as David's moving lament for Saul and Jonathan. (2.Sam. 1:19-27).

Musical Instruments

Much of what is known about the instruments of the Bible comes from literary evidence: the scriptures and their earliest translations, and the descriptions and comments of the rabbis, church fathers and classical authors. Additional evidence has come from archaeological discoveries, both the remains of actual instruments and the abundant pictorial representations of instruments and musical scenes from throughout the entire Near Eastern and Mediterranean world.

In contrast to the detailed accounts of liturgical music in the Old Testament, the descriptions of the musical instruments themselves are rather scarse. Because of the injunction of the second commandment, interpreted by the Hebrews as discouraging pictorial representations, there are few drawings of Hebrew instruments. In addition of the instruments used in the temple, the Book of Daniel lists six instruments played in King Nebuchadnezzar's court[4].

Percussion Instruments

Bells, Castanets, Cymbals, Rattler - sistrum, Tabret, Timbrel and Gong.

Stringed Instruments

Dulcimer, Harp, lute, Lyre, Psaltery, Sackbut, Trigon and Viol.

Wind Instruments

Clarinet, Cornet, Flute, Organ, Pipe, Shophar, and Trumpet.

Percussion Instruments

Most of the accounts of percussion instruments are found in the early history of the Hebrew people. They were gradually eliminated from the temple orchestra, perhaps because of their association with idolatrous practices.

Bells

One kind of bell had a name 'met silloth', that came from the Hebrew word meaning to 'jingle' or to 'rattle'. This type of bell is mentioned only once in the Bible - Zech. 14:20, where we are told that the Israelites attached these bells to the bridle or breast strap of horses. Another kind of bell was a tiny, pine gold bell. It was fastened to the hem of the high priest's robe and alternated with ornamental pomegranates (Exo. 28:33-34). These bells produced a sound only when they touched one another, for they did not have clippers. This jingling sound signified that the high priest was coming before God; others who dared to enter the Holy of Holies would be slain. (Exo.28:35).

Cymbals

Cymbals were made of copper and were the only percussion instrument in the temple orchestra. They were used when the people were celebrating and praising God. They joined with trumpets and sang to express joy and thanks to the Lord.[5] Another translation of the Hebrew word cymbal as Castanets which is the same or another word to denote cymbal.

Rattler-Sistrum

This is the correct translation for 2 Samuel. 6:5. (The RSV uses Castanets, while the KJV uses *Cornet*). The Sistrum was a small 'U' shaped frame with a handle attached at the bottom of the curve. Pieces of metal or other small objects were strung on small bars stretched from one side of the sistrum to the other.

Timbrel or Tabret

Modern musicians would classify this instrument as a "membranophone" because the sound is produced by a vibrating membrane. It was carried and beaten by hand. In very early times it may have been made with two membranes, with pieces of bronze inserted in the rim.

Gong

The 'brass' mentioned in I. Cor. 13:1 was actually a metal Gong. It was used for weddings and other joyous occasions.

Stringed Instruments

Archaeologists have found fragments of harps and other stringed instruments from Egypt and neighbouring countries of the Near East. Scripture describes several stringed instruments that were used in Israel. The stringed instruments were favoured by the Jewish people. In many ancient civilizations the strings were considered the most masculine and noble (e.g. David playing the lyre); the Jews considered them most suitable for accompaniment in the temple service.

Harp

The 'Kinnor' which is regularly rendered 'harp' is the first musical instrument mentioned in the Bible[6], and is the only stringed instruments referred to is the Pentateuch. The Kinnor was a wooden instrument, David's being made probably of Cypres[7].

"The strings, the number of which is not clear, were made of sheep tripe and the sounding box was at the bottom of the instrument"[8].

The Biblical descriptions of the sound of the 'Kinnor' include 'pleasant and sweet' (Ps.81:2). It was mainly played by the shepherds (I.Sam. 16:16) and it remained silent during times of mourning. (Isa. 14:11; Ps.137:2).

Nebel

Like the 'Kinnor', the nebel was made of cypres wood, and later of almug. It is clear that David was able to play the 'nebel' as well as the 'Kinnor'. As it is commonly linked in the Bible with other musical instruments, it is generally thought to have supplied the bass.[9].

Psaltery

This word is derived from Greek 'Psalterion', which denotes an instrument plucked with the fingers instead of with a plectrum. It is generally accepted that it was a kind of harp. It is first mentioned in I.Sam.10:5. Instruments like Sackbut, Dulcimer are recorded in the Bible but they belong to the Babylonian origin, were the instruments used in the Nebuchadnezzar's orchestra recorded in the book of Daniel.

Wind Instruments

Despite their limited knowledge of metal working, the Israelites fashioned a variety of horns and other wind instruments.

Pipe

It is also called flute. The pipe was used in festival processions (Isa. 30:29), at time of national rejoicing (I.Kings. 1:40), and also in mourning at funerals (Mt. 9:23). It was used to express wild joy or ecstatic lament.

Horn

It is made out of ram's horn and it appears to have been used in Biblical times for two purposes: as a flask for carrying oil and as a kind of trumpet. In this latter sense it occurs in only three passages. Josh.6., I. Chro. 25:5; and in Dan.3. the earliest trumpets were evidently made out of the horns of animals.

Trumpet

There is frequent mention of the trumpet in the Bible. The Hebrew words used for trumpet literally means ram's horn.

Sopar

Sopar is a long horn with a turned up end, was the national trumpet of the Israelites. It was used on military and religious occasions to summon the people. The Sopar is in use still in the Jewish synagogues.

Hasosera

The Hasosera was a trumpet made of beaten silver. Moses was commanded by God to make two of them for summoning the congregation and for breaking camp. Num. 10:1-10 contains God's instructions to Moses regarding the occasions for the blowing of the trumpet. It was principally a sacred and not a martial instrument.

Cornet

Cornet was used in conjunction with the cymbals among other instruments on which David and the children of Israel played before the Lord. The root from which it is derived means 'to quiver', 'vibrate', and it is probable that the instrument was a kind of rattle.

Folk Songs in the Bible

Basing on the definitions we saw in the introductory part of this chapter, only three kinds of songs one can find in the Bible. They are:

(1) Laments.
(2) Love songs.
(3) Ballads.

Laments

Characteristic of the lament is an invocation the essence of which is a crying out of the name of the god involved. The most primitive and essential lament is the cry in distress, "My God!" (Ps.22:1). Often Biblical laments begin simply with 'Yahweh' (Ps.3:1; 6:1; 7:1). Biblical laments don't contain lengthy hymnic introductions, usually confining their invocations to a crying out of Yahweh's name, frequently specifically identifying him as 'My God' (Ps. 7:1; 8:1), and as the one in whom the lamenter 'takes refuge' (Ps. 7:1; 57:1; 71:1). Given the world from which these laments arose, the cry `My God' is more than an aboriginal exclamation. It is a specific designation of the god that the lamenter turns to for concrete action against the forces of evil and chaos. It is an identification of the god in whom the suppliant places his faith[10].

The Biblical laments can be divided in to three categories:

(1) Lament on the death of a King.
(2) Individual lament.
(3) Community lament.

Lament on the Death of a King

David's lament on the death of King Saul and his son Jonathan is the only piece of lament on the death of a King in the Bible.

"David intoned this lament ...

O prince of Israel, laid low in death !
How are the men of war fallen!

Tell it not in Gath,
proclaim it not in the streets of Ashkelon,
lest the Philistine women rejoice,
lest the daughters of the uncircumcised exult.

Hills of Gilboa, let no dew or rain fall on you,
    on showers on the uplands!
For there the shields of the warriors lie tarnished,
    and the shield of Saul, no longer bright with oil.
The bow of Jonathan never held back
    from the breast of the foeman, from the blood of the slain;
the sword of Saul never returned
    empty to the scabbard.

Delightful and dearly loved were Saul and Jonathan;
in life, in death, they were not parted.
They were swifter than eagles,
stronger than lions.

Weep for Saul, O daughters of Israel!
    who clothed you in scarlet and rich embroideries,
who spangled your dress with jewels of gold.
How are the men of war fallen, fallen on the field!
    O Jonathan, laid low in death!
I grieve for you, Jonathan my brother;
    dear and delightful you were to me;
Your love for me was wonderful,
    surpassing the love of women.
Fallen, fallen are the men of war;
    and their armour left on the field.
        ... weapons of war perished!"[11]

Individual Lament

Many laments of the Old Testament concentrate on supplication. Ps.102, according to the rubric in the Hebrew Bible, is 'A prayer to be used by a sufferer when he is languishing and word pour out his lament before Yahweh'.

"For my days go up in smoke,
And my bones are aglow like a furnace.
Like blighted grass my heart is dried up,
For I neglect eating my food.
I am weary with loud groaning,
My flesh sticks to my bones.
I look like a desert lizzard,
Have turned into an owl in a desert ruin.
Lying awake, I've turned in to a bird,
All alone on the house top"[12].

These verses seek to draw Yahweh's attention to physical suffering, but Biblical laments, also insist that in the distress of a sufferer death and chaos are at work in opposition to Yahweh's creative sovereignty over the cosmos. This is apparent in Ps.88, a relentless lament full of allusions.

"Yahweh! my saving God!
By day I cry out, At night I'm in thy presence.
My prayer comes before thee,
Incline thine ear to my cry"[13].

This is an excellent example of the short invocation characteristic of Biblical laments. Then there follows a description of the state in which the suppliant finds himself:

for I have had my fill of woes, and they have brought me to the threshold of Sheol.
I am numbered with those who go down to the abyss and have become like a man beyond help, like a man who lies dead or the slain who sleep in the grave, whom thou remembrest no more because they are cut off from thy care.[14].

Another lament is in Ps.102:23-24.

My strength is broken in mid course; the time allotted to me is short. Snatch me not away before half my days are done, for thy years last through all generations.[15]

The essence of such laments is manifest in the invocation to Ps.69, especially in light of the Cosmic myth we discovered underlying the hymns:

Save me, O God; for the waters have risen up to my neck.I sink in muddy depths and have no foothold; I am swept in to deep water, and the flood carries me away.[16]

Such laments, and others, are characterized by concentration upon suffering in terms of cosmic order though they seem to imply specific illness and physical pain. In other laments the integrity and reputation of the suppliant is alleged to had been challenged in such a way as to threaten his standing in the social order through which he participates in the larger order of the cosmos. He protests his innocence, calling upon Yahweh to be the judge by whom he is vindicated.

Hear, Lord, my plea for justice, give my cry a hearing, listen to my prayer, for it is innocent of all deceit. Let judgement in my cause issue from thy lips, let thine eyes be fixed on justice.[17]

The Biblical laments, however, once the suppliant protests his innocence, go on to allude to accusers, and convey the impression that they are essentially appeals for vindication from false charges of wrong doing. Psalm.17, expresses it:

They have stifled all compassion;
their mouths are full of pride;
they press me hard, now they hem me in,
on the watch to bring me to the ground.
The enemy is like a lion eager for prey,
like a young lion crouching in ambush.[18]

Psalm 35 is even more explicit.

Malicious witnesses step forward;
they question me on matters of which I know nothing.
They return me evil for good,
lying in wait to take my life. And yet when they were sick,

I put on sackcloth,
I mortified myself with fasting.
When my prayer came back unanswered,
I walked with head bowed in grief as if for a brother;
as one in sorrow for his mother
I lay prostrate in mourning.
But when I stumbled, they crowded round rejoicing,
they crowded about me;
nameless ruffians jeered at me
and nothing would stop them.[19]

The third emphasis of the lament proper is upon God himself. The suppliant asks why God does not act, or be rebukes God for having permitted his faithful to endure suffering and wickedness. That is why the "How long?" is characteristic of many laments. The 'How long?' motif is common in Biblical laments[20].

My God, my God, why hast thou forsaken me
and art so far from saving me,
from heeding my groans?
O my God, I cry in the day-time
but thou dost not answer, in the night
I cry but get no respite [21].

The suppliant some times accuse God of being responsible for disaster, implying that Yahweh has abandoned his steadfast trust worthiness for the fickleness characteristic of deities of neighbouring people:

I have eaten ashes for bread and
mingled tears with my drink.
In thy wrath and fury thou hast taken me up
and flung me aside[22].

There is a long list of individual laments. They are:

Psalms: 3-7; 13,14,17, 25-27; 1-14; 28; 35, 38-40; 42-43, 51-55, 57, 59, 61, 64, 69-71; 77; 86, 88, 102,109, 120, 130, 139-143. Another section of lament is:

Community Laments

The Jerome Bible commentary finds atleast a dozen national or communal laments. The standard format of these Psalms includes the following elements: (a) the invocation of God's name; (b) a description of present need; (c) prayer for help and deliverance, frequently with an imperative ('hear', etc.); (d) reasons why God should help the one praying; (e) vow to offer praise or sacrifice when the petition is heard; (f) grateful praise to God[23].

Psalms of trust and thanks giving are two subtypes related to and perhaps developed from the lament. Like the laments from which they originated, Psalms of trust can be individual or communal. It is not always easy to distinguish as Psalm of trust from a lament, or a thanks giving psalm from a hymn of praise. However, if employed with out rigidity, the classification of Psalms of trust and of thanks giving can be helpful.

The following are the communal laments -

Psalms: 12, 60, 74, 79, 80, 83, 85, 90, 94, 123, 126, 137.

For example:

O God, thou hast cast us off and broken us;
thou hast been angry and rebuked us cruelly.
Thou hast made the land quake and torn it open;
it gives way and crumbles into pieces.
Thou hast made thy people drunk with a bitter draught,
thou hast given us wine that makes us stagger.
But thou hast given a warning to those who fear thee,
to make their escape before the sentence falls.[24]

Psalm Ps.79—the people of Israel laments about the aggression of their enemies and calls God to come and help them and deliver them from their captivity.

O God, the heathen have set foot in thy domain,
defiled thy holy temple and laid Jerusalem in ruins.
They have thrown out the dead bodies of thy servants
to feed the birds of the air;
they have made thy loyal servants carrior for wild beasts.
Their blood is spilled all round Jerusalem like water,
and there they lie unburied.
We suffer the contempt of our neighbours,
the gibes and mockery of all around us.
How long, O Lord, wilt thou be roushed to such fury?
Must thy jealousy rage like a fire?
Pour out thy wrath over nations which do not know thee
and over kingdoms which do not invoke thee by name;
see how they have devoured Jacob and laid waste his homesteads.
Do not remember against us the guilt of past generations
but let thy compassion come swiftly to meet us,
we have been brought so low.
Help us, O God our saviour, for the honour of thy name;
for thy name's sake deliver us and wipe out our sins.
Why should the nations ask, 'Where is their god?'
Let thy vengeance for the bloody slaughter of thy
servants fall on those nations before our every eyes.
Let the groaning of the captives reach thy presence and
in thy great might set free death's prisoners.
As for the contempt our neighbours pour on thee,
O Lord, turn it back sevenfold on their own heads.
Then we thy people, the flock which thou dost shepherd, and repeat thy praise to every generation.[25]

Love Song in the Bible

There are two areas which are right for expression by the folk community. Most expressions fall with in this broad Canvas namely love and war. For one thing love has to be expressed discretly and by nature it has to veiled and indirect. The parties which are directly concerned in the act of love can alone understand the true import and content of communication. One of the best means of communication in love is by songs. It may be the song of the lovers or of the parents or of friends or general public. But the focus will be the love between a man and a woman.

The Israelite folk community had immortalised a love song in the song of Solomon in the Bible. The Bible which is so spiritual does not neglect the mysterious working of the mind of lovers. The song of Solomon is an expression of pure marital love between Solomon and one of his wives a Shunamite girl. The entire song has been titled as the song of songs, since it speaks both metaphoric meaning and ordinary human love. Metaphorically it refers to the love of the divine bride groom, symbolised here by Solomon's love of the Shunamite maiden. In mundane terms, it refers to an important aspect of human relationships namely the love of a man and a woman for each other. The folk community was clear about the need for human love and eroticism usually antecedent to it. The folk literature of the Bible community was definite about the place of love against lust and asceticism. In this immortal song, they have laid the foundation for the beauty of married love.

The Shunamite maiden desires to be kissed by her lover and the daughters of Jerusalem express in a chorus that love is better than wine. An interesting conversation ensures between the Shunamite maiden and her friends. In this drama, the shepherd lover Solomon speaks. The mutual admiration that both the Shunamite maiden and Solomon have for each other gives the continuation of this song. The whole song is a dialogue imagined between the Shunamite woman and Solomon. We get from each a full length portrait of each other. The bridegroom praises her and the bride praises the groom in aside, they speak to the audience too, and thus comes out one of the most interesting love songs in the world. This can be compared with the love songs of Tamil Nadu since both contain the same element of folklore.

The following song brings out the beauty of a love song. The singers are the Bride, Bridegroom and the companions:

The girl tells of her intense love for Solomon in words which are indeed immortal in folklore communication.

I will sing the song of all songs to Solomon
that he may smother me with kisses.
Your love is more fragrant than wine,
fragrant is the scent of your perfume.

The communication between lovers takes place in the presence of the friends of the girl. Yet the conversation is directly between the lovers. This is one of the features of folklore communication wherever there is an audience, the message is directed only to the concerned person. One of the important features of the folklore communication is its stark realism.

I am dark but lovely, daughters of Jerusalem,
    like the tents of Kedar
    or the tent-curtains of Shalmah.
Do not look down on me; a little dark I may be
    because I am scorched by the sun.

The lover immediately praises her beauty. Since the lovers are in a garden or forest the environment is given a reference in the conversation.

    Like an apricot-tree among the trees of the wood,
so is my beloved among boys.
To sit in its shadow was my delight,
and its fruit was sweet to my taste.
    He took me into the wine-garden
and gave me loving glances.
He refreshed me with raisings, he revived me with apricots;
    for I was faint with love.
His left arm was under my head, his right arm was round me.

There is much action in the love song, besides references to natural phenomenon.

Rise up, my darling;
my fairest, come away.
For now the winter is past,
the rains are over and gone;
the flowers appear in the country-side;
the time is coming when the birds will sing,
and the turtle - dove's cooing will be heard in our land;
when the green figs will ripen on the fig-trees
and the vines give forth their fragrance.
Rise up, my darling;
my fairest, come away.

The love song becomes practical when the dialogue is continued by the lovers on the one side, and the friends on the other. The friends have noticed that there are some difficulties which should be surmounted to enable the love to succeed.

Catch for us the jackals, the little jackals,
that spoil our vineyards, when the vines are in flower.
My beloved is mine and I am his;
    he delights in the lilies.
While the day is cool and the shadows are dispersing,
    turn, my beloved, and show yourself
a gazelle or a young wild goat
    on the hills where cinnamon grows.

The girl had gone to sleep. Perhaps because of the comfortable climate that might have been met with and Solomon charges the friends with the task of keeping a watch over his sweet heart.

I charge you, daughters of Jerusalem,
by the spirits and the goddesses of the field:
Do not rouse her, do not disturb my love
    until she is ready.

The friends intervene to continue the dialogue and the import of their conversation is an eulogy of Solomon.

The palanquin which King Solomon had made for himself
was of wood from Lebanon.
Its poles he had made of silver,
its head-rest of gold;
its seat was of purple stuff,
and its lining was of leather.

Now, the song turns into a soliloquy. Which immediately reminds a well known dramatic device usually adopted in social dramas. The soliloquy is entirely a reminesence of Solomon's intense love for the girl and comparisons are extremely erotic. To cite a few instances of descriptions of physical beauty, Solomon's words are intensly passionate.

How beautiful you are, my dearest, how beautiful!
Your eyes behind your veil are like doves,
your hair like a flock of goats streaming down Mount Gilead.
Your teeth are like a flock of ewes just shorn
which have come up fresh from the dipping;
each ewe has twins and none has cast a lamb.
Your lips are like a scarlet thread,
and your words are delightful;
your parted lips behind your veil
and like a pomegranate cut open.
Your neck is like David's tower,
which is built with winding courses;
a thousand bucklers hang upon it,
and all are warriors' shields.
Your two breasts are like two fawns,
twin fawns of a gazelle.

Perhaps sometime passed by, and the lover meet. A tragic dream sequence is narrated in the song. The girl falls aleep and dreams that her lover came and he goes away. In the folklore this is another feature which is often cited. Some element of tragedy, either imagenary or real is usually interposed in folklore communication.

I sleep but my heart is awake.
Listen ! My beloved is knocking:

'Open to me, my sister, my dearest,
    my dove, my perfect one;
for my head is drenched with dew,
    my locks with the moisture of the night'.

'I have stripped off my dress; must I put it on again?
I have washed my feet; must I soil them again?'

When my beloved slipped his hand through the latch-hole,
    my bowels stirred within me.
When I arose to open for my beloved,
    my hands dripped with myrrh;
the liquid myrrh from my fingers
    ran over the knobs of the bolt.
With my own hands I opened to my love,
    but my love had turned away and gone by;
my heart sank when he turned his back.
I sought him but I did not find him,
I called him but he did not answer.

The tragic element is further heightened by a dialogue with the friends of the lover, and the companions try to comfort her from her dream sequence of tragedy.

Now, Solomon appears on the scene and repeats in more enchanting terms his passion for the beauty of the girl he loves.

How you love to gaze on the Shulamite maiden,
    as she moves between the lines of dancers!

How beautiful are your sandalled feet, O prince's daughter!
    The curves of your thighs are like jewels,
    the work of a skilled craftsman.
    Your navelisa rounded goblet
    that never shall want for spiced wine.

Your belly is a heap of wheat
fenced in by lilies.
Your two breasts are like two fawns,
twin fawns of a gazelle.
Your neck is like a tower of ivory.
Your eyes are the pools in Heshbon,
beside the gate of the crowded city.
Your nose is like towering Lebanon
that looks towards Damascus.
You carry your head like Carmel;
the flowing hair on your head is lustrous black,
your tresses are braided with ribbons.
How beautiful, how entrancing you are,
my loved one, daughter of delights!
You are stately as a palm-tree,
and your breasts are the clusters of dates.
I said, 'I will climb up into the palm
to grasp its fronds'.
May I find your breasts like clusters of grapes on the vine
the scent of your breath like apricots,

The girl is completely enchanted by this bold expression of love and she succumbs to the delight of love making which leaves her with a sort of nostalgia and stupor. The song reaches its climax with the dialogue between first the companion of the girl and Solomon and finally between the bride and the bride groom. The scene is that of Solomon coming along with his sweet heart which is witnessed by his friends.

I am my beloved's, his longing is all for me.
Come, my beloved, let us go out into the fields
to lie among the henna-bushes;
let us go early to the vineyards
and see if the vine has budded or its blossom opened,
if the pomegranates are in flower.
There will I give you my love,

when the mandrakes give their perfume,
and all rare fruits are ready at our door,
fruits new and old
which I have in store for you, my love.

The companions say :

Who is this coming up from the wilderness
    leaning on her beloved?

The best of the folk communication is to convey the message of bliss and total happiness which comes in the wake of lovers achieving a climactic experience.

I am a wall and my breasts are like towers;
so in his eyes I am as one who brings contentment.
Solomon has a vineyard at Baal-hamon;
    he has let our his vineyard to guardians,
and each is to bring for its fruit
    a thousand pieces of silver.
But my vineyard is mine to give;
the thousand pieces are yours, O Solomon,
and the guardians of the fruit shall have two hundred.

Thus, the song of songs is extremely rustic but beautiful. It is direct at the same time with concealed meaning. It is erotic but at the same time very sensible. It is descriptive but at the same time not revelatory. These are the central features of folklore communication.

Ballads

A ballad is a story and a form of narrative folk song. Of the four elements common to all narrative action, character, setting and theme - the ballad emphasizes the first ie. narrative action. Setting is casual; theme is often implied, characters are usually types and even when more individual are undeveloped, but action carries the interest. The action is highly dramatic, often startling and all the more impressive because it is unrelieved. The ballad practices a rigid economy in relating the action; incidents antecedent to the climax are often omitted, as are explanatory and motivating details. The action is usually of a plot sort and the plot often reduced to the moment of climax, that is of the unstable situation and the resolution which constitutes plot, the ballad often concentrates on the resolution leaving the listener to supply details and antecedent material.

This type of folk song varies considerably with time and place, but certain characteristics remain fairly constant and seemingly fundamental:

(1) A ballad is narrative.
(2) A ballad is sung.
(3) A ballad belongs to the folk in content; style and designation.
(4) A ballad focuses on a single incident.
(5) A ballad is impersonal, the action moving of itself by dialogue and incident quickly to the end.[26]

Ballad-Definition

Ballad is a short poem that tells a story of some heroic deed, romance or event in history or legend. Ballad originated among common people. No one knows who wrote them. Originally ballads were meant to be sung. They often contain a chorous or repeat certain lines as a refrain. The typical ballad consists of stanzas which repeats a regular pattern. Various changes in the pattern take place as the story progresses. Ballads are usually written in simple language. People remember them but do not write them down.[27].

S. Sakthivel says:

> "Ballad may be an origin for an epic. What ever may be the origin ballad should undergo the progress of oral transmission for sometimes in order to attain its perfect

> form. Culture is the main foe for the origin of Ballads. In India drylands and backward areas are rich in ballads than the wet lands and forward areas. A nation's natural surroundings psychology of the races and behaviour of caste play an important role in the origin of Ballads.[28]

Malcolm Laws Jr. defines Ballad like this:

> "First of all, I will be dealing with a kind of narrative folk song. The story element is vital. If the folk song does not actually tell a story from beginning to end, I do not call it a ballad. If we find a poem that tells a story but is never sung, again I would not call it a ballad... To be called a ballad, the song must have a traditional life, that is, it must live primarily in the memories of the people and be passed by word of mouth from one singer to another"[29].

Following are the nature of a folk Ballad.

(1) Describes only one event.
(2) Originates from actual incident.
(3) Local theme.
(4) Prominence of heroism.
(5) Simple plot.
(6) Any body can become hero.
(7) Dialogues.
(8) Repetitions.[30]

Narrative Basis

Typically, the folk ballad tells a compact little story that begins eruptively at the moment when the narrative has turned decisively toward its catastrophe or resolution. Focusing on a single, climatic situation, the ballad leaves the inception of the conflict and the setting to be inferred or sketches them in hurriedly. Characterization is minimal, the characters revealing themselves in their actions or speeches; overt moral comment on the characters' behaviour is suppressed and their motivation seldom explicitly detailed [31].

Whatever description occurs in ballads is brief and conventional; transitions between scenes are abrupt and time shifts are only vaguely indicated crucial events and emotions are conveyed in crisp, poignant dialogue. In short, the ballad method of narration is directed toward achieving a bold, sensational, dramatic effect with purposeful starkness and abruptness. But despite the rigid economy of ballad narratives, a repertory of rhetorical devices is employed for prolonging highly charged moments in the story and thus thickening the emotional atmosphere.

Oral Transmission

Since ballads thrive among unlettered people and are freshly created from memory at each performance, they are subject to constant variation in both text and tune. Where tradition is healthy and not highly influenced by literary or other outside cultural influences, these variations keep the ballad alive by gradually bringing them into line with the style of life, beliefs and emotional needs of the immediate folk audience. Ballad tradition, however, like all folk arts, is basically conservative, a trait that explains the references in several ballads to obsolete implements and customs, as well as the appearance of words and phrases so badly garbled as to show that the singer does not understand their meaning though he takes pleasure in their sound and respects their traditional right to a place in his song.

The new versions of ballads that arise as the result of cumulative variations are no less authentic than their antecedents. A poem is fixed in its final form when published, but the printed or taped record of a ballad is representative only of its appearance in one place, in one line of tradition, and at one moment in its protean history. "The first record of a ballad is not its original form, merely its earliest recorded form, and the recording of a ballad does not inhibit tradition from varying it subsequently into other shapes, because tradition preserves by recreating rather than by exact reproduction"[32].

Ballads in the Bible

Ballads in the Bible deal mainly the story of the liberation of the Israel from their oppressors. The first of this kind, we find in the 15th chapter of Exodus.

The Hebrews, suffered a great humiliation and torture in their bondage at the hands of the Egyptians. So the God of Israel, YHWH wanted to liberate them and told Moses to liberate his people.

> "Then the Lord said (to Moses), 'I have observed the misery of my people who are in Egypt; I have heard their cry on account of their task masters. Indeed, I know their sufferings, and I have come down to deliver them from the Egyptians... The cry of the Israelites has now come to me; I have also seen how the Egyptians oppress them. So come, I, will send you to Pharaoh to bring my people, the Israelites out of Egypt"[33].

Then the Lord sent ten kinds of Plagues on the Egyptians and at the end the Israelites were allowed to leave Egypt by the king of Egypt. But when they were on the shore of the Red sea, the King sent his army with the chariots. Then the God of Israel divides the Red sea and made the Israel to cross the Red sea on a dry land and when the Egyptian army came and he drowned them in the sea. Thus the deliverance of the Israelites happened. Moses in the following ballad sings this story.

The Song of Moses

"I will sing to the Lord, for he has triumphed gloriously; horse and rider he has thrown into the sea.The Lord is my strength and my might, and he has become my salvation; this is my God, and I will praise him, my father's God, and I will exalt him.

The Lord is a warrior; the Lord is his name.

"Pharaoh's chariots and his army he cast into the sea; his picked officers were sunk in the Red Sea. The floods covered them; they went down into the depths like a stone.

Your right hand, O Lord, glorious in power your right hand, O Lord shattered the enemy.

In the greatness of your majesty you overthrew your adversaries; you sent out your fury, it consumed them like stubble.

At the blast of your nostrils the waters pilled up, the floods stood up in a heap; the deeps congealed in the heart of the sea.

The enemy said, 'I will pursue, I will overtake, I will divide the spoil, my desire shall have its fill of them. I will draw my sword, my hand shall destroy them'.

You blew with your wind, the sea covered them; they sank like lead in the mighty waters.

"Who is like you O Lord, among the gods? Who is like you, majestic in holiness, awesome in doing wonders?

You stretched out your hand, the earth swallowed them.

"In your steadfast love your led the people whom you redeemed; you guided them by your strength to your abode.

The peoples heart, they trembled; pangs seized the inhabitants of Philistia.

Then the chiefs of Edom were dismayed; trembling seized the leaders of Moab; all the inhabitants of Canaan melted away.

Terror and dread fell upon them; by the might of your arm, they became still as a stone until your people, O Lord passed by, until the people whom you acquired, You brought them in and planted them on the mountain of your own possession, the place, O Lord, that you made your abode, the sanctuary, O Lord, that your hands have established.

The Lord will reign forever and ever".

Ballad on the Defeat of King Sihon

The second Ballad is recorded in the book of Numbers, chapter 21:27-30. This tells about the victory of the Israelites on the King Sihon.

There fore the ballad singers say,

> "Come to Heshbon, let it be built; let the city of Sihon be established. For fire came out from Heshbon, flame from

> the city of Sihon. It devoured Ar of Moab, and swallowed up the heights of the Arnon.Woe to you, O Moab! You are undone, O people of Chemosh! He has made his sons fugitives, and his daughters captives, to an Amorite king, Sihon. So their posterity perished from Heshbon to Dibon, and we laid waste until fire spread to Medeba".

The Song of Deborah

The third ballad is recorded in Judges. 5:1-31. The story is the cry for liberation come from the Israelites to God. The King Jabin of Canaan oppressed them, through the commander of his army Sisera. The oppression went on cruelly for twenty long years. At that time Deborah the prophetess, with the help of Barak, by the command of God took steps for the liberation of the Israelites. The war broke out and Sisera could not stand before the army of the Lord led by Barak fled away. Barak was chasing him. In under to escape Sisera asked for the asylum from Jael wife of Heber, an Israelite. She gave him shelter and when Sisera was sleeping Jael took a tent peg, and took a hammer and drove the peg into his temple, and thus the liberation was achieved.

This story was sung as a ballad by Deborah the Prophetess.

"When locks are long in Israel, when the people offer themselves willingly bless the" Lord! Hear, O kings; give ear, O Princes; to the Lord I will sing, I will make melody to the Lord, the God of Israel." Lord, when you went out from Seir, when you marched from the region of Edom, the earth trembled, and the heavens poured, the clouds indeed poured water.

> The mountains quaked before the Lord, the One of Sinai, before the Lord, the God of Israel. "In the days of Shamgar son of Anath, in the days of Jael, caravans ceased and travellers kept to the byways.The peasantry prospered in Israel, they grew fat on plunder, because you arose, Deborah arose as a mother. When new gods were chosen, then was in the gates was shield or spear to be seen among forty thousand in Israel?

My heart goes out to the commanders of Israel who offered themselves willingly among the people.

Bless the Lord. Tell of it, you who ride on white donkeys, you who sit on rich carpets and you who walk by the way. To the sound of musicians at the watering places, there they repeat the triumphs of the Lord the triumphs of his peasantry in Israel. Then down to the gates marched the people of the Lord.

"Awake, awake, Deborah! Awake, awake, utter a song!

Arise, Barak, lead away your captives, O son of Abinoam. Then down marched the remnant of the noble; the people of the Lord marched down for him against the mighty. From Ephraim they set out into the valley, following you Benjamin, with your kin, from Machir marched down the commanders, and from Zebulun those who bear the marshal's staff; the chiefs of Issachar came with Deborah, and Issachar faithful to Barak, into the valley they rushed out at his heels. Among the clans of Reuben there were great searchings of heart.

Why did you tarry among the sheepfolds, to hear the piping for the flocks? among the clans of Reuben there were great searchings of heart. Gilead stayed beyond the Jordan; and Dan, why did he abide with the ships? Asher sat still at the coast of the sea, settling down by his landings. Zebulun is a people that scorned death; Naphtali too, on the heights of the field." The kings came, they fought; then fought the kings of Canaan, at Taanach, by the waters of Megiddo; they got no spoils of silver.

The stars fought from heaven, from their courses they fought against Sisera. The torrent Kishon swept them away, the on rushing torrent, the torrent Kishon. March on, my soul, with might! "Then loud beat the horses' hoofs with the galloping, galloping of his steeds."

"Curse Meroz, says the angel of the Lord, curse bitterly its inhabitants, because they did not come to the help of the Lord, to the help of the Lord against the mighty"

"Most blessed of women be Jael, the wife of Heber the Kenite, of tent-dwelling women most blessed. He asked water and she gave him milk, she brought him curds in a lordly bowl. She put her hand to the tent peg and her right hand to the workmen's mallet; she struck Sisera a blow, she crushed his head, she shattered and pierced his temple. He sank, he fell, he lay still at her feet; at her feet he sank, he fell; where he sank, there he fell dead." Out of the window she peered, the mother of Sisera gazed through the lattice: Why is his chariot so long in coming? Why tarry the hoofbeats of his chariots?' Her wisest ladies make answer, indeed, she answers the question herself: Are they not finding and dividing the spoil?- A girl or two for every man; spoil of dyed stuffs for Sisera, spoil of dyed stuffs embroidered, two pieces of dyed work embroidered for my neck as spoil?' "So perish all your enemies, O Lord! But may your friends be like the sun as it rises in its might".

As a folk community the Israelites were blessed with the folk arts and forms. And they were also rich with the talent of music and song. One of such talent is proved by the ballads.

Conclusion

The natural expression of the Israelies by their songs and music give us the knowledge of their life and customs. As a folk community the Israelies were gifted with their talents of music, songs and dances. Music as we know it has become quite complex, a luxury and entertainment, music in antiquity however, was a functional expression of daily life work and a worship and it is true with the Israelite folk community.

NOTES

1. Alexander H. Krappe, '*The Science of Folklore*'. (New York. The Norton Library. 1964) p. 153.
2. Paul J. Achtemeir, *Harper's Bible Dictionary* (Bangalore. Theological Publications in India. 1990) p. 665.
3. Ibid. p. 667.
4. Walter A. Elwell (Ed), *Baker Encyclopedia of the Bible*. Vol.II. (Michigan Baker Book House. 1995) p. 1509.
5. I. Chro. 15:14; 16:5,
6. Gen. 4:21.

7. 2. Sam. 6:5.
8. Walter A. Elwell, *Baker Encyclopedia of the Bible*. Vol.II. (Michiga. Baker Book house. 1995) p. 1509.
9. 2.Sam.6:5; I.Kings. 10:12; Neh. 12:27; Ps.57:8; Amos.5:23.
10. Harvey H.Guthrie, Jr, *Israel's Sacred Songs*. (New York: The Seabury Press. 1966) p. 120.
11. 2. Sam. 1:19-27.
12. Ps. 102: 3-7.
13. Ps. 88: 1-2.
14. Ps. 88 3-5.
15. Ps. 102:23-24.
16. Ps. 69:1-2.
17. Ps. 17: 1-3.
18. Ps. 17:10-12.
19. Ps. 37:11-15.
20. Ps. 6:3; 13:1-2; 74:10; Jer.12:4.
21. Ps. 22: 1-2.
22. Ps. 102:9-10.
23. Raymond E. Brown (ed), *The New Jerome Biblical Commentary*. (Bangalore. Theological Publications in India 1992) p. 525.
24. Ps.60:1-4.
25. Ps.79: 1-13.
26. Maria Leach (ed), *Standard Dictionary of Folklore: Mythology and Legend* (New York: Funk & Wagnalls, 1972) p. 106.
27. *The World Encyclopaedia.* Vol. II P134
28. S. Sakthivel, '*Nattupura Iyal Aayvu*' (Chennai: Manivasagar Pathippagam. 1992) P.73.
29. Tristram Coffin, *American Folklore*. (Washington. Voice of America Information Agency. 1974) P.93.
30. Ibid. p. 81.
31. *Encyclopaedia Britanica* Vol. 2. p. 641.
32. Ibid. p. 642.
33. Exo. 3:7-10.

9

FOLK MEDICINE IN THE BIBLE

Introduction

Disease and sickness have plauged man since God cast Adam and Eve out of the Garden of Eden says the Bible.

> "By the sweat of your face you shall eat bread Until you return to the ground, for out of it you were taken; You are dust and to dust you shall return".
>
> - *Gen. 3:19*

The Hebrews believed that illness was caused by sin in the individual, which God had to punish (Gen. 12:17, prov. 23:29-32), may be the sin of a person's parents (2 Sam. 12:15); or seduction by Satan (Matt. 9:34; Luke. 13:16), However, some Biblical verses show that there is not always such a simple explanation for disease. (Job 34:19-20).

Health and Disease Defined

The difficulty of defining disease is implied in the very structure of the word 'disease'. So many different kinds of disturbances can make a person feel not at ease and lead him to seek the aid of a physician that the word ought to encompass most of the difficulties inherent in the human condition.

It seems reasonable at first sight to define health as the absence of disease.... The preamble of the charter of the World Health Organization attempts to convey this Utopian Ideal in the following words:

"Health is a state of complete physical, mental and social well being and not merely the absence of disease or infirmity"[1].

Folk Medicine

Medicine is older than doctors. Hence Oswald A. Enrich defines it:

> "Folk Medicine is the substance of all the traditional view points on sickness and the healing methods applied against disease which exist among the people"[2].

Of folk medicine there are essentially, two branches:

(1) Natural folk medicine.
(2) Magico-religious folk medicine.

The first of these represents one of man's earliest reactions to his natural environment, and involves the seeking of cures for his ills in the herbs, plants, minerals and animal substances of nature. Natural medicine, which is some times called rational folk medicine, and some times herbal folk medicine because to the predominance of herbs in its medica, is shared with primitive cultures, and in some cases some of its many effective cures have made their way into scientific medicine.

The second branch of folk medicine is the magico religious variety, some time called "occult" folk medicine, which attempts to use charms, holy words and holy action to cure disease.

Natural or herbal folk medicine is undoubtedly as ancient as occult folk medicine and has been widely practised. This type of healing in its commonest from is old fashioned, domestic, household medicine, the kind our mothers and grand-mothers normally practised.

S. Sakthivel gives various names for folk medicine, They are:

"Folk medicine, Ethno medicine, popular medicine, popular health culture Ethnoatry, Ethnoiatrics"[3].

Don Yoder divides Folk Medicine into two major categories as Natural Folk Medicine and Magico-Religious Medicine. Under the Magico-Religious Medicine, following reasons are given for the sickness and treated by the Magico-Religious Medicine. They are diseases due to the wrath of god and godesses, Evil spirits, witch craft, evil eye and breach of taboos.

The Natural folk medicine is divided into two categories as treatment for human beings and animals, and the medicine, are given both for internal and external use. The medicines are mainly herbs and shrubs.

G. Shanthi says:

> "Sickness is the result of wrong doing, sins and fault. If one has indulged in such acts in this (or) in the past life, he has to suffer from sickness and deprivations, the degree of which depends upon the extent of his sinfulness. Through one's sinful acts, one, not only sickness up on oneself, but also on the members of one's family or community"[4].

Since the Biblical community is a folk community, it also had the same belief as all the other folk communities were having.

The Biblical Outlook on Disease

The topics of suffering and disease in the Bible, are closely bound up with the questions of the nature and origin of evil itself. Suffering is a human experience, and diverse causes, and is one of the results of human sin. In the case of suffering from diseases the link is not usually obvious, though sometimes the illness is directly connected. From the account of the fall of man in Genesis it is clear that soon afterwards man knew insecurity, fear and pains (Gen. 3:16,17) and then mental anguish (Gen. 4:13). The direct connection between sin and suffering becomes rapidly more complex, but nations which obeyed God were, in general promised freedom from disease[5].

On the other hand pestilence is one of the three sore judgements on the people of God[6] and on other nations. eg. Philistines (I samuel. 5:6), and Assyrians (II Kings. 19:35). There are passages such as Ps. 119:67, when the sinner himself is involved, and the case of disabled man healed, recorded in Jn. 5:1-16, where his own fault implied (v.14)

"Afterward Jesus found him in the temple, and said to him, 'See, you are well; Sin no more, that nothing worse be fall you".

Jn. 5:14

David's sin involved the afflictions of others[7].

On the whole, human suffering, from disease or from any other cause, is the effect on the individual of the spiritual analaise of the human society of which he is an integral part.

In Job.1. some thing is seen of the activity of Satan. This is also apparent in Acts. 10:38, where the sick one spoken of as 'all that were oppressed by the devil', and in the suggestive parable of the wheat and tares (An enemy has done this; Mt. 13:28). Again Christ himself spoke of this women, whom Satan bound..." (Lk. 13:16).

Now let us see the diseases recorded in the Bible.

Diseases in the Bible

Many of the more common diseases of the Ancient Middle East are listed in Deut. 28 among the punishments destined to strike Israel is that nation turned away from God. In the catalogue provided below are : wasting disease (probably tuberculosis), fever (including malaria, typhoid, typhus), inflammation, boils and tumour, festering sores and itch (probably scabies, caused by a tiny burrowing insect), Madness such as Saul's Paranoia (I. Sam; 16:14-23) and Nebuchad - nazzar's insanity (Dan. 4), blindness and confusion of the mind and plauges (including bubonic).

Leprosy, mentioned often in each Testament, served as the general name for a variety of skin conditions. Blindness was common, and is mentioned sixty times in scripture. In hot, dusty Palestine, eyes were specially susceptible to a variety of infections.

The Gospels mention a woman with a serious menstrual disorder which caused her to hemorrhage chronically for twelve years (Lk. 8:43-48). Other physical problems described are paralysis (Mk.2:1-12) and epilepsy (Mt. 17:14-18).

Indentifying Diseases

In Old Testament times, the Hebrews associated healing with God. For e.g. Malachi, the prophet spoke of the sun of righteousness rising with healing in his Wings (Mal.4:2); and David praised God as the one 'that heal all thy diseases'. (Ps.103:3).

Types of Diseases, and Ailments

Aphasia

This is the temporary loss of speech, usually caused by a brain lesion but sometimes attributes to an emotional upset. This happened to the prophet Ezekiel (Ezek. 33:22). When an angel told Zacheriah that he was going to be the father of John the Baptist, the old man came out of the temple and could not speak. (Luke. 1:22).

Apoplexy

This term refers to a rupture or obstruction of a brain artery, causing a stroke. When Abigail told Nabal of his insult to David and its dire-consequences, Nabal's heart died within him, and he became like a stone, ten days later he died (I. Sam. 25:37-38). These symptoms suggest that he suffered an attack of apoplexy. The same rate may have be fallen Uzzah, who touched the ark of covenant (2 Sam. 6:7), as well as Ananias and Sapphira (Acts. 5:5, 9-10).

Blains

This terms probably refer to authrax, a disease that can be transmitted to humans by cattle, sheep, goats and horses. The disease is caused by a rod shaped bacteria that forms spores. These spores in turn can infect humans, who develop a boil like lesion with pusture (blain). In the sective stage, the blain is called a malignant pustule. Blains are mentioned only once in the Bible in Ex. 9:9-10. God inflicted them on the Egytians when the Pharoah refused to let the Hebrews go to the promised land.

Blemishes

This general term refers to any bodily defects such a blindness, lameness, a broken bone, extra fingers or toes (Poly dactylism), a humped back and so on. A person with blemishes could not offer sacrifices to God (Lev. 21:16-24), nor was he permitted to go beyond the veil of the temple or come near the altar, for this would defile the sanctuary. Imperfect animals could not be used for sacrifices (Ex.12:5).

Blindness and Hearing Loss

Three types of blindness are mentioned in Scripture, sudden blindness caused by flies and aggravated by dirt, dust and glace, the gradual blindness caused by old ages; and chronic blindness. Paul suffered temporary blindness on the road to Damascus (Acts. 9:8). Scripture often refers to the old persons whose eyes "grew-dins" (Gen. 27:1, 48:10; I.Sam.4:15). But the Bible more often refers to chronic blindness.

The Israelites had compassion for the blind. Infact, God placed a curse upon those who made the blind wander out of their way (Deut. 27:18). Jesus ministered to many people who were blind. He said, God has anointed me, to preach the gospel to the poor, he has sent me to heal the broken hearted, to preach deliverance to the captives, and recovering sight to the blind (Luke. 4:18). Jesus healed a man born blind (John 9:1-41), a blind man whose healing was gradual (Mark. 8:24), two blind men sitting by the way side (Matt. 20:30-34) and a great number of others (Mark. 10:46-520 Luke 7:21).

Blindness was often understood to be a punishment for evil doing. We find examples of this at Sodom (Gen. 19:11); in the

Syrian army (2 Kings. 6:18); and in the case of Elymas at Paphos (Acts. 13:6-11).

The New Testament occasionally refers to persons who had lost the ability to speak (Matt. 9:32; 15:30; Luke. 11:14). This often was the result of hearing loss.

Boils

This term refers to any inflamed ulcers on the skin, such as those caused by a staph infection. They may have been confused with 'blains' or authrax. Boils (Shechin in Hebrew) one first mentioned in Exo 9:9, when the Pharoah refused to let the Israelites leave Egypt, and boils broke out upon the people. Satan was permitted to afflict Job with boils from the top of his head to the tip of his toes (Job 2:7). King Hezekiah also was afflicted with boils (2 Kings. 20:7), which Isaiah cured by applying a poultice of figs. A fresh fig poultice has a drawing effect. Before the advent of antibiotics, this type of treatment for boils was common.

Cancer

Hezekiah was very sick and the Lord told him to prepare to die (2 Kings. 20:1). The Lord inflicted an incurable disease upon Jehoram, and after two years his bowels fell out (2 Chro. 21:18-19). Biblical scholars believed these men may have suffered some type of cancer though chronic dysentry would also have produced Jehoram's symptoms. However, the Bible does not refer to the cancer by name, because the disease had not been identified in Biblical times.

Consumption or Tuberculosis

Moses warned the rebellious Isralites, that Lord shall smite them with consumption and with a fever, and with an inflammation and with an extreme burning... (Deut 28:22).

Dysentry

This is a disease that in its advanced stage, rots the bowls (2. Chro. 21:15-19). The fibrine is separated from the inner coating of the intestines and is expelled.

The New Testament refers to a severe form of dysentry as the bloody flux. The father of a christian named Publius lay sick with the bloody flux (Acts. 28:8). Paul came in and prayed for him and the man was healed.

Edema (Dropsy)

This describes an abnormal accumulation of serum fluid in the body's connective tissue or in a serious cavity and is a symptom. The accumulation causes swelling. Jesus met atleast one victim of 'edema' in a certain Pharisees home. Asked by Jesus if he thought it lawful to heal on the sabbath, the pharisee declined to answer. Jesus then healed the sufferer. (Lk. 14:1-4).

Endocrine Disturbances

The law of Moses did not permit a dwarfed person to enter the congregation of God's people (Lev.21:20). Modern science has shown that dwarfism is caused by disturbances in the endocrine glands.

The Bible also mentioned a number of giants such as Goliath (I.Sam.17:4). True giantism is caused by excessive secretions of the pituitary gland. However, many tall persons inherit their tallness from their forefathers.

Epilepsy

This is a disorder marked by eratic electrical discharges of the central nervous system and mainfested by convulsive attacks. A certain man brought his epileptic son to Jesus for help (Mk 9:17-29). The King James Version of the Bible says that the boy had a 'dumb spirit'—Jesus healed him.

An ancient theory held that epilepsy was caused by the moon; people referred to epileptics as being 'Moon stroke'-Ps. 121:6 may reflect this idea where it says 'the sun shall not smite thee by day, not the moon by night'.

Female Disorders

According to the Mosaic Law, a woman suffering from menstrual disorders was to be considered unclean (Lev. 15:25). One such women who had suffered for twelve years (Lk. 8:43-48) touched the hem of Jesus garment and because of her great faith, she was healed immediatly.

Fever

The King James Version uses the word ague to describe a burning fever. Moses warned the rebellious Israelites that, "he will never appoint over you terror, panic, consumption and the burning ague that shall consume the eyes (Lev. 26:16)". When Jesus found Peter's mother-in-law ill with this symptom, he rebuked the fever and she was able to rise from her bed and wait on the disciples (Lk.4:38). On another occasion, Jesus healed the son of a Government official (Jn.4:46-54).

Many diseases in ancient Palestine would have been characterised by high fevers; the most common of which were Malaria and Typhoid. A plague broke out when the Philistines placed the ark of God in an idol's temple (I.Sam 5:2, 9,12). The out break was associated with mice.

Gangrene

This disease is mentioned only once in the Bible. "And then talk will spread like gangrene"—2.Tim. 2:17. Normally it spreads rapidly and eats up tissue.

Gout

Excessive uric acid in the blood causes this kidney ailment that manifests itself through painful inflammation of joints. 2 Chro 16:12 says that King Asa had a foot disease which apparently was Gout. Later he died out of it [8].

—2. Chro.16:12

Lameness

Scripture describes many persons who were lame, the most memorable case being recorded in Acts 3:2-11, where we read about a man (born lame) who was carried daily to beg. One day the begger saw Peter and John entering the temple and beseeched them for money. Instead, the apostles invoked the name of Jesus to heal the man. Peter lifted up the beggar who began to walk. Jesus healed many persons who were lame (Matt.15:30-31).

Leprosy

One of the most dreaded diseases of the world, leprosy in caused by a bacillus and is characterised by formation of modules that spread, causing loss of sensation and deformity. Now treated with sulfone drugs, leprosy perhaps the least infectious of all known contagious diseases. Hensen's Disease, as it is more properly known, was often misdiagnosed in Biblical times. People believed then, that it was highly contagious and hereditary. Lev. 13:1-17 condemned leprosy as a 'plague'.

On the basis of a hair in a scab, a pimple, or a spot on the skin that had turned white, the priest would declare a person to be a leper and should expel him for seven days. If no changes in the spot occurred by then, the expulsion would be extended another week. At that time if the spot had started to fade, the leper would be pronounced cured and returned to his normal life. However, if the spot remained or had spread, he was declared unclean and banished.

Leprosy was very common in the Near East. If a Hebrew was healed of leprosy, he was expected to offer certain sacrifices and engage in rites of purification (Lev.14:1-32). Jesus healed lepers on numerous occasions (LK.5:12-13; 17:12-17).

Malaria

This infectious disease was caused by protozoa of the "genus plas modium". These one, called animals can live in the blood of human beings and animals or in the female Anopheles mosquito. Once Malaria is in the system, it recurs. St. Paul may have been referring to malaria, when be spoke of his "thorn in the flesh"[9].

Mental and Nervous Disorders

King Saul Seems to have had symptoms of manic depression (I.Sam.16:14-23), and the Bible mentions others who may have suffered from mental or nervous disorders, king Nebuchadnezzar is an example. (Dan. 4:33).

Palsy

It is a total paralysis. The Gospels record a well known incident in which Jesus healed a paralysed man at Capernaum (Mark. 2:1-12). The book of Acts describes how the apostles healed people with palsy (Acts. 8:7; 9:33-34).

Plague

Our English versions of the Bible may use this word to denote any epidemic disease. It is also used in a general sense in Exo.7-10, where it refers to the hardships that God inflicted upon the Egyptians.

Epidemics hit the Israelites three times during their wandering in the wilderness. The first time was when they were eating the Quail that God sent to satisfy their longing for meat (Num. 11:33). The second time, 'a plague' claimed the lives of spies who discouraged the Israelites from entering the promised Land

(Num.14:37). The third epidemic came as God's punishment upon the Israelites. Aaron stopped this plague by offering incense to God (Num.16:46-47). On another occasion, Phinah as saved the Israelites from an epidemic by killing a man who brought a Midianite woman into their midst. Nevertheless 24,000 people died (Num 25:8-9).

The Old Testament describes many cases in which God sent 'Plagues' to chastise his people. One example is found in 2 Samuel where king David says, "Build an alter unto the Lord that the plague may be stayed from the people"—2 Sam.24:21.

The King James version also uses plague to refer to any painful affliction. When the woman with a chronic hemorrhage was healed, she felt that she had been healed of a 'plague' (Mk 5:29). We have no evidence that the Bible ever refers to bubonic plauge, which would claim millions of lives in medieval Europe.

Polio

This is the common name for infantile paralysis which usually affects children. I. Kings. 17:17 tells of a woman who brought her son to the prophet Elijah. The boy was so sick that there was no breath in him; this symptom suggests that he may have had polio, although it also may have been a form of 'meningitis'. Elijah revived the boy through the Lord's intervention in answer to his prayer. However, scripture does not tell us if the boy was completely cured. The men described in Matt. 12:9-13 and Jn. 5:2 may have had Polio.

Skin Disorders

The Bible refers to many kinds of skin disorders such as the 'itch' or ring worm (Lev.13:30; 21:20). Lev. 13:39 probably refers to Vitiligo, which was confused often with leprosy. Rather the reference in Lev. 21:20,22 refers to an itching or scabing condition caused by fungus.

Small Pox

Some Bible scholars believe that the Hebrew word Maquq (literally 'waste away') refers to small pox. The King James version usually translates this word as 'pineaway' which suggests emotional despair, "And they that were left of you shall pineaway" (Lev. 26:39).

"Ye shall not mourn nor weep, but shall pine away for your iniquities". (Eze. 24:23). In one instance the KJV understands Maquq to denote a 'corruption' of the skin. "My wounds stink and are corrupt because of my foolishness". (Ps.38:5).

Sunstroke

Isaiah may have referred to sunstorke or heat prostration when he said 'neither shall heat nor sun smite thee'. (Isa. 49:10). I Kings describes a youngman who was working among the reapers when he said to his father, "My head, my head". He was carried into the home, where he died (2 Kings. 4:18-20). Sunstroke was a common malady in the hot summer of the Near East.

Syncope

Arrested heart action or the sudden lowering of blood pressure is normally called syncope. When Jacob learned that his son Joseph was still alive, his father 'fainted'. (Gen. 45:26), probably a reference to syncope. When Eli heard that the ark of the covenant had been captured, be fell backwards off his seat, broke his neck and died (1 Sam 4:18). This may have been another instance of heart failure or syncope.

Venereal Disease

There are some evidences that venereal diseases were common in Bible times. For e.g. Zech.11:17, warns the shephered who leaves his flock saying that his arm will be dried up and his right eye will go blind. These symptoms indicate a disease of the spinal cord, probably venerael disease. Some believe that Leah had an eye condition that could have been the result of hereditory syphlis (Gen.29:17).

Worms

Isaiah warned that the rebellious people of Israel would be afflicted with worms (Isa. 51:8). He also predicted this fate for Babylon (Isa. 41:1). This parasitic disease could be fatal because no medical remedies were available. Scripture says that 'an angel of the Lord' smote Herod, the Great. Worms ate him up and he died. (Acts. 12:23).

The Treatment of Disease

The therapeutics of the Bible are these of the time, and are described in general terms.

> "A cheerful heart is a good medicine"
>
> *Proverbs. 17:22.*

Local applications are frequently referred to for sores. (Isa.1:6; Jen.8:22, 51:8), and a 'Cake of figs' is recommended by Isaiah for Hezekiah's boil (Isa. 38:21). The Good Samaritan used wine and oil as a local treatment (Lk.10:34). Such treatment is often ineffective, however, as in the case of the woman with the issue of blood (Mk.5:26), or conditions, are apparently intrinsically incurable, as in the case fo Mephibesheth (2.Sam 4:4).

In Deut. 28:27 there is a note of despair about some illnesses.

> "The Lord will smite you with the boils of Egypt, and with the ulcers and the scurvy and the itch, of which you cannot be healed".
>
> "The Lord will smite you with madness and blindness and confusion of mind; and you shall grope at noon-day, as the blind grope in darkness".
>
> *Dent.28:27, 28*

It is not surprising that treatment is sometimes bound up with superstition, such as the attempt by Leah and Rachel to use mandrakes to increase sexual desire in infertility (Gen. 30:14-16).

Wine is twice mentioned as a medicament and stimulent (Pre.31:6; I.Tim.5:23).

The word physician is rarely used, but implies much the same as 'doctor' in English today (e.g. Exo. 15:26; Jer. 8:22; Mk 5:26; Lk.8:43). Asa is condemned (2 Chro. 16:12) for consulting 'physicians', but these may have been magically minded; and worthless, and not really deserving the name of physician. The point of condemnation is that he did not seek the Lord. Job condemns his conforters as 'worthless physicians' (Job. 13:4). In the New Testament, physicians are twice mentioned proverbial by Christ (Lk 4:23, 5:31). There are mentioned in the incident of the woman who had an issue of blood (Lk.8:43). Luke is referred to by Paul as 'the beloved physician' (Colo. 4:14).

The Jewish religion differed from many non-Jewish religions in that there was almost no confusion between the offices of priest and physician. Declaration of dignosis of, and freedom, from, leprosy is an exception (Lev.13:9-17; Lk.17:14). Prophets were consulted about progresses (e.g. I. Kings. 14:1-13; 2 Kings 1:1-4, 8:9, Isaiah 38:1,21). A primitive form of bone setting is mentioned is Ezekiel 30:21.

Natural Folk Medicine

Natural folk medicine are usually of home remedy or a patent medicine. Herbal folk-medicine is the main part of natural folk-medicine. Herbs, plants, minerals of nature and animals substance of nature are considered as the Herbal folk medicine[10].

> "Herbs and spices considered in the popular sense of edible culinary, or some times medicinal. Plants although strictly a herb is a non-weedy plant with seasonal foliage and varying expectation of life in the root"[11].

In the Old Testament the Hebrew word dese normally denotes grass, hasir, e seb and the less common yaraq (Deut. 11:10; I Kings.21:2, Pro 15:17) may mean grass, and also herbs or vegetables. Herbs and spices such as cummin, dill Cinnamon and mint were employed in the preparation of food (Ezek.24:10) and the flavouring of wines. The manufacture of the sacred incense necessitated the base of frankincense, stacte, galbanum, onycha and sweet cane (Exo.30:34), while substances such as cassia, aloes and spikenard were used as unguents for cosmetic purposes. (Esther.2:12; Mk 14:3; Jn.12:3)[12].

When bodies were being prepared for burial it was customary for spices to be placed in the grave clothes as a form of embalming. They included mixtures of myrrh and aloes. (Jn.19:39), or more generally, spices and ointments. (Lk.23:56) (For The burial of Jesus).

> "Nicodemus, who had at first come to Jesus by night, also came, bringing a mixture of myrrh and aloes, weighing about a hundred pounds".
>
> —*Jn. 19:39*

> "Then they returned, and prepared spices and Eintments".
>
> —*Lk.23:56*

Medicinal Herbs Mentioned in the Bible

Following are some of the herbs which were used as medicinal herbs:

Aloes

Jn.19:39 refers to a liliaceons plant 'aloe barbadense', wild in the Yemen and now widely naturalized. The juice of its fleshy, sword like leaves is bitter and was used for embalming.

Balm

This herb is celebrated for healing properties (Jer.46:11) and often used for cosmetic purposes, it was used also to symbolize deliverance from natural distress. (Jer. 8:22; 51:8)

Coriander

Indigenous to the Mediteranean area, this small umbelliferous annual (coriandrum satirum) is known to have been used as early as 1550 BC for culinary and medicinal purposes.

Dill

An annual umbelliferous plant with firmely divided leaves and small greenish yellow flowers. The seeds and leaves were widely used for culinary and medicinal purposes inantiquity (Mt.23:23).

Rue

It grows in the rocky places of Palestine, Rue was highly prized for its medicinal value, having alleged disinfectant and antiseptic properties (Lk.11:42).

Saffron

It is a native of Greece, and in antiquity saffron was used for dying and colouring food stuff. It was also a therepeutic agent, being used as an emmenagegue, stimulant and anti spasmedic.

Oil was also used as medicine.

I. Sam.1:6 says:

> "From the sole of the feet even to the head, there is no soundness in it, but buries and seres and blessing wounds; they are not pressed cut, or bound up or softened with oil".

Mark 6:3 says:

> " ..... and anointed with oil many that were sick and healed them".

James:5:14 says:

> "Is any among you sick? Let him call for the elders of the church and let them pray over him, anointing him with oil in the name of the Lord ....."

Wine

Wine was also used for the remedy both internally and externally.

Luke: 10:34 says:

> "..... and went to him (the wounded person) and bound his wounds, pouring on oil and wine".

I. Tim. 5:23

Paul says to Timothy

"No longer drink only water, but use a little wine for the sake of your stomach and your frequent ailments".

Treatment of Fractures

Ezekiel 30:21 says:

> "The word of the Lord came to me—"Son of man, I have broken the arms of Pharoah, king of Egypt; and lo; it has not been bound up, to heal it, by binding it with a bandage, so that it may become strong to wield the sword".

Treatment of Infection

Treatment of infection is recorded in Leviticus 15:5

> "And any one who touches his (i.e. the unclean persons) bed shall wash his clothes and bathe himself in water".

Magico-Religious Folk Medicine

In ancient times, it was believed that some mystical powers resided in the medicinal herbs, hence they cure diseases. The Medical man was, therefore, almost a migician. Vetter, George, B. in his work '*Magic and Religion* (p.146) says:

> "These magicians who are experts in art of magic are well equipped with considerable bag of tricks, combination of medical skill and practical knowledge with an impressive ritualism, bolstered by an imposing array of devices for deceiving the eye"[13].

The Physician-Magician administered to a medicine a rite or a set of bodily actions to cure a deadly disease. He was sure to afflict an enemy with pain or death. The disease was also considered to be an enemy or caused by spirits or ghosts who were more dangerous than the enemies, but the herb with magical spells; also was not considered adequate enough to cure or expel them from the body of the patient, hence a sort of offensi:.e magic was through to be a necessary accompaniment of the medicinal herbs.

The primitive man was not aware of the curative properties contained in herbs. He thought the herbs to be a sort of spirits not malevolent but benevolent. However, they had to be invoked or coaxed to be kind to the patient and drive away the devil of disease from him. Hence spells in the forms of prayers were addressed to herbs to come to help. The diseases as demons personified, were invested with attributes signifying the symptoms of the diseases. Therefore, the medicine is made really effective after the spells were pronounced over it. It was believed that herbs accompanied by spells and suitable rites were sure to cure the diseases. Thus the role of the physician was almost the same as that of the magician but it was chiefly the herb or the plant on which the physician depended.

Beni Gupta says:

> "Magic was only a helper, but a pure magician had nothing to do with the medical skill".[14]

Demon Possession

The singular phenomenon of demon possession, rarely paralleled since Epostolic times. It is recorded as having occurred at the time of Christ more frequently than at any other time. The account of Saul—'an evil spirit from the Lord troubled him' in I. Sam 16:14-15 is probably to be regarded as a statement of his metal disorder rather than as a theological explanation of its origin. It seems likely that Satan was particularly active at this time in an attempt to counter the effect of the miracles of Christ and his apostles. Demon possession was real and cannot be 'explained' simply as the current interpretation of purely physical or mental disorders by ignorant (but sincere) people. Jesus himself made this diagnosis and accepted it when made by others. He was never deceived by contemporary error.

These who were demon possessed could be used as a mouth piece by the possessing spirit; they often had accompanying physical manifestations such as cleanliness.

Epilepsy or Mental Disorder

Particularly they were also to recognize the divinity of Jesus and knew they were able to recognise the divinity of Jesus and knew they were subject to his authority. However, demon possession is definitely not synonymous either with epilepsy or with mental disorder in general, and is clearly distinguished by the Synoptists and in Acts 5:16;

> "A great number of people would also gather from the towns around Jerusalem, bringing the sick and these formented by unclean spirits, and they were all cured".
>
> —*Acts. 5:16*

Different degrees of involvement were recognized as is shown (Mt.15:22) by a girl 'severely possessed by a demon'.

There is no significant difference between the man with an unclear spirit (Mk.5:2), the demoniac (Mk 5:15-16) or the man who had been possessed with demons as the same man, is variously described.

Miracles and Healing

What is a Miracle? This is some thing supernatural-beyond to the power and understanding of human beings.

Paul J.Achtemeier defines Miracle as follows:

> "Miracles, special interventions by God on behalf of his people"[15].

John L.Mckenzie defines it"

> "as a phenomenon in nature which transcends the capacity of natural causes to such a degree that it must be attributed to the direct intervention of God"[16].

Healing means the restoration of one to full health who had been ill in body or mind or both. This includes recovery resulting from medical treatment and spontaneous remission of a disease. It includes the improvement in a patients' outlook on his condition even if no physical cure is possible, and even a correction of a patients misconception of the nature of his illness. In psychological disorders, the term is used to describe an improved mental state.

It is important that those different facts of the meaning of the word be realized, because the Biblical miracles of healing (apart from cases of demon possessing) show healing in its primary medical sense of the restoration to normal in cases of organic disease. There are of course, natural recoveries from illness, as well as miracles recorded in the Bible, and in fact probably most recoveries other than the miraculous ones were natural because of the almost complete ineffectiveness of therapy in ancient times.

Healing—Its Author

God is the one who heals all our diseases.

> "...Who (God) forgives all your iniquity, who heals all your diseases".
>
> —*Ps 103 : 3*

St. Peter says;

> "And his name, by faith in his name, has made this man strong whom you see and know; and the faith which is through Jesus has given the man this perfect health in the presence of you all."
>
> —*Acts. 3:16*

Even today, when medical and surgical skill is so developed, God is the healer, using men to do his work for Him. We can see people going on pilgrimages to the holy shrines of gods seeking the miraculous healing.

Healing—the Use of Means

Even in Biblical times, when so few treatments for disease existed, people were encouraged and expected to use the means that were available both in Old Testament (e.g. the fig polutice for Hezekiah's boil) and New Testament times.

> "Now Isaiah had said, `Let them take a cake of figs, and apply it to the boil, that he may recover".
>
> —*Isa. 38:21.*

And in the New Testament times—Paul's advice to Timothy—

> "No longer drink only water, but use a little wine for the sake of your stomach and your frequent aliments".
>
> —*I. Tim.5:23*

True faith in God gladly and gratefully uses such means as are available, whether medicines, blood transfusions or surgical operations to prevent death, as much as life jackets to prevent drowning.

Faith Healing

Various terms are currently used to describe healing that occurs without the use of means and in response to faith. Because all true healing comes from God, the term divine healing is not helpful to distinguish this especial from. E.J. Chandran Job says that in order to experience the divine healing from God, one should follow him. He says:

> "God directly intervenes in the sickness of the human body and brings divine healing in a miraculous way for those who follow him"[17].

Spiritual healing suggests more the restoration of health to the spirit than the body and more over, may be confused with the work of spiritists who, in the name of the devil, can produce spurious healing. Faith healing is a helpful term so long as the object of faith is clear it by no means always God.

Faith and prayer are two conditions given in the Bible for faith healing.

James 5:14,15 says:

> "Is any sick among you let him call for the elders of the church, and let them pray over him, anointing him with oil in the name of the Lord. And the prayer of faith shall save the sick, and the Lord shall raise him up; and if he have committed sins, they shall be forgiven him".
>
> —*James. 5:14,15*

Jesus, when he healed a woman who was suffering from haemorrhages for twelve years, says:

"Daughter, your faith had made you well, go in peace".

—*Luke 8:48*

Another condition given is the forgiveness of sins. Wade H.Boggs. JR. in his book *Faith Healing and the Christian Faith* says:

> "The confession of our moral debts to God is the only solution to the problem of guilt which can destroy mental peace and adversly affect the body in a variety of ways"[18].

So sin affects both body and mental ability is the conclusion of the Bible.

The Psalmist says:

> "When I declared not my sin, my body wasted away through my groaning all day long. For day and night they hand was heavy upon me; my strength was dried up as by the heat of summer".

—*Ps.32:3-4*

We find, Jesus, when he performed healing miracles on some people he said:

> "Your sins are forgiven".

An incident is narrated in Lk.5:17-26.

Jesus heals a paralytic man. He saw some men carrying that man to Him to be healed; by seeing their faith He says:

> "Friend, your sins are forgiven"

—*Lk 5:20*

Psalm 103:3 says:

> "Who forgives all your sins and heals all you diseases".

Psycho-somatic illness is now an accepted diagonosis of various diseases. It seems as though Jesus was able to diagnose a symptom as arising from a mental state of remorse or feeling of guilt from sin or transgression - 'Mens sano corpore sano' (a sound mind in a sound body) seems to put the cart before the horse. For a sound body is largely believed to be the result of mental and emotional health. Where could a man get the mind cleared of its burden? Perhaps this was a general understanding of folk remedies in many therapeutic remedies we come across in the Holy Bible.

Faith Healings in the Old Testament

A number of Hebrew, Aramaic and Greek words are used in the Bible to refer to the activity in nature and history of the living God. They are variously translated as 'miracles, wonders, signs, mighty acts, powers'.

The working of miracles is directed to a deepening of Man's understanding of God. It is God's way of speaking dramatically to those who have ears to hear. The miracle stores are intimately concerned with the faith of observers or participants (eg. Exo.14:31; I.Kings.18:39) and with the faith of those who will hear or read them later (John. 20:30-31). Jesus looked for faith as the right response to his saving presence and deeds; it was faith which 'made whole', which made the difference between the mere creation of an impression and a saving communication of his revelation of God.

It is important to observe that faith on the part of human participants is a necessary condition of a miracle in the sense that God by himself is unable to get without human faith. Mk.6:5 is often quoted to support such a view,

> "And he could do no mighty work there, except that He laid His hands upon a few sick people and healed them"—Mark.6:5

But Jesus could do no mighty work in Nazareth, not because the people's unbelief limited His power—Mark tells us that He healed a few sick people there-but rather because He could not proceed with His preaching or with the deeds which proclaimed His gospel in action where men were unready to accept His good news and His own person.

(1) Recovery of Moses—an unknown disease which was dangerous enough to kill him.

> "At a lodging place on the way the LORD met him and sought to kill him. Then Zipporah took a flint out off her son's foreskin and touched Moses' feet with it, and said 'surely you are a bridgroom of blood to me'. So he left him alive. Then it was that she said, you are a bridgroom of blood, because of the circumcision".
>
> —*Exo. 4:24-26.*

(2) Numbers 12:1-5 records the healing of Miriams Leprosy. Which came to her because of her rebellion against Moses, the servant of God and was cured as she repented.

(3) 2 Kings 5:8-14 records the cure of Naaman through Elisha, the prophet. Naaman—a military officer of the Assyrian Empire is cured from his leprosy by Elisha by making him to take dip in the Jordan river.

(4) Healing of Jeroboam's suddenly paralysed hand is recorded in I Kings,13:4-6.

(5) The recovery of the Israelites bitten by the serpents. Because of the rebellion of the Israelites against God, God sent serpents to bite the Israelites. When the people cried for mercy to Moses, be prayed to the LORD, and the LORD asked him to make a serpent's image in bronze and instructs who ever looks up to the serpent will live. Here individuals are not mentioned.

—*Numbers.21:6-9*

(6) The recovery of Hezekiah.

King Hezekiah's sickness to the point of death is healed by the word of the prophet Isaiah-using the cake of the fig.

—*2 Kings 20:1-11.*

Faith Healings in the New Testament

This can be divided into two parts:

(1) By Jesus.
(2) By the disciples and others.

By Jesus

(1) Demoniacs healed :

Demons are pictured as inferior to the power of God and Jesus. So they obey the Lord Jesus and as soon as he orders them leave the possessed men and women. They cause dumbness and deafness some times.

(a) Demoniac in the Synagogue:

—Mark: 1:26; Luke 4:35

(b) Demoniac healed - a dumb spirit:

—Mathew 12:22; Luke 11:14, Matt. 9:32

(c) Demoniacs of Gadara:

—Matt. 8:28; Mark: 5:1; Luke 8:26

(d) Daughter of the Canaanite woman a demoniac:

—Matt. 15:22; MK.7:25

(2) Healing of the blind:

Healing of the blind men is recorded in four separate places in the Bible.

They are—Matt. 9:27-29 where Jesus looks into their faith, touches them and they are healed. Second one is recorded in Mark. 8:23-25.

Where in a place called Bethsaida, people brought a blind man and requested Jesus to touch him and he was healed.

The third event is recorded in John 9:1-7

Jesus sees a blind man by birth. A question of the belief of the Israelites is asked to Jesus here—i.e. 'Rabbi, who sinned, this man or his parents, that he was born blind?' Jesus answered, 'it was not that this man sinned or his parents, but that the works of God might be made manifest in him'. Then Jesus says, 'I am the light of the world'. Then He spat on the ground and made clay of the spittle and anointed the man's eyes with the clay, and asked him to go to the pool of siloam and wash it. He did and came seeing.

The fourth one is recorded in Matt. 20:30 and Mark. 10:46

On the way to Jericho, Jesus was stopped by the cry of a blind beggar, called Barthemaeus. He wanted to receive his sight. Then Jesus said to him, "Go your way; your faith has made you well".... And immediately he received his sight and followed Him on the way.

—Mark.10:51-52

(a) The Gospels have record a lot of healings by Jesus apart from the above few.

(b) The Gospels have recorded a lot.

They are:

(1) Peter's Mother in law's fever is healed:

—Matt. 8:14; Mark. 1:31; Luke 4:38

(2) Cleansing the leper:

—Matt. 8:3; Mark. 1:41, Luke 5:13

(3) Paralytic healed:

—Matt. 9:2; Mark 2:3; Luke 5:18

(4) Invalid healed :

—John 5:5

(5) Shrivelled hand healed:

—Matt 12:10; Mark 3:1; Luke 6:6

(6) Centurian's servant is healed:

—Matt. 8:5; Luke 7:2

(7) Bleeding of a woman healed:

—Matt. 9:20; Mark 5:25; Luke 8:43

(8) Deaf and Dumb healed:

—Mark 7:33

(9) Afflicted child healed:

—Matt. 17:14; Mark. 9:26; Luke 9:37

(10) Ten Lepers healed:

—Luke. 17:12

(11) Heals a woman with the spirit of infirmity:

—Luke 13:11

(12) Man with dropsy is healed:

—Matt. 20:30; Mark 10:46

(13) Malchus' cut ear is healed:

—Luke 22:51

Faith Healings in Apostalic Times

Healing power is one of the gifts promised to the followers of Christ. Mark 16:18 reads like this:

> "..... they will lay their hands on the sick, and they will recover".
>
> *—Mark. 16:18*

The book of the Acts of the apostles gives several accounts of individual miracles.

The Lame Man in Jerusalem Acts 3:1-11

The crippled beggar, was seeking some alms from Peter and John, the disciples of Jesus. He was asked to look up. "... Peter said,

> 'I have no silver or gold, but what I have I give you; in the name of Jesus Christ of Nazareth, stand up and walk'. And he took him by the right hand and raised him up; and immediately his feet and ancles were made strong. Jumping up, he stood and walked".
>
> —*The Acts 3:6-8*

The Lame Man in Lystra Acts 14:8-10

A similar thing happened in Lystra. But this time it was Paul and Barnabdas-who were not among the disciples of Jesus-but His follower performed this miracle.

> "In Lystra there was a man sitting who could not use his feet and had never walked, for he had been crippled from birth, he listened to Paul as he was speaking. And Paul, looking at him intently and seeing that he had faith to be healed, said in a loud voice, 'Stand up right on your feet'. And the man sprag up and began to walk."
>
> —*The Acts. 14:8-10*

The Paralytic Healed : Acts 9:33-38

In a place called Lydda, Peter heals a man who was own in bed for 8 years out of Paralysis.

His name is Aeneas. He was totally paralysed for eight years and 'Peter said to him, Aeneas, Jesus Christ heals you; get up and make your bed; And immediately be got up'.

—*Acts 9:34*

The Publican's Father's Dysentry (Blood Flux)

Paul had to reach the shore of Malta having his ship wrecked. There was a leading man of Island called Publius.

Acts 28:8 says:

> "It so happened that the father of a Publican lay sick in bed with fever and dysentry. Paul visited him and cured him by praying and putting his hands on him".
>
> —*Acts. 28:8*

Multiple Healings

Multiple healings are recorded in Acts. 5:15-16, and the unique case of the use of clothing taken from Acts 19:11-12

> "God did extraordinary miracles through Paul, so that when the handkerchiefs or aprones that had touched his skin were brought to the sick, their diseases left them, and the evil spirits came out of them".

So the miraculous healings recorded in the Bible are viewed totally different. They were not done through magic and sorcery since magic and sourcery are completely condemned in the Bible. Because,

> "Magic is a rival to true religoun, though it can be practised in conjunction with false religious ideas"[19].

The practice of magic like the wearing of charms, workers of magic, sorcerers and witches are all condemned in the Bible. The Bible prohibits magic clearly. The following passages prove this statement.

Exo. 22:18:

> "You shall not permit a sorceress to live".

Lev. 19:31:

> "Do not turn to mediums or wizards; do not seek them out, to be defiled by them. I am the Lord your God".

Lev. 20:27:

> "A man or a woman who is a medium or a wizard shall be put to death; they shall be stoned with stones, their blood shall be upon them".

Dent. 18:10:

> "There shall not be found among you .... anyone who practices divination, a sooth sayer, or an angur, or a sourcerer, or a charmer, or a medium, or a wizard, or a necro manch".

Hence the miraculous healings in the Bible are based purely on Faith, not on the powers of magic.

Conclusion

Thus as the people of the book, the Hebrews relied on God mostly for their healing. At the same time they also used the natural resources, herbs etc., for their curing of the sickness.

NOTES

1. DWHO - 1963 - Conference of medicine and Public Health in the Arctic and Antartic,(Geneva: Technical Report Series. No. 253)
2. Richard M. Dorson (Ed), *Folk Lore and Folk life—An Introduction*: (Article by Don Yoder: Folk Medicine) (Chicago: The University of Chicago Press. 1972) p. 194
3. Su. Sakthivel, *Nattupura Iyal Aaivu* (Madras. Manivasagam Pathipagam. 1992) p. 253
4. G.Shanthi, *Folklore survey of Thanjavur District*. (Thanjavur-Tamil University Publications 1994) p. 419.

5. Deut. 7:15
6. Jer. 24:10
7. 2. Sam. 24:14-15.
8. 2.Chro. 16:12.
9. J.I. Packer, *Nelson's Illustrated Encyclopedia of Bible Facts*. (London. Thomas Nelson Publishers. 1980) p. 461.
10. G. Shanthi, *Folklere survey of Thanjavur District* (Thanjavur, Tamil University 1994) p. 429
11. J.D. Douglus, *New Bible Dictionary*, II Edn. (Leicester. English-Inp Press 1986) p. 474.
12. Ibid. p. 474.
13. Beni Gupta, *Magical Beliefs and Superstitions*. (Delhi:Sundeep Prakashan 1979) p. 8.
14. Ibid. p. 9
15. Paul J. Achtemeier, *Harper's Bible Dictionary*. (Bangalore: Theological Publications of India.1990) p. 639
16. John.L. Mckenzie, *Dictionary of the Bible*. (Bangalore: Asian Trading Corporation. 1984) p. 578.
17. E.J. Chandran Job, *Guide to Divine Healing*, (Bombay : Published by E.J.C. Job - 1989) p. 68.
18. Wade H. Boggs, JR, *Faith Healing and the Christian Faith* (Virginia. Richamond. John Knox Press. 1956) P.161
19. Ibid p. 766

10

FOLK GAMES IN THE BIBLE

Introduction

Toiling all through the day, in the hot-sun, people normally want to have some relaxation. Thus they started to have some games just for fun and amusement in the beginning. Later some rules and regulations were introduced. Robert A.George has rightly said:

> "Play is a form of expressive behaviour common among all human beings and manifested overtly in all cultures. Like art, languages and religion, play is a complex phenomenon that cannot be defined succintly"[1].

Before going into the accounts of the games in the Bible, it is better to know the history and origin of games.

Origin of Games

Games and combats were instituted by the ancients in honour of their gods; and were celebrated with that view of the most polished and enlightened nations of antiquity. The most renowned heroes, legislators and statesmen, did not think it unbecoming their character and dignity, to mingle with the combatants, or contend in the race; they even reckoned it glorious to share in the exercises, and meritorious to carry away the prize. The victors were crowned with a wreath of laurel in presence of their country; they were celebrated in the rapturous effusions of their poets; they were admired, and almost adored, by the innumerable, multitudes which flocked to the games, from every part of Greece, and many of the adjacent countries.

The foot race seems to have been placed in the first rank of public games, and cultivated with a care and industry proportioned to the estimation in which it was held. The Olympic games generally opened with races, and were celebrated at first with no other exercise. The lists or course where the athlete exercised themselves in running, was at first but one stadium in length, or about six hundred feet, and from this measure it took its name, and was called the stadium; whatever might be its extent[2].

Isthumian Games

In Ancient Greece, a festival of athletic and musical competition in honour of the sea-god Posedion, held inspiring of the second and fourth years of each Olympiad at his sanctuary on the isthumus of Corinth. Legend attributed their origin either to Sisyphus, King of Corinth or to Theseus. Open to all Greeks, the Isthumian Games were specially popular with Athenians. The victor's prize originally a crown of dry wild celery, was changed to a pine wreath in Roman times, the pine being sacred to Posedion[3].

Similar games were held in cities like Macedonia, Egypt, Syria, Arabia, Italy and many other areas. Like Isthumian Games, Pythian Games, Namean Games were also popular.

St. Paul refers to atheletic games like this :

> "Do you not know that in a race the runners all compete, but only one receives the prize? Run in such a way that Athletes exercise self-control in all things; they do it to receive a perishable wreath, but we, an imperishable one. So, I do not run aimlessly, nor do I box as though beating the air; but I punish my body and enslave it, so that after proclaiming to others. I myself should not be disqualified"[4].

This has obvious reference to the then famous Isthumian Games held biennially at Corinth. These games were second only to the Olympic games. Apostle Paul was appalled at the indifference of the Corinthian church and readily uses the parable of athlete preparing for the Isthumian games. The discipline, training and motivation that inspired the athletes were shown as model to the christian believer engaged in a spiritual warfare. The reference to the laurel leaf crown won at the athletic meet is liable to fade while the crown won in a spiritual battle does not fade according to Paul. His parable refers to the rigorous training discipline and control shown by the athletes. The Corinthians were very familiar with Isthumian games which was usually held as a rehearsal for the Olympic games.

This is again alluded to by Paul in his second letter to Timothy. He says:

> "And in the case of an athlete, no one is crowned without competing according to the rules"[5].

In First letter to Timothy Paul says:

> "Exercise thyself rather unto godliness"[6].

The word 'exercise' in Greek is 'Gumnazo' from which the English word's Gymnasium and Gymnastics are derived. Obviously, Paul was referring to such training places existing then at Corinth.

We also infer that regular training would imply coaches, regular diet, proper hours and disciplined life. That such practices were prevalent at Corinth reinforces our influence that Corinth being the centre of Isthumian games had such training places. Paul refers to the goal of such training as 'fading crown'. He obviously refers to the crown of laurel leaves that used to be given as the gold medal of modern days. But leaves also sure to fade. However, people strive hard to win laurels, which in those days conferred many special privileges atleast for a short while.

Games in the Bible

Games, activities of varying degrees of structure and organization that are pursued for pleasure. Games in Biblical times may be categorised as mental exercises, sporting events, or board games.

The riddle proposed by Samson (Jud. 14:12-14) is an instance of a mental exercise. Riddles were widely known in the ancient Near East, but were supposed to deal with common experience or knowledge.

One reference to a sporting event in the Old Testament described in 2 Sam. 2:12-17, set twelve of Joab's men against twelve of Abner's men. The contest, which was probably intended to be wrestling, had, however, a fatal out come.

Board games, though not mentioned specifically in the Bible, have been found in a number of archaeological excavations[7].

Physical Sport

In common with their Near Eastern neighbours, the life of the majority of Hebrews left little time or inclination for physical sport. When introduced by Hellenzing Jews in the time of Antiochus Epiphanes and patronized by Jason, the high priest, the Greek love of sport was considered irreligious. Nevertheless, there can be little doubt that, despite the absence of explicit references, running, throwing and hunting were undertaken on occasions when they were not necessary. Like the Egyptians and Babylonians, the people of Palestine would have enjoyed contests at weight-lifting and wrestling.

Archery

Shooting arrow with a bow is one of the oldest skills practised by man. "From Pre-historic times, and except in Australia, the bow in its many forms was for a time, a principle weapon of war and of the hunt throughout the known world"[8]. The acquisation, improvement and retention of proficiency in its use involve many elements that characterize a sport regular practice to achieve accuracy or increase distance, the development of improving performance under pressure.

The Bible gives some instances of this game of skill aiming at fixed marks. Jonathan, the Prince of King Saul says to David:

> "I will shoot three arrows to the side of it, as though I shot at a mark"[9].

In lamentations, prophet Jeremiah laments his condition in a figure of speech by saying:

> "He bent his bow and set me as a mark for his arrow"[10].

Hunting

The narratives of the patriarchal period depict the Hebrews as occupied chiefly with the raising of flocks and other semi-sedentary agricultural activities. Hunting was seldom engaged in as a pastime, and was generally resorted to only either at the promptings of hunger or when the wild animals with which Palestine abounded in antiquity, threatened the security of the Hebrews and their flocks.

> "I will not drive them out before you in one year, or the land would become desolate and the wild animals would multiply against you."[11]

David said to Saul,

> "Your servant used to keep sheep for his father, and whenever a lion or a bear came, and took a lamb from the flock, I went after it and struck it down, rescuing the lamb from its mouth; and it if turned against me, I would catch it by the jaw, strike it down, and kill it"[12].

Certain individuals, however, were renowned for their hunting prowess, including Ishmael:

> "God was with the boy (Ishmael), and he grew up; he lived in the wilderness, and became an expert with the bow"[13].

Esau said:

> "When the boys grew up, Esau was a skilful hunter, a man of the field..."[14].

The following things were used as weapons in hunting.

Bows and Arrows

Isaac tells to his son Esau:

> "Now then, take your weapons, your arrows and your bow, and go out to the field, and hunt game for me"[15].

Clubs

> "Clubs are counted as chaff; it langhs at the rattle of javelins"[16].

Sling Stones

"Then David took his staff in his hand, and chose five smooth stones from the wadi, and put them in his shepherd's bag, in the pouch; his sling was in his hand, and he drew near to the Philistine. David put his hand in the bag, took out a stone, slung it, and struck the Philistine on his forehead..."[17].

Nets

Nets were used as traps to catch especially birds. Some times animals also,

> "Know then that God has put me in the wrong, and closed his net around me"[18].

Fowlers Snares

The hunters of birds, fowlers used to put snares to catch the fowls.

It is a method the hunters use and it is used as an example in the Bible.

> "For he will deliver you from the snare of the fowler and from the deadly pestilence"[19].

Pits for Larger Animals

To catch the larger animals like elephants, lions etc., the hunters used to dig big pits and catch the animals.

> "... they spread their net over him; he was caught in their pit"[20].

Wrestling

The Greek's love of sport was considered irreligious by the Jews. Nevertheless, there can be little doubt that, despite the absence of explicit references, running, throwing and hunting were under taken on occasions when they were not a necessity. Like the Egyptians and Babylonians, the people of Palestine would have enjoyed contests at weight lifting and wrestling.

Jacob's long wrestling match may reflect both practised ability at the sport and the recognition of rules precluding holds below the belt.

> "Jacob was left alone; and a man wrestled with him until day break. When the man saw that he did not prevail against Jacob, he struck him on the hip socket; and Jacob's hip was put out of joint as he wrestled with him"[21].

The expression 'hip and thigh' may be a technical wrestling term, like English 'Cross-buttock'.

> "He (Samson the great strong man of Israel) struck them down hip and thigh with great slaughter..."[22].

It has been suggested that the group combat at Gibeon was initiated as a wrestling match—

"Abner said to Joab, 'Let the youngmen come forward and have a contest before us'. Joab said, 'Let them come forward'. So they came forward and were counted as they passed by; twelve for Benjamin and Ishbaal son of Saul; and twelve of the servants of David. Each grasped his opponent by the head, and thrust his sword in his opponent's side; so they fell down together"[23].

Wrestling by grasping an opponent's belt being an ancient form of this sport.

Isaiah refers to this distinctive wrestling belt when speaking of Messiah:

> "Righteousness will be his belt, and faithfulness the sash around his waist"[24].

Boxing

For this kind of sport, one should have a very strong body and stamina. St. Paul refers about this game incomparison to his good to achieved in the spiritual life.

He says:

> "I do not fight like a man beating the air"[25].

Boxers wore metal studded leather straps on their hands, so opponents tried to evade rather than block blows. Paul concentrated on landing blows for the sake of the Gospel and did not 'beat the air'.

The popular Tamil Translation of the Bible uses the word 'Silambam' for Boxing. Silambam is a typical martial art, unique in Tamil Nadu, in which the person who performs the art uses either one or two sticks and performs. We do not have any other reference in the Bible regarding Silambam, neither in the text, nor in the Archaeological evidences. Since Boxing is not a popular known folk game in Tamil Nadu, probably the Bible Translators could have used the word Silambam for a better understanding of the people of Tamil Nadu.

Chariot Racing

In the ancient Near East, heavy wheeled vehicles drawn by asses were used for war a ceremonial in Southern Mesopotamia in the third millennium B.C. It is probable that the horse was introduced by the people of the South Russain steppe who precipitated many folk movements in the second millennium[26].

In the Bible, Paul may have been referring to the character who leaned forward, straining as his horses sped toward the finish line. In his letter to the Philipians Paul says:

> "... forgetting what lies behind, and straining forward to what lies ahead"[27].

In the chariot race, a backward look could be disasterous in this dangerous sport, the only safety lay in reaching the goal and claiming the prize.

This type of chariot race is being conducted in various places. In Tamil Nadu, we can compare the chariot race with the Reklaa race in our villages, in which either a horse or a bull is made to draw a light weighted cart driving by a driver. Here too the driver will never look back, and will lean forward and drive.

Animal Baiting

Jallikattu is a folk game which proves the valour of the young Tamils. 'Venatio' is a Roman game in which wild animals were baited and then matched against criminals or trained hunters. Paul in his First Letter to the Corinthians says:

> "... I fought with wild animals at Ephesus..."[28].

Some of the Biblical scholars interpret this verse as—

> "A metapher for the bitter opposition he had encountered, his life endangered"[29].

It was a common practice in the Roman Empire to let the criminals fight with the wild animals for their life. As per their rules, Paul was a criminal, preaching a different Kingdom of God, which was considered to be treason. So he could have been made to fight with the wild animals.

Foot Racing

In the New Testament, especially in the Epistles, metaphors are drawn from the games, generally, and from the foot race and the chariot race in particular.

In the First Letter to Corinthians Paul calls attention to the vigorus training of the athlete.

"Athlete exercise self-control in all things; they do it to receive a perishable wreath, but we an imperishable one"[30].

The athlete is pre-occupied not with the immediate token prize of the wreath of wild Olive, parsley, pine or laurel, but with the later reward. The Christian is like wise exhorted to strive 'for the mastery', for his reward is by contrast, an incorruptible 'crown'.

Normally, when the athletes train themselves for a sporting event, they will train themselves with heavy costumes and weights. But in the real event, they will shed all the heavy loads and participate with minimum and light weight costumes. In the Book of Hebrews it is said:

> "... Let us also lay aside every weight and the sin that clings so closely, and let us seen with perseverance the race that is set before us"[31].

In the Greek Athletic Games, a square pillar marked the finish line. The runner used to keep his eyes on that goal, for reaching it was all that counted. This imagery is used in the book of Hebrews 12:1-2.

Children's Games

Normally Children are linked with games and a few games are

alloted only for them. Games help the children in their growth. Brian Solton Smith has said:

> "Young children are trained in the art of leadership and obedience, so that they can fit in to the hierarchical social arrangements of these cultures"[32].

Archaeologists working in Palestine have found a variety of toys: tiny clay pots and furniture, wooden dolls and rattles. Some of these date from 900 B.C. Older boys undoubtedly played with slings.

When King David was a small boy, as a shepherd grazing his flock used this sling to protect his sheep from wild animals. He also used it to kill the giant Goliath. Normally, the children used this sling as our children use 'Kata-belt'. Children also played out stories of Biblical heroes and events.

Prophet Zachariah says:

> "The young played in the streets"[33].

Imitating their elders in daily life or at marriages and funerals. The boys may have imitated the Egyptian team games shown in paintings and a form of tug-of-war, while the girls practised juggling or ball games, including catch played by teams with one mounted on another's back.

The game of imitation is very well brought out in the following passage:

> "We played the flute for you, and you did not dance. We weiled, and you did not mourn"[34].

Here the play is the imitation of the act of the adults in both wedding and funeral-playing flute and dance in the wedding and wailing and mourning in the funerals.

The tomb painting of Beni Hasan c.2000 BC. also has given a picture of the Egyptian girls playing ball, keeping several balls in the air at once[35].

Leather covered balls have been found, whistles, rattles, model pots, chariots and animals—some with wheels, have been recovered.

Intellectual Games

Normally games involve physical work. But there are some which involve only intellect. Generally the adults used to play these types of games. Riddles are of such a type and popular with adults. These were intended not only to entertain, but often to instruct.

Riddle is a saying whose meaning is hidden, a puzzle to be solved. Riddles are questions that are framed with the purpose of confusing testing with of those who do not know the answer. Here is a riddle, used in the Bible as a game. This appears in the book of Judges, chapter 14. Here Samson, the great strong man makes a feast for young men who were gathered to celebrate his wedding. He puts a riddle to them with a reward. Samson said to them :

> "Let me now put a riddle to you. If you can explain it to me with in the seven days of the feast, and find it out, then I will give you thirty linen garments and thirty festal garments. But if you cannot explain it to me, then you shall give me thirty linen garments and thirty festal garments"[36].

After the challenge is accepted by the youngmen, he tells them the riddle.

> "Out of the eater came some thing to eat, Out of the strong came some thing sweet"[37].

The youngmen could not find the answer, because the riddle was not common one. It was a personal experience of Samson. He had already killed a lion few days back. He found the honey comb in the corpse of the lion and took it and ate it. This, he had formed as a riddle. The youngmen could not find the answer. So they went and persuaded a woman who was close to Samson to find the answer from him. She pestered him and got the answer and revealed it to them. On the seventh day of the feast, they revealed the answer to Samson. The answer is also in the form of a question.

> "What is sweeter than honey?
> What is stronger than lion?"[38]

Gambling

Gambling was common in the Middle East. We read, the Roman soldiers cast dice and gambled for the robes of Jesus, which was a special one, woven from top to bottom as one piece without any stitches. All the four gospel writers have mentioned this in their gospels[39].

So they said to one another, let us not tear it, but cast lots for it to see who will get it: This was to fulfil what the scripture says:

> "They divided my clothes among themselves, and for my clothing they cast lots"[40].

Diversion

For the Hebrews, of all ages feasting, song, music and especially dancing were the commonest form of relaxation. Opportunity was taken for this at every domestic rejoining. Prophet Jeremiah refers a situation like this:

> "Again you shall take your tambourines, and go for in the dance of the mersey makers"[41].

In the merry making, in harvest they used to play and dance.

> "They went out in to the field and gathered the grapes from their vineyards, trod them and celebrated"[42].
> "Go and lie in wait in the vineyards, and watch; when the

> young women of Shiloh come out to dance in the dances, then come out of the vineyards..."[43].

And also they will have the merry making at public and state functions as the royal occasion pictured here :

> "All the people went up following him, playing on pipes and rejoicing with great joy, so that the earth quaked at their noise"[44].

And at the celebration of the victory of war—
(Song of Miriam)

> "Then the prophet Miriam, Aaron's sister, took a tambourine in her hand; and all the women went out after her with tambourine and with dancing.

And Miriam Sang to them—

> "Sing to the Lord, for he has triumphed gloriously; horse and rider he has thrown into the sea"[45].

Some more passages like Jud. 11:34 and I.Sam. 18:6 also prove this.

Conclusion

As a folk community, the Hebrews had the above games for their amusement and relaxation. Some of them could have been borrowed from their neighbours, because they were shepherds mainly, who later became an agricultural community. In their history, we find that they had close contacts with their neighbours like Babylon, Egypt etc. It is a great surprise that some of their games have some common similarities with our Tamil Folk Games.

NOTES

1. Robert A.George, *Recreation and Games* (Chicago. 1972) p. 173.
2. Richard Watson, *Biblical and Theological Dictionary*. (London. John Mason Publishers. 1837) p. 422.
3. *Encyclopedia Britanica*—Vol. V.(Micropaedia) (Chicago. Helen Heming way-Benteu Publishers. 1974) p. 465
4. I. Cor. 9:24-27.
5. II. Tim. 2:5.
6. I. Tim. 4:7 (KJV).
7. Paul J.Achtemeier (Ed), *Harper's Bible Dictionary*. (Bangalore - Theological Publications in India. 1990) p. 332.
8. *Encyclopaedia Brittanica*—Vol. 1. (Macropaedia).
9. I sam. 2:20
10. Lam. 3:12
11. Exo. 23:29
12. I. Sam. 17:34, 35.
13. Gen. 21:20.
14. Gen. 25:27.
15. Gen. 27:3.
16. Job. 41:29.
17. I. Sam. 17:40, 49.
18. Job. 19:6.
19. Ps. 91:3
20. Ezek. 19:8
21. Gen. 32:24, 25
22. Judg. 15:8.
23. II. Sam. 2:14-16.
24. Isa. 11:5.
25. I. Cor. 9:26.
26. J.D. Douglus, *The New Bible Dictionary* (I Edition) (Norwich. Fletcher & Son Ltd. 1976) P.204.
27. Phil. 3:13.
28. I.Cor. 15:32.
29. *Jerome Bible Commentary*—Vol. 2. (Bangalore. Theological Publications in India. 1972) P.273.
30. I.Cor. 9:25.
31. Heb. 12:1.
32. Brian Solton Smith, *The Folk Games of the Children*. (Chicago: American Folklore 1968) p. 204.
33. Zach. 8:5.
34. Matt. 11:17.
35. J.D. Douglas, *The New Bible Dictionary*. (Leicester England. Inter versity Press. 1976) p. 451.

36. Jud. 14:12,13.
37. Jud. 14:14.
38. Jud. 14:18.
39. Matt. 27:35; Mark. 15:24; Luke. 23:24: John.19:23,24.
40. John. 19:23-24.
41. Jere. 31:4.
42. Jud. 9:27
43. Jud. 21:21
44. I. Kings. 1:39-40.
45. Exo. 15:20,21.

11 CONCLUSION

Conclusion

The twin benefit of the study ranges between the Bible and its community on the one hand and the instrument of folklore on the other. Folklore has been used in this study as a tool of analysis. So far folklore studies were hesitant to bring this analytical tool to an analysis of a religious book, a bold attempt is made in this study. The result of which is enhancement of the prestige of folklore. This enlightened approach which lifts not only subject studied to a higher level, but also improves the prestige of the instrument employed.

There is no detraction of the holiness of the Bible when it is subjected to a folklore analysis. It is an accepted axiom that the voice of the people is the voice of God[1]. The Bible is imperative about making God the speaker and people as listeners. Throughout the Bible the reader can get this impression[2]. The community of the Bible has heard God speaking on diverse occasions[3]. The Bible community has preserved much of this information in the form of oral tradition, stories, belief, proverb, riddle, event etc.

It is respectfully subscribed that the oral nature of God-man relationship is viewed as a folklore of the people of the Bible. This must have happened over a long period of time and the ravages of time must have taken a heavy toll of this pre-ignitions of God with people. This study has infact helped us to understand the heart of the message of the Bible namely that God's dialogue with man is the content of the Bible. Although, this is not the first time that folklore analytical tool is used in the study of the Bible. It makes a deep study of the different units of the Bible in one sweep. This is the contribution this study makes.

The Bible had been analysed over a long period of time under different objectives, for instance the form analysis or the content analysis or the philological analysis. This study has concentrated on one aspect namely the folks of the Bible. As folks of the Bible, they have preserved the stories, events, proverbs, riddles etc. in an oral form which, in the eighth century came to be transcribed to a written form.

The men of the Bible, assumed a shape and statue when they are looked at in the folklore angle. From Abraham to Malachi the Old Testament has thrown out many characters which lived in the memory of the people. Over long periods, communal memories are brief and halting. A whole character or a portrait does not immerge. Perhaps at a time when it was said that people would have understood the innuendo. It is likely that the character sketches of leaders, judges, men of God and Kings must have gained popularity or notoriety in the minds of the people by the prevalence of stories about them. The public would have added their own spicy aspects about their favourites or hatred personalities. This became the content of folklore repeated overtime orally transmitted. The conditions of history also underwent changes. Wars, famines and cataclysmic events were the back drop on which the people of the Bible waited the character of their leaders. All such material went in to the grist of the public mill, churning out interesting or uninteresting episodes, to be sung in ballads or written down in historical narratives. In fact, this was the flesh and bone of the long period of jestation of the Bible.

So, the folklore became the authentic source for the study of a people, their habits, their governments, their literature and what not. This study in that sense has raised to the level of folklore by making it an analytical tool employed to study the Bible. The Bible, has a mass of information which are shrouded in mystery and hidden in difficult terminology. Utilising the technique of folklore study, it is making it possible to understand the Bible better, and at the same time the study methods of folklore gained a superior measure of appreciation.

The Bible contains a variety of categories such as tales, proverbs, riddles, music and songs, medicine, games, beliefs and customs.

Folktales as formed in the Bible are really a library of information. Regarding the early history of the Bible community, tales are necessarily exaggerated statements of events and over time they gained a currency and veracity. This is revealed in the study of various types of tales that are come across in the Bible. The animal tales or tales of miracles and of supernatural events really open a window in to the life and dynamics of living of the Bible community in the distant past. There is no naive attempt to brush aside the supernatural elements, as simply concoctions. Tales as understood in the Bible from the point of view of folklore are essential cementing factor in the reconstruction of the history of the Bible community. Apart from the rich imagery and metaphoric usage of the tales of conveying essential and universal truth inconvenient and understandable words, these tales of the Bible are exemplary. The tale of the Egyptian captivity and their liberation under the leadership of Moses and the passage through the Red Sea and the Sinai Desert are parabolically to be understood as the 'march of man' as well as the 'march of God' in leading a people from sin and suffering to a life of freedom and abundance. One important aspect that is continuously stressed in the Bible is the role of God in the life of a people. Even when the Bible community became faithless, God was faithful to send his son Jesus of enable this people to lead a full life fruitfully.

Proverbs are pithy sayings containing some virtue or truth in Bible. The proverbs are statements of wisdom or philial piety, liberality, domestic faithfulness, honesty in business relationships. Certain vices are also condemned in these proverbs. They are intemperance, licentiousness, face hood, sloth, adultry, drunkenness etc. These proverbs are essentially humane and universal. If a comparison is made of these proverbs with those of other parts of the world, the universality and the cardinal nature get controlled. The wisdom sayings of the Bible are also relatively of the same stock. Proverbs must have necessarily been born of the people's ability to express some truth, wisdom or wise in a brief statement to be repeated overtime. Such is the origin of all proverbs and adages.

In the common conversation of intercourse of people, riddles were employed. Bible also has a store of many riddles. They form part of the Biblical folklore. The riddles so employed helps us to understand the people and their life in the distant past. To a large extent, riddles enable us to get a portrait of the social and economic life of the people in those days. Apart from that the nature of weapons or a largistic of the armaments of the Bible community is described.

Beliefs are repeatedly held in the minds of the people over centuries. Folklore brings out powerfully the static belief in a dynamic way by correlating beliefs with event and customary practices. The folklore of the Bible community reveals many elements of faith whose origin dates back to the dim past, and to the extraordinary experience of the people. There seems to have been beliefs and counter beliefs depending on the socio-politico circumstances. For instance 'the Saducees and Herodians who were materially rich and politically on the side of the establishment especially of the Roman imperialism, did not repose faith in spirits, angels or resurrection. While the basic Bible community normally held to these beliefs. The Judeao religious beliefs by and large came to be accepted by the Christians and variations. Certain habits were of course discontinued in the New Testament period such as circumcision for sacrifice of animals.

The Bible community followed a monotheistic concept of God, while the people who in close association with them had many different pagan and pantheon of gods. From Animism to nature worship, there were different types of worship among these people and the mission of the Bible community as revealed in the Bible is to establish the monotheistic worship as against the pagan gods and their superstitious practices. The choice of one community of people as a chosen ones gradually came to be addressed by Jesus as an universal choice of god for the same mission of knowing one God as Father and creator. The Jewish customs have proved to be extremely reticent and had persisted over time. The Bible community was dispersed by violent struggles and they were scattered all over the world but their exclusiveness and their grim determination to remain separate and aloof had remained persistent overtime, despite many fundamental changes in the history, economy and geography, these customs have remained sticky.

The songs and music found a vibrant plank of the communal life of unity. Be it a personal or individual experience or be it a communal expression. Music and songs very powerfully bring out the underlying ethos and aesthetics of a society. The Bible community seems to have had a vibrant music system, as immortalised by the Psalms in the Bible. They lead us in the innermost feelings and aspirations of a people and of their intimate understanding of the concept and nature of God. The Psalms speak to the modern community still in small soft voice, the longings of a loving God.

Overtime the Bible community had many kinds of folk medicines which were instant relief to different types of ailments. If a comparison is made of folk medicines of the Bible community is made with other societies a striking resemblance is the result. All over the world, every society appears to have had these practices of folk medicine and their belief in the efficacy of these medicines was really surprising. These folk medicines cannot be simply classified under witchcraft or occult science since herbs, flowers and leaves were used. The botony of the Bible explains how the explication of these remedies are possible.

Any community develops cohesion and unity by methods like games, communal songs and dances. The various references to aspects of sports and games in the Bible, actually reveal a rich reportire of the practice of communal games. The continuity of these game to this day makes it possible for an understanding of the folk games in the Bible, although very sparce references are found scattered in the Bible.

To conclude the folklore study of the Bible and people of the Bible has really paid a rich dividend of better understanding of the Bible on the one hand and a superior employment of the folklore analysis on the other hand.

NOTES

1. VOX Populi, VOX DI - The latin proverb which means the voice of the people is the voice of God.
2. I.Sam. 3:9
3. Heb. 1:1

BIBLIOGRAPHY

Adams, C.J. (Ed.) (1965): *Reader's Guide to the Great Religions,* Free Press, New York.

Agesthialingom, S. & Ramanathan. Aru.(Eds.) (1987): *Nattuppuraviyal Aaivukkovai* (Vol. 1 & 2): Indian Tamil Folklore Society, Annamalai Nagar.

Alavandhar, R. (1987): *Thamilar Thor Karuvikkal,* International Institute of Tamil Studies, Chennai.

Aletrino, L. (1968): *Six World Religions,* SCM Press, London.

Alexeev, V.P. (1986): *The Origin of the Human Race,* Progress Publishers, Moscow

Amirtham, Samuel (1969): *Introduction of the Old Testament* (Vol. I), TTBC, Chennai.

Anderson, B.W. (1969): *The Living World of the Old Testament,* Longmans, London.

Anderson, G.W. (1966): *The History and Religion of Israel,* Oxford University Press, Oxford

Azhagarasan, Antonyjohn V. (1977): *Nattuppura Padalum Panpadum* Chinnamalai Thangam Publications, Chennai.

Barclay, William (1972): *Introducing the Bible,* The International Bible Reading Association, Surrey.

Basham, Dan (1967): *Face up with a Miracle,* Whitakor House, Alabama.

Bearls, Ralph L. (1971): *An Introduction to Anthropology,* Macmillan Publishing Company, New York.

Beck, Harrel F. (1964): *Our Biblical Heritage,* United Church Press, Boston.

Belford, L. (1970): *Introduction to Judaism,* Association Press, New York.

Bhagwat, Durga (1958):*Proverbs and Idioms - An outline of Indian Folklore,* Popular Book Depot, Bombay.

Bharathi, Baktavatchala C. (1990): *Panpattu Manudaviyal,* Manivasagar Noolagam, Chennai.

Boggs, Wade H. (1956): *Faith Healing and the Christian Faith,* John Knox Press, Virginia.

Boyd, R.H.S. (1977): *Khristadvaita- A Theology for India,* Christian Literature Society, Chennai.

Bradley, D.G. (1963): A Guide to the World's Religions, Prentice Hall, New Jersey.

Brian, Solton Smith (1968): "*The Folk Games of the Children*", American Folklore, Chicago.

Bright, John (1970): *A History of Israel,* SCM Press, London.

Brown, Raymond E., Fitzmyer Joseph A. & Murphy Roland E. (Eds.). (1992): *The New Jerome Bible Hand Book,* Geoffrey Chapman, London.

Chellappah, W.T. (1985): *Preventive Medicine in the Bible,* CLS Publications, Chennai.

Choondal, Chummnal (1988): *Christian Folklore,* Kerala Folklore Academy, Trichur.

Clemen, Carl (1988): *Religions of the World,* Manas Publications, Delhi.

Clements, R.E. (1989): *The World of Ancient Israel,* Cambridge University Press, Cambridge.

Coffin, Tristram (1974): *American Folklore,* Voice of American Forum, Washington.

Das, N. (1993): *Folklore of Karnataka - An Introduction,* Media Exploration for Social and Cultural Advancement, Chennai.

Dharmaraj, A.K. (1970): *Manithanum Samayamum,* Tamil Theological Book Club CLS, Chennai.

Dorson, Richard M. (Ed.). (1972): *Folklore and Folklife,* The University of Chicago Press, Chicago.

Dorson, Richard M (1977): *American Folklore,* University of Chicago Press, Chicago.

Dundes, Alan (1978): *Essays on Folkloristics (Folklore Institute)*, Ved Prakash Vatuk, Meerut.

Duncan, Homer (1997): *Satan's Strategy,* Operation Moblisation of India, Mumbai.

Durkheim, Emile (1976): *The Elementary Forms of The Religious Life,* George Allen & Unwin Ltd, London.

Dyrness, William (1979): *Themes in Old Testament Theology,* Paternoster Press, Virginia.

Fohrer, George (1973): *History of Israelite Religion,* SPCK, London.

Fuller, R.H. (1974): *Interpreting the Miracles,* SCM Press Ltd, London.

Frangipane, Francis (1989): *The Three Battle Grounds,* River of Life Ministries Publications, Cedar Rapids (USA).

Frazer J.G. (1918): *Folklore in the Old Testament,* Appollodorus, London.

George, Robert A. (1972): *Recreation and Games—Folklore and Folklife-An Introduction,* Chicago University Press, Chicago.

Geus, G.H.De. (1976): *The Tribes of Israel,* (Van Gorcum), Studia Semitica Nearlandica, Amsterdam.

Gottwald N.K. (1978): *The Hypothesis of the Revolutionary of Ancient Israel,* SCM, Orbis (U.K.).

—— (1979): *The Tribes of Yahweh, Mary Knoll,* Orbis (UK).

Graham, Billy (1994): *Angels,* Suvartha Books, Tiruvalla

Grollen, Berg Luc. H. (1959): *Atlas of the Bible,* Penquin Reference Books, Middlesex.

Gunkel, Hermann (1987): *The Folktale in the Old Testament,* The Almond Press, Sheffield.

Guthrie, Harvey H. (Jr.) (1966): *Israel's Sacred Songs,* The Seabury's Press, New York.

Gutzke, Manford George (1975): Plain Talk on Genesis, Zondervan Publishing House, Michigan.

Hammond, T.C. (1965): *In Understanding be Men,* Inter Versity Fellowship, London.

Handoo, Jawaharlal (1989): *Folklore - An Introduction,* Central Institute of Indian Language, Mysore.

Hargreaves, Cecil (1989): *The Miracles of Jesus,* Indian Theological Library. CLS, Chennai.

Harlow, R.E. (1970): *Songs of Israel, Everyday Publications,* Torento.

Harrington, Wilfred J. (1976) *Key to The Bible,* Image Books. Double day and Company Inc, Newyork.

Hinson, David F. (1993): *The Books of The Old Testament,* ISPCK, Delhi.

—— (1993): *History of Israel,* ISPCK, New Delhi.

Hopkris, D.C. (1985): *The High lands of Canaan - Agricultural life in the Early Iron Age,* The Social World of Biblical Antiquity, Almond Press, Sheffield.

Hunter, A.M. (1972): *Introducing the New Testament,* SCM Press Ltd, London.

Islam, Mazhurul (1985): *Folklore - The pulse of the people,* Concept Publishing Company, New Delhi.

Jevons, F.B. (1985): *Comparative Religion,* Orient Publications, Delhi.

Jeyaraj, Jesudasan (1993): *Thirumaraiyil Deivangal,* Vacation Institute of Christian Education, Madurai.

Jhingran, Saral (1982): The Roots of World Religions, Books & Books Publishers, New Delhi.

Job, E.J.C. (1989): Guide to Divine Healing, Job Malad (W), Mumbai.

Kanal, S.P. (1984): The Philosophy of Religion, Lotus Publishers, New Delhi.

Karunakaran, K. & Handoo, Jawaharlal (Eds.) (1988): *Folklore of India. Commonness and comparisons,* Bharathiyar University, Coimbatore.

Keesing, Roger M. (1981): *Cultural Anthropology,* Holt - Saunders International Editions, Tokyo.

Kirkpatrick, Patricia G. (1988): *The Old Testament and Folklore Study,* The University of Sheffield, Sheffield.

Krappe, Alexander H. (1964): *The Science of Folklore,* The Norton Library, New York.

Lakshmanan, S.M.L. (1980): *Folklore of Tamil Nadu,* National Book Trust, New Delhi.

Lambrecht J. (1976): *Parables of Jesus,* Theological Publication in India, Bangalore.

Landy, David (1977): *Culture, Disease and Healing. Studies in* Medical Anthropology, MacMillan Publishing Co. Inc, New York.

Lewis, C.S. (1947): *Miracles,* The Centenary Press, London.

Lewis, John (1982): *Anthropology Made Simple,* William Heini Mann Ltd., London.

Lillie, V. (1969): *Introduction to the Old Testament* (Vol.II), TTBC, Chennai.

Lockyer, Herbert (1995): *All the Doctrines of the Bible,* Zondervan Publishing Home, Michigan.

Louis, Jacob (1973): *A Jewish Theology*, Darton, Longman & Todd, London.

Lourdu, De (1987): *Nattar Vazakatriyal, Nattar Vazakatriyal Aaivukazhagam,* Tinnelvely.

Luke, K. (1988): *Companion to the Bible (Vol.1,2),* Theological Pub. in India, Bangalore.

Macarthur, John (1983): *God, Satan and Angels,* Word of Grace Communications, Panorama City.

Maity, S.K., Uppendra Thakur & Narain A.K. (1988): *Studies in Orientology,* (Essays in Memory of Prof. A.L.Basham). Y.K. Publishers, Agra.

Manson, T.W. (1950): *The sayings of Jesus,* SCM Press Ltd, London.

Manuel, Albert (1972): *A Theological Word Book of the Bible,* Tamil Theological Book Club, Chennai.

Manuel,Vimala (1967): *Isravelarin Thuthi Padalgal,* T.T.B.C. (CLS), Chennai.

Marshall, Howard I. (1969): *The Work of Christ,* The Paternoster Press, Fakenham.

Mattam, Er. Zacharias (1988): *Opening the Bible,* Kristu Jothi College Publications, Bangalore.

Menezis, Allen (1987): *History of Religion,* Anupama Publications, New Delhi.

Mercatante, Anthony S. (1978): *Good and Evil,* Harper & Row Publishers, New York.

Moore, Alexander (1978): *Cultural Anthropology,* Harper & Row Publishers, New York.

Mondin, Battista (1985): *Philosophical Anthropology*, Urbaniana University Press, Rome.

Murugan, P. (1992): *Pudhia Nokkil Pazhamozhi*, New Century Book House Pvt. Ltd, Chennai.

Muthiah, E. (1986): *Nattuppura Maruthuva Manthira Sadangukal,* Annam Pvt. Ltd, Chennai.

Nasir, Ali M.A.M (1987): *Nattuppura Panpattiyal,* Ighrah Publications, Trichy.

Nigosian. S.A (1975): *World Religions,* Edward Arnold Publishing Ltd, London.

Noth, Martin (1960): *The History of Israel,* A & C Black, London.

—— (1966): *The Old Testament World,* A & C Black, London.

Noy, Dov (Ed.) (1969): *Folktales of Israel,* The University of Chicago Press, Chicago.

Osteen, John (1978): *How to Flow in the Super Supernatural,* Gospal for Asia Publications, Tiruvalla.

Packin, David (Ed.) (1977): *The Anthropology of Evil,* Prentice Hall.Inc, New Jersey.

Parrinder. Geoffrey (1961): *Worship in World Religions,* Sheldon Press, London.

Perumal, A.N. (1987): *Nattuppuraviyal Sinthanaigal,* Ainthinai Pathippagam, Chennai.

—— (1987): *Tamilil Kathaip Padal,* International Institute of Tamil Studies, Chennai.

Perumal, V. (1987): *Palanokil Pazhamozhigal,* Ilakiya Publishers, Chennai.

Pink, Arthur W. (1988): *The Anti Christ,* Kregal Publications, Michigan.

Poonan, Zac (1996): *Know Your Enemy,* New Life Literature. Katunayake.

Potter, Peter (Ed.) (1992): *All About Sin,* Universal Book Stall, New Delhi.

Prince, Derek (1990): *Blessing or Curse,* Word Publishing, Victoria.

Rad, G. Von (1972): *Wisdom in Israel,* SCM Press, London.

Radin, Paul (1957): *Primitive Religion,* Its Nature and Origin, Dover Publications, Inc, New York.

Rajeev, Rajendrakumar (1994): *World Famous Religions,* Pustak Mahal, Delhi.

Ramanathan, A. (1998): *Nattuppuraviyal Aaivugal,* Manivasagar Pathipagam, Chennai.

Richards, H.J. (1976): *The Miracles of Jesus,* Fontana Books, Glasgow

Richardson, Alan (1988): *A Theological Word Book of the Bible,* SCM Press Ltd, London.

Robinson, Gnana (1969): *Introduction to the Old Testament (Vol.III),* TTBC, Chennai.

——(1969): *Isravelarin Samayam,* Tamil Theological Book Club, Chennai.

——(1972): *A Companion to the Bible,* Tamil Theological Book Club, Chennai.

Robinson, Theodore H. (1947): *The Poetry of the Old Testament,* Duckworth, London.

Robinson, H. Wheeler (1947): *The Religious Ideas of the Old Testament,* W.C.Duckworth. London.

Roland,de Vaux (1961): *Ancient Israel (II Volumes),* McGraw - Hill Book Company, New York.

Rose, Lynda (1995): *The Devil and the Sovereignty of God,* Kingsway Publications, East Bourne (UK).

Rosenberg, Donna (1986): *World Mythology,* Harrap Ltd, London.

Rowley, H.H. (1961): *The Faith of Israel,* SCM Press Ltd, London.

——(1963): *A Companion to the Bible,* T&T Clark Ltd, Edinburg.

Ryken, Leland (1980): *The Literature of the Bible,* Zondervan Publishing House, Michigan.

Sakthivel, S. (1976): *Folklore Literature in India,* Meena Pathipagam, Aundipatti.

—— (1989): *Folklore Study of Tamil Nadu,* Tamil Folklore Association of India, Annamalai Nagar.

—— (1995): *Nattuppuraviyal Ayvu,* Manivasagar Pathipagam, Chennai.

Santhi, G. (1994): *Folklore Survey of Thanjavur District,* Tamil University Pub., Thanjavur.

Schector, S. (1946): *Studies in Judaism,* The Word Publishing Co., Meridian Books, New York.

Schmidt, Warner H. (1983) *The Faith of the Old Testament,* Basil Black Well, Oxford.

—— (1986): *The Faith of the Old Testament,* Basil Blackwell, Oxford.

—— (1992): *Old Testament-Introduction,* St. Paul's Publication, Mumbai.

Shanmuga, Sundaram S. (1988): *Nattuppura Ilakkiya Varalaru,* Manivasagar Pathipagam, Chennai.

—— (1989) *Nattuppuraiyal,* Manivasagar Pathippagam, Chennai.

Shaman, Dean (1990): *Spiritual Warfare,* Y W A M Publication, Pune.

Sharma, Ramnath (1994): *Philosophy of Religion,* Kedarnath Ramnath, Delhi.

Simpson, W.W. (1965): *Jewish Prayer and Worship,* SCM Press, London.

Skutch, Alexander F. (1970): *The Golden Core of Religion,* George Allen and Unwin Ltd, London.

Soggin, J. Alberto (1989): *Introduction to the Old Testament,* SCM Press Ltd, London.

Spragne, Ruth L. (1970): *People of the Old Testament,* United Church Press, Boston.

Starr, Chester G. (1983): *A History of the Ancient World,* Oxford University Press, Oxford.

Stith, Thompson (1981): *The Types of the Folktale,* F.F. Communications, Helsinki.

Stone, Nathan (1944): *Names of God,* The Moody Bible Institute, Chicago.

Stott, John R.W. (1993): *Understanding the Bible,* Gospel Literature Service, Mumbai.

Subramanian, P.R. (1972): *An Introduction to the Study of Indian Folklore,* PRS Publications, Tuticorin.

Subramanian, S.V. (1977): *Tamilil Vidukathaigal,* International Institute of Tamil Studies, Chennai.

Subramanian, Bala R. (1990): *Nattuppura Vazhvial,* Sathya Publications, Madurai.

Subritzky, Bill (1992): *Demons Defeated,* Dove Ministries Ltd. Auckland.

Thiyagu (1984): *Israyelin Kavalarkal (Vol. 1&2),* Loyola College, Chennai.

—— (1978): *Torah,* Nobili Press, Madurai.

Thompson, S. (1974): *The Sociological Study of Religion,* Robertson and Smith, London.

Tokarev, Sergei (1989): *History of Religion,* Progress Publishers, Moscow.

Toynbee, Arnold (1979): *An Historian's Approach to Religion,* Oxford University Press, Oxford.

Turnbell, H.Clay (1986): *Oriental Customs,* Traditions and Social Life, Mittal Publications, Delhi.

Verma, K.M.P. (1982): *Philosophy of Religion,* Classical Publishing Company, New Delhi.

Vanamamalai, N. (1992): *Pazankathaikalum Pazhamozhikalum,* New Centenary Book House Pvt. Ltd., Chennai.

Vos, Geerhardus (1985): *Biblical Theology,* The Banner of Truth Trust, Pennsylvania.

Vriezan, TH.C. (1967): *The Religion of Ancient Israel,* Lutterworth Press, London.

Walton, Robert C. (1970): *A Basic Introduction to the Old Testament,* S.C.M. Press. London.

Ward, Charles G. (1978): *The Billy Graham Christian Worker's Handbook,* World Wide Publications, Minneapolis.

Weber, Max (1952): *Ancient Judaism,* Free Press, New York.

Wellhausen, J. (1878): *History of Israel,* Geschichte Israel, Berlin.

Whyte, H.A. Maxwell (1989): *Demons and Deliverance,* Whitaker House. Springdale (USA).

Wielenga, Bastian (1988): *It's a Long Road to Freedom,* Perspectives of Biblical Theology, T.T.S. Publications, Madurai.

Wijngaards (1983): *Historicity in the Old Testament,* Theological Publishers in India, Bangalore.

Wiseman, P.J. (1977): Clues to Creation in Genesis, Marshall Morgan & Scott, London.

Commentaries

Black, M., & Rowley H.H. (Eds) (1962): *Peaks Commentary on the Bible,* Nelson Pub., Edinburgh.

Brown, Raymond E., Fitzmyer, Joseph A., & Murphy, Roland E. (Eds) (1972): *The New Jerome Bible Commentary,* Theological Publications in India Bangalore.

Guthirie, D., Motyer J.A., Stibbs A.M., & Wiseman D.J. (Eds) (1995): *New Bible Commentary,* IVP Pub., Leicester.

Laymon,Charle M. (1973): *Interpreter's (I Vol.) Commentary on The Bible,* Collins, London.

Roehs, Walter R., & Frenzmann, Martin H.(Eds) (1979) *Concordia Self- Study Commentary,* Concordia Publ. House, St. Louis.

Dictionaries

Achtemeir, Paul J. (Ed) (1990): *Harper's Bible Dictionary,* Theological Publications in India, Bangalore.

Brown, David (Ed) (1986): *The Dictionary of Life,* Sidgwick and Jackson, London.

Butterich, George Arthur., Samuel., Knox, John., & Buck, Emory Stevens (Eds) (1976): *The Interpreter's Dictionary of Kepler,* Thomasthe Bible (in IV Vols.), Abington Press, New York.

Douglas, J.D. (Ed) (1986): *New Bible Dictionary, IVP Publ.,* Leicester.

Dufour, Xavier Leon (Ed) (1973): *Dictionary of Biblical Theology,* Theological Publications in India, Bangalore.

Hastings, J. (Ed) (1963): *Dictionary of the Bible,* T & T Clark, London.

Leach, Maria (Ed) (1949): *Standard Dictionary of Folklore,* Mythology and Legend, Funk and Wagnalls, New York.

Mckenzie, John L. (Ed) (1984): *Dictionary of the Bible,* Asian Trading Corporation, Bangalore.

Richards, Lawrence O.(Ed) (1990): *The Applied Bible Dictionary,* Kings way Publications, Sussex.

Tenney, Marrill C. (Ed) (1984): *The New International Dictionary of the Bible,* Zondervan Publ. House, Grand Rapids.

Encyclopaedias

Elwell, Walter A. (Ed) (1995): *Bakers-Encyclopaedia of the Bible (Vol. I & II),* Baker's Book House, Michigan.

Packer, J.I. (Ed) (1995): *Illustrated Encyclopaedia of Bible Facts,* Thomas Nelson Publishers, Tennessee.

Translations of the Bibles Used

Scofield Reference Bible.
The Dake Annotated Reference Bible.
The Family Devotional Study Bible.
The Good News Bible.
The King James Version of the Bible.
The New English Bible.
The New International Version of the Bible.
The New Revised Standard Version of the Bible.
The Open Bible.
The Revised Standard Version of the Bible.
The Revised Version of the Bible.
The Thompson Chain Reference Bible.

INDEX

Abraham, Robert D., 27, 37. 52-54. 62-63, 70-71, 91-92, 134, 207. 208, 210. 308

Achtemeir, Patil J., 278

Adam and Eve, 53, 85, 258

Adultery and Prostitutions, proverbs on, 109-10

sexual sins, 108-110

Aetiological motifs, 84

Agesthialingam, S., 20

Agriculture, 53, 98-99

sowing and reaping, 99-100

Ancestor worship, 208-10

Ancient Egypt, polytheistic religion of, 196-97

Ancient Greece, polytheistic relations of, 199-200

Angels, 176-77

good spirits of, 177-78

Animal baiting, 299-300

sacrifice, 310

stories of, 73-74

Animatism, 206

Animism, 21

Anthropology, 20-21

Anthropological perspective, 17

Anthropomorphism, 157-59

Apocalyptic literature, 45-46

Apoplexy, 262

Apostalic times, faith healings in, 286

Aramaic, 211-12

Archery, 295

Aristotle, 134

Arithmetical riddle, 137

Asherah, 203-04

Ashtoroth, 203

Assyrian religion, 200

Atheletic games, 292

Authorities, 35

Baal, 203-05

Baalam's donkey, 73-74

Babel, tower of, 85-86

Babylonia, idol worshippers of, 198

God of, 198

worship and festivals, 198-99

Babylonian Gilgamesh Epic, 59

Babylonian myth, 62

Ballads, narrative basis, 250-51

oral transmission, 251-52

Barthemaeus, 285

Bascom, William R., 18

Beliefs, 310

regarding defilement, 182-83

regarding magic and sorcery, 188-89

regarding man, 162

Bhagwat, Durga, 137

Bhagwat Gita, 103

Battrick, George Arthur, 179

Bible, ballads of, 252-56

composition of, 35-36

diseases in, 261-62

evil spirits in, 181-82

folk games in, 291-305

folk medicine in, 258-80

folk songs in, 230-35

games in, 293-94

love songs in, 241-48

medicinal herbs in, 273-74

message of, 36-37

musical instruments in, 230-32

non-Isralite Gods in, 203-04

proverbs in, 97-98

Bible community 15-20, 34-52, 182-88, 205-20, 306-10

Biblical folklore. 16-18
Biblical laments, categories of, 235-36
Biblical prophecy, 42
Biblical riddles, 139-40
Biblical revelation, 167
Birth, life and death, 103-05, 165-67
Balains, 262
Blemishes, 263
Blessing, 102
Blindness, 263-64
Boils, 264
Bowra, 228
Boxing, 298
Brown, Raymond, 183
Browne, B., 92
Burnt offering, 217
Business, investment in, 100-101

Cain and Abel, 85
Canannite, religion of, 200-201
Canaanite Bronge Age, 209
Canaanite mythology, Baal in, 204-05
Cancer, 264
Chandran Job, E.J., 280
Chappell, L.W., 134
Chariot racing, 299
Chettiyar caste, 22
Child birth, uncleanness due to, 186
Children's games, 300-302
Christianity, 15-17
Chronicles, 40
Cleaning rituals, 186-87
Community laments, 240-41
Compassionate God, 159
Comte, August, 21
Contextual method, 30
Corinthians, 292-93, 299
Corporate ritual worship, 215
Cosmic powers, 199
Cream, Jacob, 24
Creation, story of, 61-62
Credibility, 15
Crimms, Jocob, 25
Cross-cultural method, 29
Cupbearer, dream of, 145-46

Daniel, 45
David, 294-95
Death, experience of, 167-168
 influence of, 168
Defiled animals, 184-85
 birds, 185
Deboral, songs, of, 254-55
De Geus, 51
Demons, 75-76, 170-77, 284-85
 possession, 277
Deuteronomy, 38
Dewey, John, 22
Disciplines, 19
Diseases, Biblical outlook on, 260-61
 treatment of, 271-72
Disease and ailments, types of, 262-70
Dorson, Richard M., 24, 27
Dreams, 83-84
Durkheim, Emile, 152, 189
Dysentry, 265

Ecclesiastes, 42, 94
Economy, proverbs on, 117-20
Edema (dropsy), 265
Egyptian King Merneptah, 51
Egyptian, funerary beliefs of, 197-98
 worship, 197
Eliade, Mircea, 152
Elijah, 66-69
Elisha, 68-69
Elizabeth, 72
Elon Morah, 207
Emerson, Ralph Wolds, 90
Encyclopaedia of Britanica, 17, 58, 138
Encyclopaedia of Religion and Ethics, 17
Endocrine disturbances, 265
En Mishpal, 207
Enrich, Oswald A., 259
Epidemics, 268
Epilepsy, 265, 277-78
Epinosa, Aurelio M., 19
Esther, 40
Evil spirits, 179-82
Ezekiel, Prophet, 40, 139
 riddles, 142-43
Ezra, 40

Faith healing, 280
Faley, Roland J., 183-84
Fall of Adam, 46
Feasts and Festivals, 220-22
Fellowship offering, 218
Female disorders, 266
Fever, 266
Flood Story, 62
Folk artisans, occupation of, 54
Folk Ballads, 248-50
  definition of, 249-50
Folk cultural method, 29-30
Folk Gods, 201-02
  categories, 202
  characteristics of, 202
Folk literature, 34-35
Folk medicine, 259-60, 311
Folk music,
  percussion instruments, 230
  stringed instrument, 230
  wind instrument, 230
Folk songs, classification of, 227-30
Folklore, approaches of, 17-18
  communication, 243
  current theories of, 24-25
  definition of, 16-18
  studies, 47-49
Folktales, 59-60, 309
  classifications of, 58-59
  primitive beliefs, 82
Foolish person, proverbs on, 127-29
Foot racing, 300
Fowlers Snares, 296
Fracture, treatment of, 275
Frazer, J.G., 48, 49
Freud, Sigmund, 20, 27
Fried, M.H., 52
Friendship, proverbs on, 114-16
Frustration, 130
Functional Method, 26-27

Games, origin of, 291-92
Gambling, 303
Gangrene, 266
George, Robert A., 291
German Biblical scholarship, 49
Giants, tales of, 77-78
God's complaint, 101-02
  fourfold revelation of, 153
  meaning of, 195-96
  moral attibutes, 154-56
  proverbs on, 124-25
God felt sorry, 159-60
God-a-Judge, 167-68
God is love, 153-55
Goddess Ishter, 198
Goliath, 77
Good Government, 110-12
  proverbs on, 110-12
Good Samaritan, parable of, 148-49
Gospels, 46-48, 74-76, 285-87
Gout, 267
Grain offering, 217
Guilt offering, 218-19

Habakkuk, 44
Haemorrhage, 280
Haggai, 45
Hard, Wayland D., 151
Hastings, James, 135
Healing, 278-79
  use of means, 279-80
Health and disease, 258-60
Hearing loos, 263-64
Heaven, 170-71
  develling of God, 171-72
  future house of the saints, 172-73
Hebrews, 166-67, 173
Hebrew music, origin of, 229-30
Hebrew religion, 210-11
Hell, place for sinners, 175-76
Hemispheric method, 30
Herbal folk medicine, 212
Herdsman, 53
Hero stories, 62
Hezekiah, 110
  recovery of, 283
Historical-Geographical method, 24-25
Historical reconstruction method, 25-26
Historical science, 22
Holiness, 154
Hosea, 43-44
Human sacrifice, 219-20

Humanistic perspective, 17
Hunting, 53, 97-98, 295

Ideological method, 26
Idolatry, 222-23
Immortality, 169
Individual lament, 236-40
Individnal ritual worship, 216-17
Infection, treatment of, 275-76
Intellectual games, 302-303
Inter disciplinary approach, 47
Isaac, 62, 70-71, 208-210
Israel worshipping system in, 214-15
Israelites, 38, 51-53, 63-65, 153, 158-160, 161, 163-65, 172, 180
    folk community, 242
    occupation of, 52-54
    prophecy, 42
Isaiah's song of vineyard, 143
Isthumian games, 292

Jacob, 62, 208-10
Japanese folklore, 25
Jataka tales, 25
Jehovah, 212-23
Jehovaist, Elohist, Deutronomic and Priestly (JEDP), 50
Jeremiah, prophet, 43, 303
Jerusalem, 43
    lame man in, 286-87
Jesus, birth of, 72
    hard sayings of, 146-47
    spoken word, 81
    temptation of, 75
Jewish customs, 310
Joel, 44
Jonah, 44
    fish, 74-75
Joseph vision of, 144
Joshua, 38
Jotham's feble, 141-42
Judaism, 151

Kailasapathy, 29
King David, 65
King Sihan, balled on difeat of, 253-54
King Solomon, 65-66
Kumar, Keval J., 19
Krappe, Alexander H., 91

Lameness, 267
Laments, 235-40
Lamentation, 43
Lang, Andrew, 21
Languages, 15
    proverbs on, 120-21
Late Bronge Age, 52
Laves, Malcolm, 250
Lazy person, proverbs on, 29-30
Leach, Maria, 90, 134, 227
Legion, 76-77
Leprosy, 261, 267
    uncleanness due to, 187-88
Levitious, 38
Linguistics, 23-24
Liquor, 116-17
Lord Jesus Christ, 36
Lowie, Robert, 25
Lystra, Lame Man in, 287

Magic, tales, of, 78-79
Magic-religious folk medicine, 259-60
Magico-religious folk medicine, 276-78
Mair, Lucy, 151
Malachi, 45
Malaria, 268
Malinowski, 26
Man and woman, creation of, 61-62
Marriage/women, 107
    proverbs on, 107-108
Martial songs, 229
Marx, Karl, 194
Mashal, 95
Mass cultural method, 30
Mckenzie, John, L., 188, 278
Mental disorder, 277-78
Mental and Nervous disorders, 268
Mercy, 155
Methodology, 31-32
Micah, 44
Milton, John, 162
Miracles, 278-79, 282
Moloch, 205-06

Moore, Alexander, 160
Moses, 63-65, 71-75, 110-15
 recovery of, 283-85
 songs of, 252-53
Mount Carmel, 67
Muller, Max, 24, 195
Multiple healings, 288-89
Musical instruments, 55, 230-32
Mythical tales, 60-61

Naaman, 70
Nahum, 44
Natural folk medicine, 259, 272-74
Nature, proverbs on, 102
Nazarite, 63, 116
Nebuchadnezzar, 81
Nehemiah, 40

New Jerusalem, 172, 173
New Testament, 35-38, 46, 59, 90, 109, 137, 153, 169, 171-74, 177, 279, 310
 faith healigs in, 284-85
Non-oppositional proverbs, 93-94

Obediah, 44
Occupation, 52-53, 97
Oedipus complex, 19
Offerings, 216-17
Old Testament, 35-37, 40, 45, 46-48, 59-60, 84-86, 90, 94, 103, 107, 116, 137, 153, 156, 158, 163, 167-69, 173-75, 177, 205, 213-15, 221-23, 269, 308
 animism in, 206-08
 anthropomorphism, 158
 faith healings of, 282-83
 folk Gods in, 206-07
 folklore research, 49-50
 laments of, 236
 liturgical music in, 230
 wisdom, concept of, 96
Olympic games, 292-93
Oppression, 39
Oral formulaic method, 28-29
Oral Transmission, 50
Ornaments, proverbs on, 101

Palani-Murugan, 208
Palsy, 268
Parables, 147
Paralytic healed, 287
Paramasivanandhan, A.M., 18
Parent-child relationship, 112-14
Patriarchs, 62
Paul, Apostle, 164, 167, 292
Paul, Timothy, 293
Peacock, Kemmeth, 228
Pedagogy, 194
Pentateuch, 49, 50
Percussion instruments, 231
Persons, proverbs on, 125-26
Pharaoh's dream, 145-46
Philistines, 62-64
Philosophy, 23
Physical sport, 294
Plague, 268
Poetical books, 40
Polio, 269
Polytheism, 210-11
Polytheistic religion, 196-97
Potter, Charles Francis, 19, 100
Poverty, 130
Propp, Vladenia, 28
Prophetical Books, 42-43
Prostitution, 109-10
Proverbs, 41-42, 309
 characturistics of, 92
 classification of, 92-93
 definition of, 90-92
 structural study of, 93-94
 stylistic study of, 93
Psalms, 41, 240-42, 281-83, 311
Psalmist, 70
Psaltery, 233
Psycho-analytical method, 27
Psychology, 22
Psychological-Psycho analytical perspectives, 18

Radin, Paul, 189
Rational folk medicine, 259
Religion and God, 194-95
Relationship, 112-14
Resurrection, 166-67

Revelation, 173
Richardson, Alam, 206
Riddles, 302
    classes of, 136-38
    definitions of, 133-35
    logograph, 135-36
Right way to speak, 121-22
Rivers, streans and brooks, 207-08
Roman inperialism, 310

Sacrifice, 55, 216-17
Sakthival, S., 20, 21, 59, 93, 202, 249, 259
Samson, 63, 77, 302
    riddle of, 140-41
Samuel, 39, 110
Satan, origin and activities, 179-81
Secret place of soul, 82
Sengupta, Sankar, 19
Sexual relations, 108
Shanthi, G., 260
Sheol, 174, 175
Shepherds, 53, 100
Shunamiti maiden, 242
Sin offering, 218
Skin disorders, 269-70
Small pox, 270
Sociology, 21-22
Solomon, 110, 240-48
Song of songs, 42
Soul's location, 82-83
Sower, parable of, 147-48
Speaking serpent, 73
Spirits God and Evil, 75-76, 177
Spoken word, 80-81
Stringed instrument, 228, 230-32
Structural method, 28
Subramaniam, P.R., 18, 23, 28
Subramanian, S.V., 138
Succoth-Benott, 205
Sunstroke, 270
Syllable-riddle, 136
Syncope, 270

Tales of two cows, 74
Tamil Nadu, folklore of, 32-34
Tamil Proverbs, categories, 93-95
Teraphim, 224-25
Thomas, William John, 16
Tirupathi, 208
Totemism, 21
Townsend, W.J., 156
Toynbee, Arnold, 201, 220
Tribal organisation, 52
Truth, 155
Tuberculosis, 264

Unclean beings of water, 185-86
Uncleanness, causes of beliefs, 183-84
Unilateral and Unilineal Kinship system, 52

Vanamamalai, M., 19
Venereal disease, 270
Vetler, George B., 276

War between Devil and God's army, 77
Water unclean of, 185-86
Wind instrument, 230, 233-34
Wine, 116
Wisdom, Hebrew, 94
    literary types of, 95-96
    literature, 40-41
Wisdom and God, 96-97
Wise person, proverbs on, 125-27
Witchraft, 189
World Health Organisation (WHO), 258
Worms, 271
Worship, 54-55
Wrath of God, 156-57
Wrestling, 297
Wrong way to speak, 122-23

Yehweh, 36-39, 54-60, 63-70, 95-98, 235-40
Yodor, Don, 20, 30, 46, 260

Zarephath, 66
Zachariah, 44, 73
    prophet, 301
Zephaniah, 45
Zuni mythology, 26